Reporters for the Union

Memorial to the Civil War Correspondents,
Battlefield of South Mountain, Maryland

REPORTERS
for the Union

BERNARD A. WEISBERGER

Boston

Little, Brown and Company

LIBRARY OF CONGRESS CATALOG CARD NO. 52-12638

FIRST EDITION

Published simultaneously
in Canada by McClelland and Stewart Limited

PRINTED IN THE UNITED STATES OF AMERICA

To my parents

who were helpful in the beginning

AND

To June

for whom everything is done now

Acknowledgments

NO one who writes a book can ever really remember, much less record, what he owes to friends who, by their interest, their questions, or their objections, do much to direct his thinking. He can at least offer his thanks, however, to the librarians whose patience and knowledge are often infinitely helpful. I am glad to publicize my gratitude to the staffs of the Manuscript Division of the Library of Congress, the Missouri Historical Society in St. Louis, the Historical and Philosophical Society of Ohio in Cincinnati, the New England Deposit Library on the campus of Harvard University, the New York Public Library's Newspaper Division, the New York Historical Society, the Chicago Historical Society, and the Library of the University of Chicago.

I welcome as well the opportunity to thank belatedly the members of the Department of History of the University of Chicago, and especially Professor William T. Hutchinson, for the kind of fruitful teaching and leadership which led me into historical research.

In that connection, it is most satisfying to set down the most important acknowledgment of all, to Professor Avery O. Craven. He gave me everything in the way of direction, encouragement, stimulation and incentive that a teacher and friend can offer. In almost any sense of the term, he provided most of the means by which this book was brought into being.

Yellow Springs, Ohio B.A.W.

Preface

BETWEEN Burkitsville and Boonsboro, in Maryland, a road winds uphill around South Mountain. High up, by the side of the road, a monument stands, unique among war memorials. It is on a battlefield. The rural Sunday morning calm of Boonsboro was broken, in 1862, when a part of General William B. Franklin's corps drove a Confederate force from the mountain. The Confederates retreated sullenly westward, towards a place called Antietam. But the monument is not to Franklin, or his men.

It is a curious monument — a great arch, in natural stone, surmounted by three smaller arches. Through it a visitor can see the fat fields of central Maryland below, and can look toward Washington, some distance away to the southeast. One side of the arch is prolonged upward into a crenelated tower. Two disembodied horse heads, a Hermes, and a pair of Muses, all in stone, stare from niches cut in the west face. Over the arch, in great letters of red brick, runs the legend: WAR CORRESPONDENTS. More explicitly, a stone plaque in the north side dedicates the work

To The
Army Correspondents
and
Artists
1861–1865

Whose Toils Cheered The Camps, Thrilled The Fireside, Educated Provinces of Rustics Into A Bright Nation of Readers and Gave Incentive to Narrate Distant Wars and Explore Dark Lands

A tablet on the east face lists the names of one hundred and six writers and sixteen artists who followed the Union armies, in addition to nine Southern correspondents and twenty men described as "Army Artists." The structure is also enriched — if that is the word — by stone tablets bearing the words "Speed" and "Heed," a list of quotations appropriate to the correspondents' calling, a directory of the committee responsible for creating the work in 1896, and a rich, full-bodied poem.

O Wondrous youth
Through this grand ruth
Runs my boy's life its thread.
The General's name, the battle's fame,
The rolls of maimed and dead
I bear, with my thrilled soul astir,
And lonely thoughts and fears,
And am but history's courier
To bind the conquering years —
A battle ray through ages gray
To light to deeds sublime,
And flash the lustre of my day
Down all the aisles of time.

Probably the poem is the work of George Alfred Townsend. Townsend's name is on the list of war reporters. He was a modestly successful working journalist, regional poet and novelist when the arch was built under his direction, and he chose to locate both the memorial and his home on the old battleground.

Monuments to military leaders and events are as old, and generally as unattractive, as war itself. But a tribute in stone to one hundred-odd civilians whose martial deeds were carried out with pencils is something to raise a tourist's curiosity. What kind of war was it in which such men could be found, and in which they could be sufficiently important to have someone undertake the preservation of their names in rock?

There is an answer. It was a modern war. The Civil War does not seem remote to us after nearly a century, partly because it was in so many respects up-to-date — in its totality, its tremendous cost in real and paper wealth, its drab, impersonal destruction of half a million lives, and the bitter finality of its decision. It had a draft and photographers. It had trenches, aerial observation, and at least one submarine. It had signal officers, railroad construction troops, and engineer specialists. They have had their stories told, because in their own way they reflected and foreshadowed great things that were happening in the United States, and in the entire world of the nineteenth and twentieth centuries.

The war also had, for the first time in any appreciable numbers, correspondents. They, too, were important. This is their story.

Contents

Reporters for the Union

CHAPTER I

The Newspaper and the Reporter in the Fifties

IN 1864 the Philadelphia banking house belonging to Jay Cooke was given the job of floating a great loan to carry on the three-year-old war. Cooke was an up-to-date financier and he knew the quarter from which blew the breezes that stirred public opinion. From his home in Toledo, he proceeded to ship several lots of wine, ducks, and fish to a number of gratified newspaper editors and correspondents. It must have had a pleasing flavor of novelty for them. Congressmen were already accustomed to receive from lobbyists such small attentions as dinners of game pie, broiled oysters, mixed salads, and burgundy at blood heat. But newspapermen, whose calling had generally been thought of as less elevated, were not usually subjected to such pleasant persuasions.[1]

Yet Cooke was very much the man of the times, and was in his own way contributing to precedent. A few years after the war, the chairman of Washington's Board of Public Works, for example, found himself about to distribute

[1] Elwyn B. Robinson, "The Dynamics of American Journalism from 1787 to 1865," *Pennsylvania Magazine of History*, LXI (1937), 444; Benjamin Perley Poore, *Reminiscences of Sixty Years in the National Capital* (Boston, 1886), II, 513-514.

several million dollars worth of contracts for refurbishing the capital. He proceeded to bestow a few upon newspaper correspondents for resale, obviously well aware that there was nothing like good press relations for speeding business transactions. In the same era of enterprise, the vice-president of the Pullman Company, interested in building New York City's first elevated railroad, thought it advisable to make one of his early calls on Mr. William A. Croffut. Croffut had been a war correspondent for the *New York Tribune*, and his editorial contacts were good. He was, therefore, the very man with whom to arrange for a few articles "to create a favorable public opinion" against the day when shares in the undertaking should reach the market.[2] These arrangements represented something of an experiment with an unknown quantity. It was still decades before reporters would explore the shame of the cities or the insides of continents and cabinets for the enlightenment of a nation-wide audience. But they were clearly rising in the scale of importance.

Yet a mere dozen years before Jay Cooke opened his wine cellar in the interests of a good press, the reporter had no place in the gallery of national types. Like Cooke, himself, and the purposeful business tycoons of whom Cooke was a prototype, he was made a person of importance by the war. In the thousands of words which the war correspondents spread across the front pages of a dozen metropolitan journals daily, they furnished an avidly de-

[2] Poore, *Reminiscences*, II, 263; William A. Croffut, *An American Procession* (Boston, 1931), p. 164.

sired link between the army and the homes from which it had been drawn. It was natural that they should be thought of as equally able to make the connection between the businessman and consumer, politician and voter. All these relationships, after all, reduced themselves to one. The shape of the average man's daily life was becoming more dependent, with each tick of the clock of history, upon happenings in a world that extended far beyond the horizon of his farm or village. It was through reporters that he might learn each morning of the changes in that world.

So the correspondent was, in one sense, a participant in a revolution. The newspaper which paid his salary was a long-standing part of the American scene on the eve of the war, but it was changing with the scene, and at the same time attempting to describe the changes. For years a blanket-sized gazette, political review and advertising handbill, it had been hitched to the dynamo in the eighteen-forties. Steam presses and electric wires worked rapid alterations in its appearance and its aims. The presence of the correspondent was one of those alterations. But in the beginning, of course, he took the newspaper as he found it, tailoring his work to a pattern which could be reshaped only gradually. He began to create for himself a new profession, within an established one which was already self-important, ridden with politics, moralizing and sensational.

In the years which unfolded between the end of the War of 1812 and the crisis of the fifties, the power of the press

— a phrase the editors loved to roll upon their tongues — was one of the acknowledged commonplaces of life in America. Federal and State statutes carefully stood sentry over the liberties of print. Politicians from Jefferson's day onward lavished funds on party organs. Hand presses, as often as not manned by foot-loose journeymen printers who were the press services, advertising agencies and salesmen of their own ephemeral dailies and weeklies, followed closely behind the moving frontier line. The circulation totals of the census grew by the decades; between 1840 and 1860 alone the number of dailies in circulation leaped from 138 to 372, and in the latter year the readership ran comfortably into seven figures.[3]

To some, the tally sheet was cheering, but there were doubts. Edward Everett, who knew the influence of the press as president of Harvard, governor of Massachusetts, Senator, Secretary of State and ultimately Vice-Presidential candidate, spoke apparently for the more cautious when he referred to it as "for good or evil, the most powerful influence that acts on the public mind." The good was amply sworn to in editorial columns whenever a newspaper observed a birthday or whenever a debate over the raising of newspaper mail rates was enlivening the Congressional sessions. There was, however, a distinguished deputation to point out the evil. James Fenimore Cooper echoed a number of contemporaries when he turned momentarily from the world of the Leatherstocking Tales to

[3] Frederic Hudson, *Journalism in the United States, 1690-1872* (New York, 1873), pp. 770-772.

pose a grave question: Had the nation, escaped from the tyranny of "foreign aristocrats," unwittingly fallen under an "insupportable" dictatorship of the press? An entire volume, entitled *Our Press Gang: A Complete Exposure of the Corruptions and Crimes of the American Newspapers*, was published in Philadelphia in 1859, devoted to bilious affirmatives.[4]

The foreign visitors who, notebook in hand, paraded successively around the circuit of major cities, seemed to be surprised at the importance, in America, of the periodically printed word. Alexis de Tocqueville, in his full-length X ray of American democracy, thought that with its "immense" influence and its ability to "summon the leaders of all parties to the bar of public opinion," the newspaper's power was "only second to that of the people." Dickens, returned from his first tour of the United States in the forties, doubted the self-advertised virtues of a nation where the press "had its evil eye in every house and its black hand in every appointment in the state." His lampooning of that press lost no time in finding its way into *Martin Chuzzlewit.* In 1861 the London *Times* sent its ace Crimean War correspondent, William Howard Russell, over to do what would come to be called "background studies" on the divided sections. He reserved a special dose of Piccadilly contempt for the press of the North. "Talk of the superstition of the Middle Ages," he snorted, "if you desire to understand how far faith can see and trust among . . . peo-

[4] Lambert A. Wilmer, *Our Press Gang: A Complete Exposure of the Corruptions and Crimes of the American Newspapers* (Philadelphia, 1859); the quotations from Everett and Cooper are on page 64.

ple consider themselves . . . civilized and intelligent . . . you will study the American journals." In the major cities, he confided to his London audience, men spoke of "the chiefs of the most notorious journals very much as people in Italian cities of past time might have talked of the most infamous bravo or the chief of some band of assassins." [5]

The infamous bravoes, contentedly planning the purchase of new and bigger presses, were not perturbed. Abuse was part of their professional diet, and they not only expected it as a hazard of journalism but control it by bold plunges into politics. They could, in fact, have hardly avoided the subject, for the adolescent republic seemed to breathe the atmosphere of the stump and the ballot box. Not only were there the major parties, reaching down to village level, but the reformers who flourished on the scene could not long preach the virtues of free land, women's rights, temperance, fiat money, or abolition without organizing a party to advance the cause at the polls. The "common man" of Jacksonian democracy was extraordinarily willing to sit on hard benches through campaign harangues lasting for hours, and he often bombarded his Congressmen with requests for speeches, committee reports and other governmental tracts in deadening numbers. Some of this civic consciousness was grounded in practical cir-

[5] Alexis de Tocqueville, *Democracy in America*, ed. Henry S. Commager (New York, 1947), p. 107; Dickens, *American Notes*, quoted in Frank L. Mott, *American Newspapers, 1690-1940* (New York, 1941), p. 303; William H. Russell, *The Civil War in America* (Boston, 1861), pp. 52-53; *My Diary, North and South* (Boston, 1863), p. 102.

cumstance; literary and social opportunities were rare in the hinterlands.

Whatever might be the reasons, newspapermen were no different from their contemporaries in living for politics. News — a potpourri of stale clippings — ran second to election disputations in their columns. Outright party ownership or subsidy was expected. An important lever in the ruling political machine of every State was a loyal editor, for whom the spoils of victory were printing contracts, special advertising or legislative tips on which to speculate. By 1859, Lambert A. Wilmer, the vitriolic compiler of *Our Press Gang*, publicized his belief that American newspapers were "supported almost entirely by . . . office-holders or office-hunters," and three years later James Gordon Bennett, lord of the mighty *New York Herald*, directed a well-publicized sneer at the "country editors" who lived at State capitals enjoying "free paper, pens and ink, free drinks and chewing tobacco, free board at the hotels, free travel by railroad." [6] But twenty years before, when the *Herald* itself had been a six-year-old enterprise hustling towards its place in the sun, New York's onetime Mayor Philip Hone had observed that it was "understood to be the champion" of Whig President John Tyler, and that its Washington representative had "the run of the presidential kitchen" in return for doing "the dirty jobs about the palace" — which meant, apparently, slandering the disloyal

[6] Wilmer, *Our Press Gang*, p. 195; *New York Herald*, April 5, 1862. For comment on the relative importance of news and opinion in the pre-Civil War newspaper, see Will Irwin, *Propaganda and the News* (New York, 1936), pp. 24-26.

opposition. Tyler was evidently a newspaper-minded chief executive; he was rumored to have attracted "by a lavish distribution of the advertising patronage of the Executive Departments, an 'organ in nearly every State,' " and was not above scolding a minor official as far away as New Orleans for throwing an advertisement to an opposition journal.[7]

Whether or not editorial loyalty was bought, it was outspoken. The first issue of Horace Greeley's *New York Tribune* pledged the paper to the Whig Party's support with the sweeping announcement that

> the political revolution which . . . called William Henry Harrison to the Chief Magistracy of the Nation was a triumph of Right, Reason and Public Good over Error and Sinister Ambition,

which was the kind of statement that the *Democratic Review* undoubtedly had in mind when, in 1852, it sourly held that the nation's presses were "in continual danger of becoming the mere tools of public men"—an opinion seconded by a Philadelphia journal which feared that its entire profession had become "nothing more than the vehicle of partisan intemperance."[8] Yet partisan intemperance was, perhaps, less sinister than a new kind of venality which was creeping into the newspaper world by the time of Jay Cooke's attentions to the press. In 1860, the Pennsylvania Railroad had been waging a legislative battle against a new

[7] Hone is quoted in Don C. Seitz, *The James Gordon Bennetts, Father and Son* (Indianapolis, 1928), p. 92; Poore, *Reminiscences*, I, 289-290.
[8] Hudson, *Journalism in the United States*, p. 523; Mott, *American Newspapers*, p. 253; Robinson, "Dynamics of American Journalism," p. 440.

State tonnage tax, and it had enlisted some of its editorial support by a generous distribution of advertising. At almost the same time the State's iron manufacturers, whose yearning for a high tariff was perennial, were noted by Salmon P. Chase to "do much toward controlling public sentiment in Pennsylvania." In 1864, editor Bennett received a letter from the New York office of a Colorado mining company, thoughtfully announcing a gift of fifty shares to him — a token which it was probably intended that he should remember on some useful occasion. The dyspeptic Wilmer, among his other charges against the press, claimed that certain journals kept agents at Washington ready to negotiate with applicants for contracts, solicitors of private bills, lobbyists, or others who might "stand in need of newspaper assistance." [9]

The shop talk of an editor's office, then, was apt to be supercharged with references to delegations, doubtful counties, committee appointments and postmasterships. Yet in the midst of this intensely practical gossip there was a strain of something else that seemed inconsistent on the face of it — a brand of effusive idealism so outspoken that it is hard to recognize in the pre-Civil War newspaperman an ancestor of the reporters caricatured in the boozy city-room wags of *The Front Page*. In this, too, journalism bore what was almost the trade-mark of an era. The America of the first half of the nineteenth century was in a per-

[9] Robinson, "Dynamics of American Journalism," pp. 443-444; James Gordon Bennett Papers, Library of Congress, George Manley & Co. to Bennett, March 24, 1864; Wilmer, *Our Press Gang*, p. 196.

petual seethe of Utopia-building. It went on incongruously blending spiritual concern with hardfisted acquisitiveness, year after year, affected both by its intellectual legacies and the day-to-day realities of its expanding life. Americans, forever wresting new cities out of the grip of the Western wilderness, could hardly help believing that tomorrow would always be better, granted a tolerable amount of good faith and hard work today. In the isolated rural world of dawn-to-dusk work that most Americans then knew, the drabness of life needed and found some counterweight in passionately emotional religion; brimstone sermons stung more sharply after six dusty days in the plow-furrows. Schools fed their pupils the comfortless, warmed-over homilies of Puritanism, enthroning duty: "Satan finds work for idle hands to do"; "learn to labor and to wait"; "improve each shining hour." Less direct influences left their stamp on the literate classes who were aware of them — humanitarianism, which snatched man from under the shadow of Calvinistic damnation and even dreamed that he might be perfect; romanticism, with its stress on the individual, its rich, dark colors, its love of violent clash, its unashamed sentimentality; the idealism of the German universities, in its American transcendental homespun, looking for the soul of the universe, and making of some of its practitioners judges to interpret a Higher Law that could override certain merely human statutes. Under such stars, the articulate American was frequently dogmatic, bounded by absolutes, and incurably right-thinking. He felt certain that right and wrong could be forever distinguished from each other, and that progress, a state of affairs perpetuated by divine orders, consisted in the winning of the world to right. When he spoke for others, he was inclined to think in romantically egocentric terms. Holding the center of a great stage, he exhorted his followers to rise and go forward in the names of God and duty. This gave his politics a rather magnificent effect. Heaven on the side of bran bread or the Free Soil ticket made for potent oratory, though lesser issues might be seen in warped perspective.[10]

The journalists worked within the shadow of this compulsive progressivism. It was not enough to provide a daily diet of information or observe the antics of mankind with good-humored detachment. James Gordon Bennett was a canny Scot who knew that one purpose of a newspaper such as his *Herald* was the enrichment of its owner, but he had been raised on a diet of Scottish Calvinism, Burns, Wordsworth, Scott, Byron, Carlyle and sundry metaphysicians.

> What is to prevent a daily newspaper [he asked] from being made the greatest organ of social life? Books have had their day — the theatres have had their day — the temple of religion has had its day. A newspaper can be made to take the lead of all these in the great movements of human thought and of human civilization. A newspaper can send more souls to Heaven, and save more from Hell, than all the churches or chapels in New York — besides making money at the same time. Let it be tried.[11]

[10] See particularly the first chapter of Henry S. Commager, *The American Mind* (New York, 1950), and Roy F. Nichols, *The Disruption of the American Democracy* (New York, 1948), Chapter II.
[11] Quoted in Mott, *American Newspapers*, pp. 232-233.

Horace Greeley, who displayed in the *New York Tribune* the virtues and vices of the crusading editor in their most virulent degree, once wrote that he who had not "corrected long-standing errors, or thrown forward a more searching light in the path of progress," had "never tasted the luxury of journalism." When the side-whiskered Henry J. Raymond, New York-born and Vermont-educated, began the *New York Times* in 1851, his first editorial dedicated it hopefully to the support of "Morality, of Industry, of Education and Religion." Raymond also declared that the *Times* would uphold "every just effort to reform society, to infuse higher elements of well-being into our political and social organizations, and to improve the condition and character of our fellow men." The paper's guiding stars would be "Christianity and Republicanism," words which seemed occasionally interchangeable. In the same year, Samuel Bowles, of the Massachusetts *Springfield Republican*, laid out an even more exhilarating prospectus for his colleagues.

> The brilliant mission of the newspaper is . . . to be, the high priest of history, the vitalizer of Society, the world's great informer, the earth's high censor, the medium of public thought and opinion, and the circulating life blood of the whole human mind. It is the great enemy of tyrants and the right arm of liberty, and is destined, more than any other agency, to melt and mould the jarring and contending nations of the world into that one great brotherhood which, through long centuries, has been the ideal of the Christian and the philanthropist.[12]

[12] Quoted in Willard G. Bleyer, *Main Currents in the History of American Journalism* (Boston, 1927), pp. 233, 240, 257; Oliver G. Carlson, *James Gordon Bennett, The Man Who Made News* (New York, 1942), p. 236.

It was undoubtedly breath-taking for a flesh-and-blood editor even to think of getting out three hundred and sixty-five issues yearly of a newspaper with such glittering pretensions, but there were those who held such ideas in more than lip-service esteem. Their columns were not apt to balance issues judiciously, under the sign of objectivity. They had more of the camp meeting than of the forum about them.

So much righteousness was bound to be at least slightly truculent, and there were plenty of examples to spur newspapermen into the embattled tone which enlivened their densely printed pages. Honor was quick and touchy, opinions heady, and political gatherings in the back country often awash with whiskey before the evening wore well on. In the West, a tinge of the cow town on Saturday night or of the trading post when the trappers were there colored public activities. The cities were already the home of a restless and disrespectable lesser class, ready to demonstrate on a number of pretexts. The South seemed almost to enjoy advertising its factually infrequent duels. This fever warmed the editorial offices, from whose cluttered desks the melters and molders of the jarring and contending nations of the world (according to editor Bowles) belabored each other with the full resources of rich vocabularies. "Pimp," "liar," "blockhead," "leper," "thief" and "blackleg" were terms which fell with practiced ease from editors' pens, and, by the fifties, "villain" and "scoundrel" had spent their offensive power. In New York alone, Raymond rarely referred to

Bennett except as "Old Satanic," Greeley recognized Raymond officially as "The Little Villain," and Bennett completed the circle by styling the *Tribune's* editor "Massa Greeley," in uncharitable recognition of the paper's abolitionism. The tourists from abroad were apparently used to more seemly conduct on the part of their own papers. At any rate, they were scandalized. Tocqueville shuddered at the "open and coarse appeal to the passions of the populace" which marked the journalism of American democracy. Dickens christened some of the newspapers in *Martin Chuzzlewit* with such names as the *New York Sewer*, the *New York Stabber* and the *New York Plunderer*. As for William H. Russell, whose own prose often rolled with the somnolent gravity of an after-dinner speech, he felt that he had seen the bottom touched when, just before the outbreak of the war, a Union general showed him a press clipping from a small-town Kentucky journal, which, even allowing for the passions of war, was sensationally un-Christian. It described the general as "a miserable hound, a dirty dog, . . . a treacherous villain, a notorious thief, a lying blackguard," accused him of keeping "his hide continually full of Cincinnati whiskey," and concluded: "In him are embodied all the leprous rascalities, and in this living sore, the gallows has been cheated of its own." [13]

Under such conditions, the adventures of editorship were more than intellectual, especially when language alone became too frail a container for the passions generated

[13] Tocqueville, *Democracy in America*, p. 106; William H. Russell, *Pictures of Southern Life* (New York, 1861), p. 133.

by such salty exchanges. An Arkansas Congressman once caned Horace Greeley on the steps of a Washington hotel. One morning, Bennett received a bomb in the mail, labeled as "native ore from the mountains of Cuba." (Fortunately for him, his managing editor, a suspicious Yankee, distrusted the looks of the package, soused it in the traditional pail of water and sent for the police.) The editor of the *Cincinnati Commercial*, leaving his office on the 15th of September, 1856, was accosted by a journalistic confrere from the rival *Enquirer*, who rushed at him swinging a stick and crying "God damn you! You will keep lying about me" — or "something similar." The *Commercial* editor retreated and wrote up the incident fulsomely for the next day's issue. There was, perhaps, not so much exaggeration after all when the terrible-tempered Lambert A. Wilmer listed no fewer than twenty-one editorial duels in his book attacking the press; not such a great degree of artistic license in Mark Twain's *Journalism in Tennessee*, wherein a cub reporter was told: "In case of accident, go to Lancet, the surgeon, downstairs. He advertises; we take it out in trade."

It was this kind of high-minded, strident, election-conscious journalism which, in 1835, literally began to feel an electric stirring. The appearance of the telegraph, in that year, unlocked the door to the entire country for the newspaperman. Until it came, current news was the property only of the city room; a story with a fresh dateline could come from whatever point a reporter's shoe leather and curiosity could reach in a day. News from places beyond had to be rummaged from the mailbag, and while the steam locomotive sliced helpfully into the mailbag's travel time, it could not keep up with dots and dashes. "This agency," wrote James Gordon Bennett at the time, "will be productive of the most extraordinary effects on society, government, commerce and the progress of civilization." [14] Bennett liked to hurry along an effect, and he promptly dropped his existing venture, scraped together five hundred dollars, and founded the *Herald*. Along with his borrowed money, Bennett had a borrowed idea to go on. A New York contemporary named Moses Beach was at that time attempting to sell his paper, *The Sun*, at the reduced price of a penny a copy. His idea was to establish a workingman's paper, an objective which was announced with the usual dithyrambs about the elevation of the laboring classes. He was also seeking for that "mass market" which was shortly to become the Holy Grail of American industry.

Bennett took up this notion, and bringing to the *Herald* his own considerable energy and craggy personality made it the foundation of a revolution. He never feared inconsistency, and was armor-plated against abuse. The *Herald*, from its birth, was as peppery as a Mexican supper, and as intimate as a bathrobe. Its pages were soon blooming with police-court reports, details of murders and offenses against morality of an interesting nature, blow-by-blow write-ups of bare-knuckle prize fights, stock market reports, gossip,

[14] William A. Dill, "Growth of Newspapers in the United States," *Bulletin of the Department of Journalism of the University of Kansas* (Topeka, 1928), p. 53.

and the most up-to-date news that money could procure. Bennett hunted feverishly and with brassy publicity for news, and he showered his irreverent comment on politicians, reformers, and issues so unceasingly that the entire newspaper profession rapidly came to hate him for the tonic which he was forcing down their throats. Late in the forties, a New York manufacturer of printing equipment, Richard M. Hoe, made a vast addition to the swelling popularity of the newspaper. His invention of a rotary press which quadrupled the rate at which sheets could be gotten out helped to spread the penny paper to Boston, Philadelphia, and Baltimore.

But while that was happening, Bennett had found a new world to conquer. There had been newspaper correspondents in Washington since Jackson's administration — men of a certain top-heavy and didactic stamp, "neither eavesdroppers nor interviewers," as one of them put it, "but gentlemen, who had a recognized position in society, which they never abused." Erastus Brooks, who covered the capital in Old Hickory's time for the *New York Express*, was one of the editors of the paper, a dual role which would have appeared rather pleasant to a later generation of reporters who had no position in society to abuse. Samuel Knapp, of the *Boston Gazette*, was trained as a lawyer; Matthew L. Davis was a wealthy, retired South American trader.[15] They were all presumably of sufficiently high caste to merit invitations to Congressional dinner tables, but a ruling lobbied through by Washington newspapers barred the

[15] Poore, *Reminiscences*, I, 57, 60, 260, 400.

House and Senate galleries to reporters from offices outside the District. In 1841 Bennett wrote to Henry Clay, asking for the distinguished Senator's help in removing the "illiberal and injurious" rule. Clay, a master politician, perhaps guessed that already the *Herald* was useful to have on one's side. He went to work and the rule fell. *Herald* reporters, followed by others, soon moved in and the solons rapidly accustomed themselves to orating for a national audience. Within a few years, telegraphic correspondence from Washington was making the morning edition of every metropolitan journal.[16]

The notion that a reporter on the end of a wire to a distant and newsworthy spot was a profitable investment quickly took root in the minds of those editors whose establishments were fortunate enough to afford expenses of a novel kind. What could be done in Washington could be done elsewhere, and there were places in plenty which ranked with it in news appeal. War with Mexico, the rush to the gold fields, constant harassing outbursts of near warfare between British and Americans in Central America, revolutions and conflicts in Europe — all these were tests of the enterprise of newspapers. Bennett, Greeley and others were presently seeing fit to arrange for regular letters, and wires when possible, from continental parliaments, Western mining camps and roving naval squadrons. In 1850, the *New York Tribune* had three regular corre-

[16] Carlson, *Bennett*, pp. 206-207; see also, for a discussion of this process of expanding the limits of journalistic cognizance, Charles H. Levermore, "The Rise of Metropolitan Journalism," *American Historical Review*, VI (1900-1901), 446-465.

spondents in Washington. It had signed agreements for periodical letters with two residents of California, and one each in Philadelphia, Baltimore and Boston. These were supposed to watch politics and markets for New York readers. It had four agents in European capitals, two in Canada, one in Mexico, another in Cuba, and one who roamed through Central America. Expenses shot upwards so quickly that by 1858 New York City's papers had already formed a local Associated Press in an effort to lower the cost of the service. Two years later, Bennett boasted that his bill for one September week's special dispatches came to $1275, and that his telegraph expenses for the year would run to more than $50,000. That was precisely one hundred times what he had laid out a quarter of a century before to begin the paper.[17]

Inside of twenty years the collection of news had already become the central and dominating task of journalism. But new outlooks and new ambitions had not changed the traditions of the profession overnight. The average newspaper still thought of itself politically as the life of the party. It still counted an occasional bloody nose as part of the normal cost of reform, and it still cherished the notion that God had a particular interest in its success in spurring on progress. When the reporter, a new man, joined its staff, he picked up these ruling ideas along with his assignments, an elementary knowledge of printing, and his thin

[17] Bleyer, *Main Currents in American Journalism,* p. 221; *New York Herald,* September 17, 1860.

wages. It could be expected that he would move with events as well as chart them, take a few liberties with the lesser truths in pursuit of the larger ones, and pass unrepressed partisan judgments upon affairs with considerable *élan.* His writing was florid; it jingled with euphemisms and its clauses were strung together like the joints of a caterpillar, but there was enough sting in his ideas to make his stories stimulating reading.

Issues and events were being prepared for him to meet. Every morning, new names were transcribed from the telegraphers' penciled scrawl, and turned into small type packing the eight-column pages — Oregon, California, Mexico, Nicaragua. Each was a log on the blaze of sectional argument. A young man who served his apprenticeship as a shorthand reporter or printer in the early eighteen-fifties entered on the duties of a reporter with glowing opportunities to put political awareness, idealism, and vigor to work.

National elections came in 1856 — automatically a year ripe for trouble. At the very beginning of it, ominous stories were appearing from the territory of Kansas, opened to settlement since 1854. There had been elections for a legislature, bad blood between factions divided on the inescapable issue of slavery, angry claims of fraud, and then shootings. Patently, things were happening once more in the West. Editors swung around in their chairs and scribbled notes; reporters boarded trains and steamboats and headed West to cover Kansas.

CHAPTER II

Kansas: Tryout for the Reporters

THE Kansas story was an old production with a new cast. Americans had been crowding into open lands to the west for more than three centuries, following the lure of fresh soil and the bent of their spirits. But in the opening of Kansas, in 1854 a new set of characters had joined the troupe. There were politicians, aiming to manufacture a President or Presidents, as there were sharp-eyed promoters, aiming to manufacture a railroad. Besides the traditional land-starved and trigger-happy frontiersmen there were New England parsons and editors who sensed that there was a new Canaan to wrest from the Jebusites and Hivites of Missouri. There were firebrands of the Southern variety, seeing in Kansas the last test of whether or not the Union would "protect them in their rights." In a setting of tent-and-shanty towns and bare prairies dotted with sod houses, the forces opposed to each other measured their strength — the South, rural, conservative and paranoiac over its threatening race problem, and the North, rushing ahead on the current of industrialism and centralization, its social structure wracked by tremors of unrest and reform.

The drama gained force in the sultry atmosphere of its performance. At stake were political and economic dominations and powers, but Americans of the fifties were not accustomed to fit institutions and events — nullification, the tariff, California, the Fugitive Slave Law — into their economic and social context. They were prone to see them against a background of Christianity, progress or sin. The age took its tone both from Walter Scott and *The Pilgrim's Progress.* In the blaze of argument, complex notions of human, legal and social rights, federalism and constitutional government were melted and recast, to appear in the shape of figures as readily comprehensible as Christian and Faithful and Mr. Worldly-Wise — the Slave Power, Uncle Tom, Hosea Biglow.

Under such lowering skies, happenings in Kansas threw grotesque shadows. Genuine clashes of a small civil war were difficult to separate from the claim jumpings, the lynchings, the horse thefts of the "ordinary" frontier. The newly born profession of journalism might have discovered here a chance to throw light on affairs, to restore perspective as it dispelled the shade, in which the intensely practical and frequently amoral horse trading of democratic politics could no longer be conducted. But the challenge was not taken. The reporters sent to Kansas by the metropolitan journals wrote amid the time-hallowed insanity of an election year, and under the weight of their own upbringing. They wrote as actors, not spectators, and many believed that truth *could* be put to flight in a free and open encounter unless it received at least some assistance. They sallied forth to depict a contest between freedom and tyranny in the impressive arena "beyond the Mississippi." The results boded ill for the caving Union.

One calls the roll of Kansas reporters, looking vainly for the cool, mature detachment of the skilled and experienced observer. One finds, instead, men like James Redpath. Redpath was twenty-one in 1855 when he came to the territory. Already he was the author of fervid articles damning slavery in a Detroit paper, and this training together with a mastery of printing apparently commended him as Kansas correspondent to the editors of the St. Louis *Missouri Democrat*, *Chicago Tribune* and *New York Tribune*.[1] When he got to the contested area he made connections which resulted in his being chosen as "reporter" and apparently as a delegate (for he spoke unstintedly on at least one motion) to the first two conventions of the Free State faction. He became an intimate of Charles Robinson, chosen "governor" by the Free State men, who was so impressed with his young friend's qualities as an "indomitable friend of the oppressed" that when guerrilla fighting flickered across the territory, in the summer of 1856, he commissioned him a "major" in the Free State army.[2] In this capacity he met (and came to worship) John Brown and served for a time as "adjutant" to James H.

[1] Charles F. Horner, *The Life of James Redpath and the Development of the Modern Lyceum* (New York, 1926), p. 17.
[2] Daniel W. Wilder, *The Annals of Kansas* (Topeka, 1886), pp. 84-85; *New York Tribune*, January 29, 1856; Charles Robinson, *The Kansas Conflict* (New York, 1892), p. 182; Horner, *James Redpath*, p. 96.

Lane, picturesque political freebooter who carried fire and sword to the proslavery counties of Missouri. Three years later, the youthful warrior explained why. "I believed that a civil war . . . would ultimate in [slave] insurrection and that the Kansas troubles would probably create a military conflict," he wrote. "Hence I . . . went to Kansas; *and endeavored, personally and by my pen, to precipitate a revolution.*" (When the Civil War finally came, Redpath edited a newspaper in Boston and meekly preached that it was "not the blood of the slaveholder, but the blood of the Redeemer" that would free the slave.)[3]

That was one Kansas reporter. One looks further and finds William A. Phillips, bellwether of Horace Greeley's flock. The Scotch-born Phillips had tried law and editing before he moved on to the more stimulating atmosphere of Kansas, to become a Free State knight-errant and the correspondent of the *New York Tribune*, which, with a circulation of some 170,000, shook opinion throughout the free States with its broadsides. The *Tribune* had no illusions about the objectivity of its man; he was in Kansas "not only to write well, but . . . to fight well," it once asserted. Phillips's letters to the paper were hastily gathered into a volume, *The Conquest of Kansas by Missouri and Her Allies* (the Democrats in Congress), dedicated to freeing the territory from the "iron grasp" of slavery. It was published opportunely for the Republican campaign of 1856.

[3] James Redpath, *The Roving Editor; or, Talks with the Slaves in the Southern States* (New York, 1859), p. 300, italics supplied; St. Louis *Missouri Republican*, January 10, 1862.

Phillips's reward came after the war, in a Congressional seat from Kansas.[4]

One finds Thomas Wentworth Higginson, corresponding for the *New York Tribune* over the signature "Worcester." Harvard Divinity School and a spell of preaching in Massachusetts had apparently prepared him for a contemplative life. But in those days God was sending down to the pulpit curious instructions for the improvement of society, and presently Higginson was participating in a Boston riot to free a captured fugitive slave, and then posting to Kansas where, in addition to journalistic chores for Greeley, he shepherded Free State settlers across the border for the Massachusetts Emigrant Aid Society. Despite his journalistic preoccupations, he kept a diary to which he could confide, on a September day in 1856, that things then looked "discouragingly safe," and the settlers in his care feared "marching in without a decent excuse for firing anything at anybody."[5]

Or one finds Richard Hinton, penning passionate stories from Kansas, under the nom de plume of "Kent," for the *Boston Traveller*, *Chicago Tribune* and *New York Post.* An emigrant from London (he would always mention his origin in "Hold Hingland" on introduction, snorted an old settler who found his letters "sensational" years later),

[4] Kansas State Historical Society, "Memorial Proceedings on Colonel William A. Phillips," *Transactions,* V (1889-1896), 100-113; Jeter A. Isely, *Horace Greeley and the Republican Party, 1853-1861* (Princeton, 1947), p. 338; *New York Tribune,* January 26, 1856; William A. Phillips, *The Conquest of Kansas by Missouri and Her Allies* (Boston, 1856), p. 414.

[5] Wilder, *Annals of Kansas,* p. 139; Mary T. Higginson (ed.), *Letters and Journals of Thomas Wentworth Higginson, 1846-1906* (Boston, 1921), pp. 140-141.

Hinton soon became a member of the Free State legislature, which contended for recognition as the sole legitimate government. It suited him. He and Redpath were devoted to the task of "fighting slavery with every weapon obtainable."[6] So dedicated, as well, were two professional colleagues, Richard Realf and John H. Kagi. Realf was still another Englishman, twenty-two years old in 1856, a writer of verses, midway through a life clouded by domestic bitterness and religious insecurity. In Kansas he took a part apparently far out of character, as a roughly dressed trooper of James Lane, and corresponded for several Eastern papers. He was drawn by his work into the fatal orbit of John Brown. Both he and John Kagi, three years his junior, were to have cabinet posts in the republic of freed slaves and their friends that was planned by Brown. Kagi, an ex-schoolteacher, marched with Brown and Lane while covering Kansas for the *Washington National Era* and the *New York Post*, edited by the aging but sturdy William Cullen Bryant. Realf was not on Brown's last raid, but Kagi died, at twenty-four, in a crackle of gunfire in the streets of Harpers Ferry.[7]

One scans the list further to find Samuel F. Tappan, a self-described Massachusetts abolitionist and "mechanic,"

[6] Wilder, *Annals of Kansas,* pp. 165, 171; Eli Moore, Jr., "The Naming of Osawatomie, and Some Experiences with John Brown," Kansas State Historical Society, *Collections,* XII (1911-1912), 345; Richard B. Hinton, *John Brown and His Men* (New York, 1894), pp. 40-42.

[7] Rossiter Johnson, "Richard Realf," *Lippincott's Magazine,* XXIII (1879), 293-300; James Redpath, *The Public Life of Capt. John Brown* (Boston, 1860), p. 231; Thomas Featherstonhaugh, "John Brown's Men: The Lives of Those Killed at Harper's Ferry," Southern History Association, *Publications,* III (1899), 288-289.

corresponding for the four-year-old *New York Times.* Writing for the same paper were James M. Winchell and William Hutchinson. Winchell was a Republican of such priestly caste that in 1864 he was to lead a brief Presidential boom for Salmon P. Chase, whom he found to be a more faithful party servitor than Lincoln. Hutchinson, a Vermonter, was sent back to the East by Free State officials in November of 1856, when burnt offerings grew lean, to pass the hat and recruit settlers among the friends of Freedom. [8]

These were some of the men through whose eyes metropolitan readers witnessed Kansas. (In small towns, editors waited hopefully to reprint the letters of local emigrants.) They had, many of them, a talent for gusty prose, and infinite sincerity. But they were writing from a frontier, and the frontier was a place of short tempers, argued claims, flouted laws, violent political bombast, and magnificent exaggerations. As interpreters of it, New York and New England abolitionist schoolteachers, lawyers, preachers and pamphleteers, some with the fuzz of adolescence hardly off their cheeks, could offer zeal in plenty but little true insight of a kind to cut through a complex tangle of economic and social conflicts.

Certain editors, with an eye on the approaching elections, were content to have it so. "We cannot admit Kansas as a

[8] Wilder, *Annals of Kansas*, pp. 85, 142-143, 164, 261, 281; Richard J. Hinton, "Pens That Made Kansas Free," Kansas State Historical Society, *Collections*, VI (1897-1900), 371-382; William Hutchinson, "Sketches of Kansas Pioneer Experiences," Kansas State Historical Society, *Transactions*, VII (1900-1901), 392; Burton J. Hendrick, *Lincoln's War Cabinet* (Boston, 1946), pp. 410-415.

State. We can only make issues," Greeley wrote to his managing editor on one occasion. In making issues, he was willing to extend the boundaries of the news column to no small degree. Correspondent Hutchinson of the *New York Times* was somewhat dejected to find that his employer, Henry J. Raymond, placed journalistic duty above his solid mid-road Republicanism. He would not "tolerate any tincture of liberalism" in Kansas stories, being "just the antipodes of Greeley." (Several of the missives returned by Raymond to Hutchinson found a home in Boston papers where "liberalism" was more highly esteemed.) When Greeley visited Kansas in 1859 he advised Hutchinson to keep trying. "The *Times*," he explained, was "read by a class of people who need enlightening." Readers of the *Tribune* were "right already," and required "no converting." [9] The president of the Free State "central committee" begged settlers who could use a pen to bombard newspaper offices with tales of the "atrocities" they had endured. In 1859, one of the original Free State inner circle, George W. Brown (who edited the "official" newspaper, the *Herald of Freedom*, in 1856) named Realf, Kagi, Phillips and Hinton as dangerous extremists, a fact which could not have been entirely unsuspected by the publishers for whom they wrote.[10] It could be useful, at times, to have the Free State case laid before public opinion by extremists.

[9] James Malin, *John Brown and the Legend of Fifty-Six* (Philadelphia, 1942), p. 89; Hutchinson, "Kansas Pioneer Experiences," p. 395.
[10] Malin, *John Brown and the Legend of Fifty-Six*, pp. 221, 257-258.

Hence the Kansas story unwound from the newspaper columns ("Our Latest Intelligence") in a twisted skein, the truth, the half-truth, the rumor, the accusation, the morsel of artistic license all tangled together. First came the amateurs — the local settlers such as Cole McCrea, who wrote to the *Chicago Tribune* in June, 1855, to tell of how, at a meeting controlled by proslavery men, he had raised his voice in opposition and been beaten with a plank so severely as to break his collarbone; or such as the nameless correspondents on whose testimony the editors of the same paper assured readers that the Missourians who had drifted over the State line in sufficient numbers to swing early territorial elections away from the Free State forces were guilty of "ruffianly violence, threats, brutalities, stabbings, shootings and gougings." [11] By December, however, the stage was set for the more professional efforts of men like Redpath, or one of his co-workers for the St. Louis *Missouri Democrat.* In a series of kidnappings and raids known as the "Wakarusa War" the proslavery settlers briefly blocked access to Lawrence, the Free State capital. A siege was palpably the stuff of romance, and the newspaper public had vicariously (and safely) enjoyed that of Sevastopol for a year past. Now the *Democrat* carried the tale of a brace of daring Free State ladies who had ridden through the "lines" unchallenged by the "ruffian" Missourians, visited friends and returned. Their petticoats had, however, been hung with powder bags and their stockings bulged with per-

[11] *Chicago Tribune,* June 14, May 5, 1855.

cussion caps when they were welcomed home by the defenders. For color such a story even overtopped that of a *New York Tribune* scribe who reported the tarring of a Free State resident and asked that rifles (paid for by subscription) be rushed into Kansas by the portentous date of "the 'ides of March' next." It lent more sting to the *Chicago Tribune's* "headline" (of standard one-column width) over a story filed at Lawrence, "IMPORTANT FROM THE SEAT OF WAR!" [12]

Redpath knew, too, the value of an atrocity story rendered at first hand. In April he sent in, with one of his own stories, the letter of one, Reverend Pardee Butler, recently tarred and feathered at Atchinson for voicing what some Missourians considered dangerous thoughts on slavery. His tormentors, Reverend Butler revealed with a pardonable shudder of retrospect, had worn "the look of a Cuban bloodhound, just ready . . . to seize a panting slave in a Florida swamp." Accounts of such flesh-creeping deeds were at home in the files of news from Kansas, where tales were told of armed ruffians robbing merchants' wagons, searching travelers, looting homes and even, in one instance, allegedly falling on an emigrant with knives and hatchets and spitting tobacco juice into his eyes as he lay dying.[13] Greeley's paper, pillar of "liberalism" that it was (as the furore of the Presidential campaign heightened), was preeminent in coverage of events of this kind. Stories from Kan-

[12] *Missouri Democrat,* quoted in *Chicago Tribune,* January 4, 1856; *New York Tribune,* January 14, 1856; *Chicago Tribune,* February 18, 1856.
[13] *Chicago Tribune,* April 10, May 15, 22, 1856; *Cleveland Herald,* quoted in *New York Herald,* May 27, 1856; *New York Tribune,* May 26, 1856.

sas increased during the spring, elbowing other news in among the patent medicine advertisements, and a topical joke told of the elderly lady who vainly tried to identify a back number she desired with a triumphant cry: "I think it had something about *Kansas* in it!"

When the occurrence in the territory itself rose above the murderous commonplaces of partisan warfare the reporters' stories took on scope and artistry. On the 21st of May, 1856, a proslavery posse, joined by several irregular "militia" units, entered Lawrence, dismantled the presses of the two Free State newspapers and tumbled them into the Kaw River, looted the home of "Governor" Robinson and set fire to the empty Free State hotel, headquarters of many incoming emigrants and the itinerate editors, politicians and Congressional investigators visiting Kansas on behalf of freedom that year. Liquor flowed, and some shops and homes were broken into. It was hoodlums' work, poorly dignified by political origins and the writ of a "court" established by the proslavery territorial government. Nevertheless, there were only two casualties — both accidental — and relatively slight damage.

In the lurid paragraphs of the Kansas correspondents, however, the "sack of Lawrence" ranked high in the record books of barbarity. One *New York Tribune* reporter claimed to have galloped out of town, "his midnight pathway . . . lighted by a pyramid of fire." Others among his journalistic co-workers spoke of Missourians "firing at the houses with their artillery," of residents "disarmed, robbed, plundered and shot down," of attackers firing "by platoons" at the hotel, heedless of "the women and children fleeing in every direction." One had "no doubt" that the town was "in ashes and many of its inhabitants butchered." A pious newsman, one of a breed then more common, lamented "that God's beautiful earth contained such savages," and the prolific Redpath counted not only two cases of rape but two hundred stolen horses — a matter almost equally serious on the empty frontier of plains where a man without a mount was completely helpless.[14] Redpath was also one of several who recorded the alleged remarks of onetime Missouri Senator David Atchison, who was present, urging the proslavery warriors into the breach.

> Faint not as you approach the city of Lawrence; but, remembering your mission, act with true Southern heroism, and at the word, spring like your bloodhounds at home, upon that damned Abolition hole. . . . Yes, Ruffians! draw your daggers and bowie-knives, and warm them in the heart's blood of all those damned dogs that dare defend that dammed [*sic*] breathing hole of hell. . . .
>
> Boys! do the Marshal's full bidding . . . and for it you shall be amply paid as United States' troops, besides having an opportunity of benefiting your wardrobes from the private dwellings of those infernal nigger-stealers. . . .
>
> Are you determined? Will every one of you swear to bathe your steel in the black blood of some of those black sons of B——s?
>
> Yes, I know you will; the South has always proved itself ready for honorable fight, and you who are noble

[14] *New York Tribune,* May 30, June 2, 5, 1856; *Missouri Democrat,* quoted in *New York Tribune,* May 30, 1856; *Chicago Tribune,* quoted in *New York Tribune,* June 9, 1856.

> sons of noble sires, I know will never fail; but will burn, sack and destroy until every vestige of these Northern Abolitionists is wiped out!

Atchison, by no means the last man to have the albatross of a newspaper story hung about his neck, was still attempting to deny that speech years later. Even *Tribune* reporter Phillips charitably judged that all printed versions of it were "more or less incorrect." [15]

The effect of these stories, falling like showers of coal dust into the furnace of election debate, was probably immense. In Kansas itself, the "sack" set off a new train of cruelties, beginning on the night of May 24th when John Brown and a group of his men murdered five proslavery settlers in cold blood. At least one *New York Tribune* reporter sent in a version of the killing in which it was made to appear that half a dozen or more of the "enemy" had been caught in the act of lynching a Free State resident, and that the five deaths had occurred in the ensuing skirmish. Meantime, reporter Phillips's letters had gotten him an unenviable renown among the Missourians, and he wrote to his paper to reveal that he was in hiding for his life — "proscribed and hunted like a wild beast." While he palpitated in seclusion, other journalistic pens outlined what Redpath, with some lack of originality, described as a "Reign of Terror." In their outpourings, rings were snatched from the fingers of Free State womenfolk, men

[15] *Chicago Tribune*, July 15, 1856; Phillips, *The Conquest of Kansas*, pp. 295-296; Atchison is quoted in James C. Malin, "The Proslavery Background of the Kansas Struggle," *Mississippi Valley Historical Review*, X (1923), 304, in his denial.

were bound and left on the prairie to die of thirst, and anti-slavery farmers were robbed of their livestock, dragged from their homes, and pulled up on tiptoe at ropes' ends until they promised to leave Kansas. Free State prisoners from one clash were marched twenty-five miles afoot, under a blazing sun, loaded with chains; and on the wide Missouri, armed "Ruffians" turned back Kansas-bound steamboats — proving (according to one correspondent) that the North was "*subjugated* and *subdued*." [16]

The summer of 1856 was often cruel — cruel as the incidents of a civil war conducted without rules could make it; and cruelty, truthful or exaggerated, leaped from each morning's newspaper pages, as Eastern readers unfolded them, adding what was to become a familiar note to popular journalism. There was a story of three "Ruffians" who had killed an emigrant by stamping on his belly with their boots. There was another of "Ruffians" who cut down a Free State man with ten bullets and then slit his throat. There was one horrible tale told of a German farmer who was shot dead in the streets of Leavenworth by a proslavery man. The murderer then scalped him, and, according to one version, paraded his sticky trophy through the town on a pole. An account of the capture of Frederick Brown (John Brown's son) said that, as he writhed on the ground in the agony of his mortal wounds, a gun was jammed into his mouth and fired. Still one more letter filed from the terri-

[16] *Chicago Tribune*, quoted in *New York Tribune*, June 12, 1856; *New York Tribune*, June 5, 13, 14, 16, July 7, 1856; *Worcester* [*Massachusetts*] *Spy*, quoted in *New York Tribune*, July 9, 1856.

tory told of a young Indiana woman who, while returning from what delicacy styled "one of the outbuildings in the rear of the house" one night, was seized, ravished, kicked viciously in the abdomen and left for dead. This last outrage, according to the reporter of it, showed the hollowness of the claim "that negro slavery elevates the character of the whites." [17]

The proslavery press, in its Kansas coverage, was not nearly so shrill, voluminous or stimulating. This was not altogether the result of a nicer regard for truth. The more hustling metropolitan journals were concentrated in the rising cities of the North. Then, too, the Southern position had it that most of the Kansas agitation was manufactured by "fanatics" specifically for purposes of publicity. Even if the territorial body politic was somewhat restless, it was far from convulsive, and entirely undeserving of the anxiety focused upon it. Hence, as one editor pointed out two years after the worst of the troubles, "the republicans [*sic*] . . . enjoyed a monopoly of the manufacture of Kansas news." [18]

The Kansas correspondents of the more excitable North-

[17] *Chicago Tribune*, August 16, September 5, 1856; *New York Tribune*, August 21, 29, September 8, 1856; *New York Tribune*, quoted in *Chicago Tribune*, September 9, 1856; *Missouri Democrat*, quoted in *Chicago Tribune*, September 8, 1856; *Rochester Democrat*, quoted in *New York Tribune*, September 15, 1856; *Missouri Democrat*, quoted in *New York Tribune*, August 30, 1856.

[18] *New York Herald*, February 27, 1858. The occasion for the comment was the dispatch by the *Herald* of a reporter to Kansas. The *Herald*, which had not lacked for resources in 1856, confessed its error. "Had the democratic organs in the North," it said, "had the energy and enterprise to send correspondents of their own to Kansas, the agitation might long since have been checked."

ern papers used their "monopoly" not only in politically rewarding attacks on public sensibilities through their vigorous tales of violence, but in a general defamation of a postulated "Southern character." The proslavery settlers were sketched with all the features of the comic hillbilly of a subsequent day — hard-drinking, picturesquely unlettered and mortally fearful of work. But the humor was a thin casing around an explosive charge. Readers educated to a gospel of willing industriousness and self-improvement were apt to feel that lazy, self-indulgent and ignorant opponents dwelt too uncomfortably close to damnation for laughter.

There were, therefore, seeds of civil war in the letters of correspondents who, between paragraphs of blood-and-thunder rhetoric, described the "Missourians" as "hard-featured and whiskey-flavored . . . obscene, depraved, brutish . . . ignorant and unpolished." The nameless reporter who declared that "an incalculable amount of whiskey" had been provided for an incoming group of Southern volunteers for the "war" was in his own way contributing to what Greeley might have styled the "enlightenment" of public opinion. It was to be expected that Redpath would have a story on the subject, and in May he submitted an account of a curious odyssey up the Missouri on a steamboat with a full passenger list of what he described as "scions of the first families of South Carolina, Alabama [and] Louisiana," all "educated to despise labor." Their entertainments had consisted, according to the chronicler, in unabated drinking, sham combat with the bowie knife, and the occasional discharge of a pistol into the still frontier air. It was presumably these same scions, disembarked in Kansas to contest the soil with the Free State emigrants, who were described by other reporters as "lazy, loafing, cursing and whisky-swilling," living "an indolent camp life . . . abominably filthy." [19]

To judge by the correspondents, this represented a successful adjustment to Missourian mores, for the river towns which they surveyed from steamboat decks in their journeys to Kansas were inhabited by "dirty, unwashed, unshaven and unshorn scamps," and "groggery hangers-on." One newsman of more than ordinary descriptive power summarized matters:

> They are a queer-looking set, slightly resembling human beings, but more closely allied, in general appearance, to wild beasts. An old rickety straw hat, ragged shirt, buttonless corduroys with a leather belt and a coarse pair of mud-covered boots constitute a "full dress." They never shave or comb their hair, and their chief occupation is loafing round whiskey shops, squirting tobacco juice, and whittling with a dull jack-knife. They drink whiskey for a living, and sleep on dry goods boxes — are all "national democrats," and delight in robbing hen roosts. . . . They generally carry a huge bowie-knife and a greasy pack of cards, and . . . frequently spend the night . . . in some convenient mudhole. Their conversation is interspersed with original oaths, and generally ends in a free

[19] *Chicago Tribune*, January 5, March 25, May 16, 1856; *New York Tribune*, March 21, 1856; *New York Times*, February 25, 1856; *Chicago Democratic Press*, quoted in *New York Tribune*, May 10, 1856; *New York Tribune*, June 13, August 16, 1856.

> fight. They are "down on" schools, churches and printing offices, and revel in ignorance and filth.[20]

Clearly an audience which believed with reasonable solidarity in the divine origin and responsibility of mankind would have qualms over delivering Kansas into hands such as these.

Events took their course in Kansas and Washington, and, as the months passed, the troubles in the territory shrank into proportion against the threatening background of larger sectional deadlocks. Meantime, however, ominous images, sketched in part by the reporter, waxed in the public mind. Was every Southerner a slave-beater or the drunken tool of one? Did every "Yankee" keep a set of false scales and a picture of John Brown on his mantelpiece? Conceptions fully as unrealistic took deeper root as editors bartered off pride and confidence in the Union, bit by bit, for election advantages, and propagandists transformed countrymen of other sections from quarrelsome next-door neighbors into enemies of all that was worthwhile in the human spirit.

The Kansas correspondents who traveled westward already dedicated to abolition principles, prepared to find torture, murder and fire, had played a significant role. They had helped to cut the crumbling ground from beneath the few harried moderates of 1856. In a young America fizzing with impulsive conceit, romantic hopes and implacable evangelism, the prospects of moderation were dispiriting at best, but it was doubly certain that no

[20] *Chicago Tribune*, March 25, April 13, 14, 20, 1857.

long-range proposal of racial and economic adjustment, demanding patience and concession of all parties, could spring from soil scorched by hate propaganda. The stories marshaled in the Kansas news columns had riveted more firmly in some minds the notion that the sections were at odds over issues of pure right and wrong. The notion was a wall, confronting any compromise set in motion.

It was not altogether correct for a New York journal to charge Greeley with the blame "*for the blood which has been shed in Kansas . . . and for all that is bitter and ferocious in the modern school of politics.*" [21] Still, the Kansas reporter, in his muddy boots and coarse shirt — the Kansas reporter who had buttonholed impatient politicians in the dirt streets of Leavenworth and Topeka and Lawrence — the Kansas reporter who had been a thrilling visitor to thousands of New York and New England breakfast tables, had made what resembled a professional name for the newspaper writing that had been something of an avocation. It was not altogether an enviable name, nor one to provoke distaste. Given time, it might grow and assume character, and time and opportunity were at hand. ". . . *all that is bitter and ferocious.*" Bully Brooks, Lecompton, Harpers Ferry — soon these names, freshly inked on the front page, would be part of the daily consciousness of millions. There was work for reporters to do.

[21] *New York Express,* quoted in Albert J. Beveridge, *Abraham Lincoln, 1809-1858* (Boston, 1928), II, 407.

CHAPTER III

The Reporters Become Professionals

ONE April day in 1858, the *New York Tribune* broke a story that must have greatly satisfied its editor, Horace Greeley, a fierce competitor and a man of more than ordinary self-righteousness. The city's Board of Supervisors had voted a two-hundred-dollar "gratuity" to seven metropolitan reporters for certain nebulous "services rendered to the Common Council." No *Tribune* man was involved, which enabled the paper to be comfortably outraged. It spoke sharply of "bribery," and ran a letter signed "A Reporter," the burden of which was that this was nothing new. "A Reporter" had known at least one colleague who had accepted "a golden-headed cane from a used up politician" to palliate in print "a gross and unjustifiable assault committed at the Capitol"; a gold watch from "a Tombs lawyer to place his name conspicuously before the public"; and a weekly salary, plus free passes, from the proprietor of one of the city's theaters. There was even, he declared, "a regular and well-organized system of blackmail" worked by the unscrupulous newsman on the officials of the Court of Sessions, from the District Attorney through the clerks of the courts, all of whom were supposedly willing to shore themselves up against adverse publicity by such payments.[1] A moment in journalistic history was thus frozen into the record; the reporter was making his way into the inner circles of municipal politics and business.

It was only part of a professional education that was proceeding amid cloudy circumstances. The constant alarms and excursions on which the maturing press fed, and which demanded coverage as never before, furnished lessons both in the organization of news services and the uses of propaganda. In the nation at large, the labored processes of political adjustments between sections were grinding to a stop. North and South, the political bosses, the professors, the lawyers, the socially awakened ministers and the articulate businessmen mouthed the old slogans and dug the last ditches. Events were becoming meaningless in themselves, and noteworthy only as they symbolized to each side the other's native wickedness. Newspapermen, under any circumstances, would have had trouble enough in attempting to fix the shape of happenings as they really were. And yet they themselves were caught in the collapsed scaffolding of national unity. At the same time, the instruments of their trade were changing form in their hands; newspapers were hiring more men, sending them further, buying more machines, swallowing more capital, making more readers. In part town criers, in part pamphleteers, and in part managers of modern business enterprises, the editors had enough trouble viewing themselves in perspective, let alone national affairs.

[1] *New York Tribune*, April 28, 1858.

Their confusion was felt throughout their organizations, not yet too overgrown for them to control entirely. Few could be more sensitive to it than the reporters, who, as newcomers, had no status on which to fall back in an argument. It was not a question of writing as they pleased. If they did not please, they might not have the chance to write at all. Their entry into journalism was somewhat sidelong. Some of them began, apparently, as constant readers whose notes to the editor were good enough to earn an offer of payment for more. Some were fortunate enough to live in regions which suddenly flowered into newsworthiness; they were sought out by metropolitan journals on the basis of their contributions to local gazettes, perhaps, and compacted with for a fixed number of chatty letters. Some had to fall back on undisguised self-promotion, like hopeful young actors buttonholing producers for the chance to do a reading.

There was, for example, the case of a young German immigrant named Heinrich Villgard, who, when he was not yet of voting age, opened a brief career in journalism by sending a letter to a New York German-language paper, the *Neue Zeit*, "at a venture." The letter described the political situation in Wisconsin, a State whose heavily Teutonic population made its fortunes a matter of large interest in the German-speaking neighborhoods of Manhattan. The report was so satisfactory that the *Neue Zeit* printed it and asked for more, at five dollars apiece. Villgard furnished them, and presently, heartened by his successes, made his way to New York and the office of Charles

A. Dana, the managing editor of the *New York Tribune*. The young immigrant, who had now Americanized his name to Henry Villard, struck a bargain with Dana to pay him twelve dollars of the *Tribune's* money for every column of news which he could supply on a visit to Minnesota. He also visited the *New York Post*, and tried to cajole it into shipping him to India to cover the great mutiny of 1857. The *Post* declined, though it helpfully offered him twenty dollars a letter if he could contrive to get himself to the scene. The twenty-one-year-old Villard turned westward again instead, and arranged with the *Cincinnati Commercial* to send him to Pike's Peak to file some stories from the newly opened mining camps there. In the next year, Villard — whose talent for making contacts was impressive — succeeded in forming a friendship with Lincoln, on the strength of which he sent to the *New York Herald* a number of stories which furnished many Eastern readers with their first detailed information about the Illinois lawyer when he became President-elect.

At the beginning of the war, Villard came into his own. He settled in Washington and became a one-man press service, turning out dispatches for the *Tribune*, *Herald* and *Commercial* at a combined weekly take of fifty dollars. Although he saw considerable action as a war correspondent, Villard was plainly too gifted a promoter to remain forever a newspaper writer; when he died, thirty-five years after the war, he was a millionaire railroad financier. His fruitful example was evidently pursued by other young writers whose judgment of the market was less acute. In the late fifties, Horace Greeley was obliged to warn youthful travelers that they could not count on financing trips across Europe by letters sent to home-town papers, and in 1860 the staid *National Intelligencer*, of Washington, begged the "patience, pardon and pity" of voluntary correspondents, for whose offerings the already glutted columns could provide no space.[2]

The self-hired correspondent was not necessarily one who devoted his entire energies to his craft. In 1857, the Federal government was involved in an acidulous dispute with Brigham Young and his followers, over the title to all the lands of Utah. Late in the year, a military expedition was sent out to uproot the Mormons from the new Zion. It spent a miserable, unsheltered winter on the plains before the spring brought a settlement. Its progress was reported intermittently in the ever-enterprising *New York Herald* by special correspondents, one of whom happened to be an infantry captain of thirty-odd named Jesse A. Gove. Captain Gove was a West Pointer from New Hampshire, whose crisp but affectionate letters to his wife showed a wholesome versatility; he studded brief commands to Mrs. Gove on the employment of her leisure time with paragraphs on botany, zoology, music and politics. He was also especially interested in attracting the attention of ex-President Franklin Pierce, a New Hampshire native son, whose acquaintance would presumably be helpful to a young officer. The *Herald* had been one of Pierce's sup-

[2] Henry Villard, *Memoirs* (New York, 1904), I, 63-64, 73-79, 98, 153-154; Horace Greeley, *Recollections of a Busy Life* (New York, 1868), pp. 325-326; *Triweekly National Intelligencer*, March 3, 1860.

porters during his trying administration, from 1853 to 1857. In addition, the New York paper must have made gratifying reading for the captain when its belated numbers reached his tent. He thought that the Mormons were "worse than the banditti of Italy"; the *Herald's* editor scorned them as part of an intellectual coterie responsible for "infidelity," "socialism" and other "ridiculous vagaries." Between guard mounts, the filling of requisition forms, and the supervision of camp details, the captain found time to take his pen in hand. Presently, letters in the *Herald* under Utah datelines, signed "Argus," were appearing—letters which, besides their news content, bristled with scorn for the "fanaticism" and "vice in its most hideous forms" of that "supreme blasphemer," Brigham Young. At the same time, letters to Mrs. Gove directed her to read the correspondence of "Argus," coyly invited her to guess the identity of the writer, and then in a burst of impatience revealed the truth and thoughtfully reminded her to send clippings to ex-President Pierce, to whom she apparently had some access.[3]

The step from the role of "Constant Reader," who occasionally echoed an editorial thunderclap in a letter, to that of a regular correspondent, at least for a transient period, was an easy one. It was perhaps natural that a reporter of such origins would march in political cadence with his employer—or depart. In 1862, the *New York World* lost one of its war correspondents, a Mr. H. L.

[3] Jesse A. Gove, *The Utah Expedition* (Concord, New Hampshire, 1928), pp. 16, 61, 68-69, 164, 190-191; *New York Herald*, February 27, March 1, 1858.

Wayland, who announced by mail that as a Republican he felt it would be "wrong to conscience and . . . sense of duty" to harvest information for a journal which, at that particular moment, had next to no use for the administration.[4] The reporter still had something of the advocate, leaping into the public prints, about him — something of the "Pennsylvania Farmer," of "Novanglus," of "Publius," appealing to the world in a just cause.

It was no wonder that a first-rank newspaper's editorial tone reverberated through almost every word in it outside of the market reports and shipping news. The reporters for the *New York Tribune*, for example, could hardly ever forget the fact that they worked for a living parcel of moral energy. Horace Greeley's child was a lusty property in 1860, with a weekly circulation running into six figures, but the Vermont-born editor had little time to count his gains or his problems. In his third-floor sanctum in downtown New York, he sat on a high stool, bent near-sighted eyes over an ink-stained pine table, and ground out dozens of letters daily, plus fragments of columns, books and almost weekly lectures. Periodically he scuttled back and forth to Albany and Washington to reassure himself that the country was going to hell by neglecting his advice. He burned with "an unexpected and intense craving for office," as an unfriendly editor phrased it, "and a petulant soreness at its non-attainment." As a reformer, he did not spare the brimstone. He meant to bring order to "an

[4] Manton Marble Papers, Library of Congress, Wayland to Marble, October 13, 1862.

atrocious world . . . permeated with Democrats, and free traders, and idle folks given to drink!" Asked once if he did not wish to save sinners from hell, he snapped "No! It isn't half full enough of them now." The effect of such a personality on an editorial staff was evidently formidable. "Until good old Horace Greeley is gathered to his fathers," wrote a New York newspaperman, Junius Browne, in the late sixties, "and some man succeeds him who can be made to believe his daily opinions are not vital to the salvation of the Republic, I look for little change in the great radical organ of the New World." Browne ought to have known; for almost two years of the war he had been a *Tribune* correspondent.[5]

If Greeley himself was not sufficient example to a fledgling newspaperman of the exhilarations of what might mildly be called critical rather than narrative journalism, the entire headquarters of the paper, located in a building at Spruce and Nassau Streets, exhaled Christian endeavor. In 1854, the staff numbered 220, of whom only 130 were "full time." Even three years after the war, when the city editor alone had thirty-two reporters working for him, no more than thirteen got salaries (ranging from $15 to $35 a week); the rest worked by the line. Among the regulars, the managing editor and ten assistants comprised a

[5] Junius H. Browne, *The Great Metropolis: A Mirror of New York* (Hartford, 1869), pp. 216-217, 307; *New York World*, April 24, 1863; Jeter A. Isely, *Horace Greeley and the Republican Party, 1853-1861* (Princeton, 1947), p. 21; John Russell Young, *Men and Memories* (New York, 1901), I, 112; Don C. Seitz, *Horace Greeley* (Indianapolis, 1926), p. 27; Frederic Hudson, *Journalism in the United States, 1690-1872* (New York, 1873), p. 548.

talented and opinion-ridden group which might have overawed any piecework writer who submitted copy to them. Stout and fiftyish George Ripley, onetime Unitarian minister who had founded the transcendentalist experiment in co-operative living at Brook Farm, was there. So was another veteran of that effort to attract mid-century intellectuals back to the soil, Charles A. Dana, who corresponded with Proudhon and Marx in moments when he was not scissoring copy. Richard Hildreth, distinguished historian and apoplectic enemy of slavery, was on the editorial panel in the fifties. There was, too, a pale young man with a slight, curling beard, named Bayard Taylor — a linguist, scholar, poet and traveler of growing reputation.

William Fry, tall, pallid and intense-looking, had a desk. He was not only a sponsor of American artistic efforts, but had personally written one of the first operas by an American. In contrast, the healthy features of the agricultural editor, Solon Robinson, were framed in flowing white whiskers. Though he resembled a good-humored Isaiah, he was a veteran of the fight for free government grants of land to Western settlers, a political contest not meant for trustful amateurs.[6]

Neutrality, plainly enough, was not going to be the long suit of a newspaper whose high command was so consecrated, and the *Tribune's* Washington correspondence was perhaps the best showcase for high-minded reporting,

[6] James Parton, *The Life of Horace Greeley* (New York, 1855), pp. 395-396, 403-405; L. D. Ingersoll, *Life of Greeley* (Chicago, 1873), p. 457; Isely, *Greeley and the Republican Party*, pp. 6-10.

as the capital itself was a laboratory exhibit in political pathology. The capital correspondents were moving up in status and influence through the years. At the beginning of 1857, an observer for the *New York Times* named James W. Simonton had established himself as a forerunner of the Congressional columnists with their "inside stories" by a neat bit of muckraking. A company founded to build a railroad in Minnesota had organized a lobby which paid improper attentions to a number of accommodating Congressmen in order to secure their votes for a gigantic handout of public land. Simonton broke the story in print, scotching the movement, and impressing the legislators with the importance of a friendly press gallery. When the House adjourned on the night of March 3, the Speaker, Nathaniel P. Banks of Massachusetts, had a brief note delivered to the assembled newspapermen thanking them for their efforts, as he sonorously expressed it, "to promote the public weal." [7]

One of the leading *Tribune* men in Washington had more than the general good will of the Speaker to help lighten his professional burden. He was James S. Pike, a Calais, Maine, businessman turned journalist, doubling as a Washington correspondent for Greeley and as one of his assistant editors. In this last capacity he enjoyed a quite companionable correspondence with such first-rank Republican members of Congress as Benjamin Wade, Salmon P.

[7] Benjamin Perley Poore, *Reminiscences of Sixty Years in the National Capital* (Boston, 1886), I, 511; Augustus A. Maverick, *Henry J. Raymond and the New York Press For Thirty Years* (Hartford, 1870), pp. 104-107.

Chase and Thomas Corwin of Ohio, William P. Fessenden of his own Maine, New York's William Seward, and the redoubtable Charles Sumner of Massachusetts. Wade wrote to him once in 1858 lamenting that a recent article had appeared too late to be made use of in a scorching antislavery speech. On the 15th of April in that year Pike received a letter from Seward suggesting "a few generous words" for those Democrats who, under the lead of Stephen A. Douglas of Illinois, were threatening to break with the administration over the handling of the still tender Kansas question. At the beginning of 1860, when Pike was not present in Washington, Representative Israel Washburn, of Illinois, wrote to the editor lamenting that in his absence there was not "a single correspondent here who has understood the ground we were travelling, or . . . has not been laboring in the interest of the 'opposition' party rather than of the Republican party." [8]

The "news" columns from Washington, usually unsigned except by pen names, reflected this happy unconcern with any responsibility for presenting both sides of a story. Democratic Congressmen absorbed most of the close-in blows. The grandeur of the *Tribune* reporters' prose as it cascaded into the type sticks is unappreciable in anything except direct quotation. In March of 1858, for example, Senator Robert Toombs of Georgia made a speech advocating the admission of Kansas under a strongly proslavery constitution framed by what the Free State men

[8] James S. Pike, *First Blows of the Civil War* (New York, 1879), pp. 385, 410, 417, 483, 526.

described as a "rump government" at Lecompton. The speech was reported in the *Tribune* of the 23rd of March by "Index," who wrote in part:

> It is a sad instance of the wretched effect which the Africanization of the South has had upon even her strongest minds, that a man like Mr. Toombs should feel himself compelled to rise as he did to-day, in the face of the American Senate and the American people, and debase himself by prostituting his powers of speech and argument to the vain task of proving that to be true which he knows to be false, and that to be sound which he knows to be rotten. . . . He palpably had no confidence in his own arguments, and went through his pettifogging talk with the air of an attorney who has undertaken for a fee to defend a desperate criminal whom everybody knows to be guilty.

Nearly a year later, when a bill to provide free homesteads for settlers had passed the House in the face of sixty Democratic "nays," a nameless Washington scribe for Greeley asked the reason for the opposition and rousingly answered his own question:

> Because the Southern "Democracy," so called, is hostile to the hard hand and sweating brows of Free Labor. It sneers at free laborers, free lands, free schools, free speech, free presses and free men.[9]

Ten days after this appeared, another letter from a Congressional eyewitness described the part played by Louisiana's Senator Judah P. Benjamin in the contest over the purchase of Cuba, a scheme whose ultimate result (if not

[9] *New York Tribune,* February 4, 1859.

whose aim) — increasing the slave territory of the country — sent the Republicans into frenzies. Benjamin was described as

> small in stature; dresses carefully and neatly; has a soft, catlike step; a fawning, sinister smile; a keen, snaky eye; a look and address now bold and audacious, and then cringing and deprecatory; his whole air and mien suggesting a subdued combination of Judas Iscariot with Uriah Heep.

His speech, of course, was "false to truth, to humanity and to decency." [10] When Senator Toombs rose to speak on the same subject, his oration, *Tribune* readers learned as they rustled the crisp sheets, was the ravings of a drayman on the dock, the cursings of a common drab in a dirty alley.

> In the midst of this gust of passion, the fire-eater might be seen shaking his clenched fist and curly locks at the New York Senator, who was leaning against the doorway of the cloak-room, quietly smoking his cigar and calmly eyeing Toombs. It was a *tableau* indeed.[11]

The correspondents seemed equally capable of reversing gears and reporting the "right" speeches with an enthusiasm unpruned by any censor's scissors. A speech by Wade of Ohio, for example, emerged as

> full of marrow and grit, and enunciated with a courage which did one's heart good to hear. No mealy-mouthed phrases . . . but strong and stirring old English, that had the ring of the true metal.

[10] *New York Tribune*, February 14, 1859.
[11] *New York Tribune*, March 1, 1859.

And almost any Republican pronouncement received the same cordial description as one by Owen Lovejoy, Representative from Illinois, on the necessity of confining the further expansion of slavery. Wrote an enraptured newsman:

> For all who desire to be informed what Slavery is, and what is the answer to the various sophisms by which it is defended, Mr. Lovejoy's speech tells the story. And it does it in such a graphic and emphatic way that nobody can fail of comprehending the subject. . . . And the whole is so vitalized . . . that the pictures blaze with a fervent heat that melts the soul of the beholder.[12]

It was not particularly to be wondered at that the observation of Artemus Ward was accepted in substance by newspapermen with a somewhat attenuated appreciation of the literary arts:

> Shakspeer rote good plase, but he wouldn't hav succeeded as a Washington correspondent of a New York daily paper. He lackt the rekesit fancy and imagginashun.[13]

Outside of Washington, certain amateur reporters for the *Tribune* were also working through their journeyman years as propagandists. The news from Kansas continued hot and sputtering in Greeley's columns, although the actual fighting had given way to more conventional political reactions by 1858, and when, in 1859, the editor himself visited Lawrence on a spine-jarring, dust-caked stagecoach

[12] *New York Tribune,* March 16, 1858, April 9, 1860.
[13] Charles F. Browne, *The Complete Works of Artemus Ward* (New York, 1898), p. 28.

trip over the prairies, he was disgusted to find a rising Democratic faction with whom the Kansas Republicans were intermittently willing to deal on local matters. Greeley was stung by the "ingratitude" of the "One-Horse politicians" whom he had described as heroes of freedom some years before.[14] There was, however, plenty of stimulating reading in the copy baskets of the *Tribune* office, much of it contributed from both regular and transient correspondents in the South, ready for the presses.

The *Tribune*, more than almost any other newspaper, exulted in parading the iniquities of slavery. In part this was because opposition to the system was quite literally part of the religion of its editors. In part, it was a political stock in trade. In the North at large, abolitionism enjoyed nothing like popularity. Millions of voters — not all of them Democrats, either — regarded slavery as an unpleasant anachronism, beyond the reach of anything but time to cure. Some believed it the best possible adjustment between Southern whites and Negroes, accepting uncritically the idea of the slaves' racial inferiority; others were hopeful that it would wither away if it did not get a foothold in the new lands of the West; a few even lent their energies to well-intentioned schemes to buy the Negroes free and transport them to Africa, obviously a segregated district designed by God himself. All these Northern groups opposed immediate or violent action, but, on the other hand, not one of them numbered more than a fistful of believers in the doctrine of some extreme Southerners that

[14] *New York Tribune*, June 2, 1859; Greeley, *Recollections*, pp. 360-367.

slavery was a positive good and a molder of civilization — a gospel to which they clung like drowning men to a spar while the waves of the nineteenth century broke over them. North of the Mason Dixon line, hardly a soul would argue the nonexistent moral case for slavery.

This meant that for politicians the question was that miracle of rare device, a safe issue. It was easier to hammer the palpable evil of slavery than to discuss the tariff, credit, the ten-hour day, the price of land or Federally sponsored public works. But in the late fifties this satisfying option was open only to Republican politicians. They led an all-Northern aggregation. Democratic orators in the free States could not open fire too freely on slavery and keep close contact with their Southern allies. They could only invoke "reality," condemn "exaggerations," and try prayerfully to keep the whole subject out of politics. Men like Greeley had no intention of allowing that to happen.

The *Tribune's* pages were usually a haven for stories of outrages committed on Southern Negroes, most of them carefully clipped from Southern papers or else packaged as hearsay. But occasionally a *Tribune* correspondent was enlisted to file a story from the heart of darkness itself. In those reports, the writers showed a skill in the choice of symbols and appeals that was creditable in a pre-loudspeaker age. There was, for example, the lady who brought back certain unerasable souvenirs of a trip to a plantation and shared them with the *Tribune's* audience in October of 1859. She recalled the "driver" who had confided his remedy for unruly Negroes:

> Just take the nigger alone — tie him — blindfold him — bare his back — and then take some sticks of sealing-wax and a candle and let the burning wax drop all over his back. He'll think he is being dissected alive! You *never* have to wax a nigger but *once*. It does no harm — only works upon him powerfully, and he never knows what was done to him.

For the mid-century ladies, there were shivery hints of sex. In one cabin, sick to death, lay a "nearly white" child of a slave and the overseer. The reporter in skirts, being shown about by the plantation owner's daughter, murmured properly that she hoped it would die — presumably in preference to growing up to be the love toy of some master. "What do you mean?" snapped the hostess. "It will be the most valuable nigger on the plantation." [15] The well-bred shudders of the readers must have rattled the pages. Another *Tribune* operative in the South wrote in to say that he had there heard the history of a Georgia planter with a pair of fair mulatto daughters. His death-bed request to his son had been to take care of them, but the young man had succeeded in acquiring such an impressive number of debts that he shortly "shook off all qualms, and, by coining his sisters' flesh and blood, restored in part the waning substance of his fortune." He sold the girls, and it was "not likely they were bought for purposes of toil." [16]

The most focal point of attack on slavery, however, was the auction block, and the *Tribune's* most artful piece of writing on the subject was that which appeared anony-

[15] *New York Tribune*, October 22, 1859.
[16] *New York Tribune*, April 12, 1860.

mously in the paper in March, 1859, giving an account of the sale of slaves of Pierce Butler at Savannah, early that year. It struck almost every possible chord in the hymnal of popular sentiment, beginning with nostalgia. For all the slaves, it would be the first time away from home.

> Here have they lived their humble lives, and loved their simple loves; here were they born, and here have many of them had children born unto them; here had their parents lived before them.

Soon, however, they would be scattered through the cotton fields of Alabama, grown children leaving their parents "to wear out their weary lives in heavy grief, and lay their heads in far-off graves over which their children might never weep," and lovers wrenched apart with "loves . . . as yet unconsummated by marriage."

Then there was a touch for the mothers, in the picture of "pickaninnies" crawling under the feet of buyers, clinging crablike to the legs of the older men, and cheerfully submitting to being knocked down, rolled over or otherwise disturbed in their travels. Family loves led to pitiful efforts on the part of slaves already sold to have their nearest bought in parcel with them.

> "Show mas'r yer arm Molly — good arm dat mas'r — she do a heap of work mo' with dat arm yet. . . . Come out yer Israel, walk aroun' an' let the gen'lm'n see how spry you be."

There was sex again, in chaste wrappings of morality. The buyers included old gentlemen in gold spectacles and white neckcloths, moving softly among the women and "tormenting" them with "questions which, when accidentally overheard by the disinterested spectator, bred . . . an almost irresistible desire to knock somebody down." And there was the colloquy between two Southern gentlemen over one female slave.

> "Well, Colonel, I seen you looking sharp at shoemaker Bill's Sally. Going to buy her?"
>
> "I think not. Sally's a good, big strapping gal . . . but it's five years since she had any children. She's done breeding, I reckon."

Perhaps these were the same chivalrous bidders who objected when Daphney, a young woman two weeks out of childbed, was permitted to wrap herself in a blanket as a protection against the chill air.

Young love was personified by Jeffrey, a twenty-three-year-old prime field hand, and Dorcas, a slave girl. They had, said the correspondent, about whose words a scent of lavender hung thickly:

> exchanged their simple vows . . . and who shall say that in the sight of heaven and all the holy angels, these two humble hearts were not as closely wedded as any two of the prouder race that call them slaves.

But Jeffrey was sold. Trembling, and hat in hand, he stood before his new owner and pleaded:

> "I loves Dorcas, young mas'r, I loves her well an' true; she says she loves me; and I know she does; de good Lord knows I loves her better than I loves any one in de wide world — never can love another woman half so well.

> Please buy Dorcas, mas'r. We're be good sarvants to you as long as we live. . . . We loves each other a heap — do, really, true, mas'r."

But the new owner could not meet the bidding on Dorcas, and the star-crossed two were separated after all. The story ended with swelling organ notes and light streaming through the church windows.

> That night, not a steamer left that Southern port, not a train of cars sped away from that cruel city, that did not bear each its own sad burden of those unhappy ones . . . some of them maimed and wounded, some scarred and gashed by accident, or by the hands of ruthless drivers — all sad and sorrowful as human hearts can be.
>
> But the stars shone out as brightly as if such things had never been, . . . as if Man had never marred the glorious beauty of earth by deeds of cruelty and wrong. All nature was as wondrously beautiful and glorious as in that earlier day when "all the sons of God shouted for joy, and the morning stars sang together," and the burden of that celestial song was Freedom to Mankind.[17]

The entire episode showed a striking likeness to that chapter in *Uncle Tom's Cabin* entitled "Select Incidents of Lawful Trade." The *Tribune's* stories on slavery were generally cast in the patterns of contemporary fiction. The horrors which they described may have been actual ones, or they may have been visioned from a perspective no better than that afforded by the windows of the bustling Manhattan offices of the paper. In any event, the impor-

[17] *New York Tribune,* March 9, 1859.

tant thing was that correspondents assigned to the subject could be as mawkish, as passionate and as positive in their convictions as they liked, almost never reproved by editorial pens. The line between reporter and propagandist was almost invisible, and the propaganda was aimed at an audience that believed unhesitatingly in its sermons, and wept over the death of Little Eva.

Not all of the torrid reporting came from the antislavery side. The *Tribune's* neighbor, the *Herald*, was in many ways the product of a more modern outlook on journalism. The *Herald's* copy desks were not manned by a team of artists and lay preachers such as the *Tribune's*. The paper's managing editor, Frederic Hudson, was a Massachusetts Yankee who joined the paper at the age of eighteen, stayed with it for thirty years, and gave his days unremittingly to the pursuit of news.[18] Yet a paper owned by James Gordon Bennett could not be colorlessly neutral. Bennett was pure activity personified. He had begun his million-dollar paper in a basement in Ann Street, New York, with a candle for light, and a board laid across two barrels for a desk, and no assistants of any description. He worked an eighteen-hour day even when he had wrung success from a world that laughed at his gangling and cross-eyed appearance and fought his vigorous kind of journalism as a brand of moral leprosy. His birth in a stern and barren Scotland made him a match for the most

[18] Frederic Hudson, MS. Diaries for 1854, 1855, 1861, in possession of his granddaughter, Mrs. Wesley P. Wilmot.

conscience-ridden New Englander sprung from the same kind of rocky ground, and while he never hesitated to put reader appeal before all, his opinions were flung at the audience in daily broadsides in the editorial columns.

His correspondents, too, were in many cases unafraid of the large and bold phrase. In the fifties, Bennett, nominally independent, was on congenial terms with President James Buchanan, who, "not insensible to the vast influence of the *Herald*," wrote the editor letters in which he rejoiced over their "friendly relations," and passed advance information, some said, to the *Herald's* Washington bureau. In response, *Herald* editorials on the Kansas question damned the slavery issue there as "a mere abstraction," and reporters on the scene described Free State leaders as "howling dervishes," wrote that the majority of Kansans were anxious to end the "agitation, misrule and disorder," and castigated the *enragés* of abolitionism — "among the most active of whom," said one observer, "have been the hired reporters of the Eastern newspaper press." That was a plain blast at the *Tribune*, guilty of "the falsification of its Kansas record from the beginning." [19]

As for the "peculiar institution," Bennett's attitude could only be described as sardonically Anglo-Saxon. Bennett's forte, indeed, was to be caustic at the expense of causes. A *Herald* reporter on the city beat was capable

[19] Oliver G. Carlson, *James Gordon Bennett, The Man Who Made News* (New York, 1942), pp. 249, 268; Don C. Seitz, *The James Gordon Bennetts, Father and Son* (Indianapolis, 1928), pp. 160-165; *New York Herald*, March 9, April 10, May 4, 15, June 26, 29, 1858.

of getting into print a story about an abolitionist meeting which began: "The claims of the ubiquitous nigger were presented in the most common place language and with no pretension to oratorical effect." There was room in the *Herald's* foreign news columns for stories from places as far off as Mauritius Island, in the Indian Ocean, in which a correspondent might claim that the natives were "not one half so well clothed as the slaves that I have seen in our Southern States." As for the iniquities of the South, *Herald* men covered slave auctions too. A reporter came away from a sale in Alabama, in 1860, to write that the Negroes did not appear "to have the slightest cause for grief or complaint." They were, in fact, "happier and less concerned about their situations than three-fourths of the white people clustered about them." The women were "neat and comfortable," the men sported gift watches "with flashy chains attached," there was no "pulling, hauling, feeling of legs, arms, *etc.*" and in general the scene seemed, if the *Herald* man could be believed, only to need the addition of a few banjos and slices of watermelon to turn it into a minstrel jamboree.[20]

A correspondent in Charleston, covering the Democratic convention of 1860, reported that the first sight to meet his eye was a Negro "who looked as if he would have gone to the devil long ago if he had not had a master to clothe, feed, and house him." A correspondent in Honduras wept (like the Walrus over the oysters) for the "old free blacks,

[20] *New York Herald,* October 21, 1858, January 17, 1859, February 16, 1860.

worn out, decrepit, halt, lame, and blind" without kind masters to provide for them in their declining years. A correspondent in Havana was shocked to see a colored militia being raised, and arms glistening in the hands of "savages . . . all but one remove from the native African." A correspondent in what was later to be the city of Colón, in Panama, saw nothing resembling progress in a city populated mainly by the "male species of the nigger . . . incurably lazy, lying and thievish"; another, in what was later to be Greytown, Nicaragua, presented a picture clearly designed to prophesy the evils of emancipation, when he described the carrying of a municipal election by "a crowd of the worst looking negroes human eyes ever gazed on, all fresh from the grog shops, armed with cudgels, whooping and yelling in the most unearthly strains, and thrusting their votes in the faces of the inspectors." A correspondent back home in Alabama, after a tour through a cotton mill on the Flint River manned by Negro hands, reported that they "wore a happy and contented look, compared with the white slaves of New England." [21]

Even the fugitive slaves, who would demonstrably seem to be the more independent and sensitive of the Negroes, did not escape the accusing eye of a *Herald* writer. An eight-column article in the issue of January 5, 1860, described the settlements of escaped "servants" in Ontario, Canada, a terminus of the underground railroad. Its conclusion was that "the fugitive slaves go into Canada as beg-

[21] *New York Herald,* April 25, 1860, March 23, 1858, July 25, 1859, May 28, January 7, March 8, 1860.

gars, and the mass of them commit larceny and lay in jail until they become lowered and debased, and ready for worse crimes." It was a charge hotly rejected by the abolitionists, although they were obliged to water the new plantings from the well of private charity frequently. (At an abolitionist center like Oberlin College, Artemus Ward reported, the day opened with prayer and reading of the *New York Tribune*, and then a "kolleckshun" was "taken up to buy overkoats with red horn buttons onto them for the indignant cullered people of Kanady." [22])

The correspondents of either side were spectators at a fateful contest. Their accounts should have mirrored the struggle. In a sense they did, but the mirrors were the curved and distorted glasses of carnivals, and the images which they presented were not amusing, at least to most of the viewers.

The story in which the reporters themselves figured most prominently as actors broke at half past one on the Monday morning of October 16, 1859, when the engineer of an eastbound Baltimore & Ohio express pulled his train to a stop in the shadows of a covered bridge across the Potomac at Harpers Ferry, Virginia, and found himself confronted by rifle muzzles. John Brown and his men had come to write slavery's epitaph. Twenty-four theatrical hours later, the old man lay bleeding on the floor of the local jailhouse, and the attention of the entire country had been wrenched into a focus on Jefferson County, a pocket of

[22] Charles Browne, *Artemus Ward*, pp. 52-53.

hills cupped between the Shenandoah and Potomac Rivers where they met. For the six weeks of trial and punishment which followed, no first-line editor worth his salary failed to keep a column open for at least secondhand news of John Brown.

The court convened at Charles Town, a hamlet of 1700 people, kept in apparently unfruitful contact with the outer world by the Winchester & Potomac Railroad. It was a hill town, and metropolitan reporters filing stories from it had a chance not equaled again until the Scopes case to exercise their wits at the expense of the bumpkins. The ill feeling was mutual. The streets were dusty parade grounds for volunteer militia companies, still uncertain that Brown's men were not the vanguard of a great army of abolition; the men twanged their suspicions of outsiders to each other as they stood guard at the flyblown courthouse, carelessly dangling muskets and challenging visitors. Reporters for outspokenly antislavery newspapers — the *Tribune* chief among them — were unable to appear except in disguise.

The chief reporter for the *Herald*, had no such professional difficulties. He was a resident of the village, and a cousin of the editor of the *Jefferson County Times-Democrat*, the local gazette. With considerable enterprise, he first got himself hired as a guard at the jail, which gave him an occasional chance to speak with Brown and his fellow prisoners, and at the execution itself — from which all reporters were to be impartially excluded — he somehow pre-empted the assignment of driving the undertaker's wagon in which Brown rode to the gallows.[23] His reports were eminently judicious. Though he may well have loathed Brown, he praised the "daring of his spirit," his "indomitable will" and his "composure, and . . . quiet, truthful manner." He had good words for the militiamen (who displayed all the "subordination . . . indispensable to the making of good soldiers") and the townsmen (guilty of no "manifestation of disloyalty to the Union"). According to the *Tribune*, nevertheless, the *Herald* reporter did not escape without one rebuke from an officer of a company on guard. He had described the morning drum roll for assembly as "asthmatic." [24]

As for the *Tribune* men themselves, they played the principals in a spy drama with courtroom trappings. One of the first things brought to light as the earliest news ticked northward on the telegraph wires was the fact that John H. Kagi, one of the raiders killed in the fighting, had been a *Tribune* correspondent in Kansas. An editorial denied this; it admitted only William A. Phillips as its regular correspondent, but acknowledged accepting "volunteer letters" from a number of people, Kagi included.[25] One of Kagi's Kansas fellow troopers, however, Richard B. Hinton, promptly made an appearance at the paper's office and volunteered to go down to Charles Town. But Hinton's fiery Free State prose had marked him, and one

[23] Richard B. Hinton, *John Brown and His Men* (New York, 1894), pp. 336-337.
[24] *New York Herald*, October 28, November 1, 3, 5, December 2, 1859; *New York Tribune*, November 19, 1859.
[25] *New York Tribune*, October 24, 25, 1859.

unnamed editor with a profound appreciation of realities answered his request with: "You d——d fool! Do you want to get yourself hanged?" Apparently Hinton did not, and the first man sent was an associate agricultural editor, Henry S. Olcott. Olcott was twenty-six years old and apparently athirst to uncover the mysteries of life; he was, in time, to become a leading disciple of Madame Blavatsky and theosophy, and a dabbler in Buddhism and Brahmanism. In his somewhat less occult mission in Virginia, he undoubtedly had some anonymous assistance. Greeley's men were marked in the South. They had to hide their identities and send their accounts back in envelopes innocuously addressed to agents in Maryland and elsewhere, who forwarded them to New York.[26]

The attitude of Greeley had been made plain as early as the second day following the raid, when he announced that he would leave it to others to "heap execration on the memory of those mistaken men." By the time the trial was imminent, he was sneering at the Old Dominion's triumph over a "broken and bewildered old man" and suggesting that the propaganda purposes of the slaveholders might be better served by putting Brown in an iron cage and parading him through the State.[27] The reporters on hand made little attempt to present Brown's case sympathetically; everyone including the old man himself recognized the entire hopelessness of matters. Rather, the New York paper's Charles Town stories were freehand

[26] Seitz, *Horace Greeley*, p. 151; Hinton, *John Brown*, p. 396.
[27] *New York Tribune*, October 18, 28, 1859.

lampoons of Virginia justice. There were word caricatures of the judge, with his feet propped on the table in front of him; of "county magistrates" cracking chestnuts in court; of the homely militiamen; of the local hotel, boasting "the delights of society — a bar-room filled with blatant boors"; of the prosecuting attorney, whose face showed "the worst marks of intemperance"; and of such visitors as the young woman who, hearing that the hanging was to be soon, girlishly asked her husband: "Oh, won't that be gay? Oh, Paul, may I be here to see?" [28]

The citizens of Charles Town hunted for their anonymous gadflies with an air of desperation, falling on possibly innocent journalists in the process. Both *Harper's Weekly* and *Frank Leslie's Illustrated Weekly*, contemporary pillars of pictorial journalism, had artist-reporters on the scene. Mr. Jewett, the *Leslie's* artist, was suspected of un-Virginian associations with Greeley, and asked to leave town. He did, drawing an irreverent sketch of himself as a terrified-looking cadaver being pointed northward by an angry and pudgy citizen. The *Tribune* mirthfully carried the story. It also complained that the *Harper's* correspondent had slanted his pictures, giving Brown and his men the "cut-throat air" of bandits. The artist was entirely capable of it. He was David H. Strother — "Porte-Crayon" by pseudonym — soon thereafter to be a Confederate officer, as became a Virginian born. He averred in print that Brown was a "fanatical serpent" leading "vulgar knaves and midnight assassins." But even a benign portrait tended

[28] *New York Tribune,* November, 5, 9, 10, 11, 12, 17, 18, 24, 1859.

to glower ferociously after it was put through the engraving processes of the period.[29]

The last touch that reporters could furnish to the Brown story was to frame a legend, and in embedding it in folk art for generations they testified to their own importance. The *Tribune's* account of Brown's final emergence from the jailhouse, on the way to the gallows, told how

> as he stepped out of the door a black woman, with her little child in arms, stood near his way. The twain were of the despised race for whose . . . elevation to the dignity of children of God, he was about to lay down his life. . . . He stopped for a moment in his course, stooped over, and, with the tenderness of one whose love is as broad as the brotherhood of man, kissed it affectionately.

Placed on canvas in academic fashion by Thomas Hovenden, the baby-kissing scene hung over Victorian mantelpieces wherever the antislavery gospel ran freely. But in 1887 Edward F. Underhill, an erstwhile correspondent for Greeley, announced in the *New York Sun* that he had written the story in the *Tribune* office — though he did claim to have gotten the facts from one J. Miller McKim, who said that *he* had heard it from a man who was there. But James Redpath, the journalistic Garibaldi of Kansas, told F. B. Sanborn, when the latter was laboring on a biography of Brown, that the original suggestion had come from Edward H. House, who had been at Charles Town

[29] *New York Tribune,* November 15, 16, 30, 1859; *Frank Leslie's Illustrated Weekly*, VIII (1859), 414: pictures of the trial are on pages 335, 342, 374-375, 378-379, 390, 394-395, 406; *Harper's Weekly*, III (1859), 712-713 721, 728-730, 902; Hinton, *John Brown*, p. 320.

for the *Tribune* throughout the trial. It was a curious assignment for him, since he was the paper's music critic, but versatility was apparently part of a correspondent's trade. Two newspapermen claimed the paternity of the baby-kissing story; the conflict was not publicly resolved.[30]

By 1860, then, the reporter's enlarging audience expected from him not only that he would be a bringer of news, but a chorus exploring its meaning. Goaded into taking up their pens either by a sense of adventure or by feelings too ardent to be repressed, and directing their letters to editors who were skilled polemicists themselves, correspondents were finding their way to standards and techniques of their own through a brisk apprenticeship as special pleaders. Theirs was the kind of reporting which had made such a sulphurous tale out of the settlement of Kansas; theirs was the kind which even outran, from time to time, the editorial enthusiasm of a Greeley. The editor once had to scold his second-in-command for allowing a reporter to "caricature and ridicule . . . as much as possible" a State Democratic convention.[31]

April of 1861 brought the final crash of the Federal Union. For the newspaper world, it was the challenge of the century; for the reporters, the story in whose coverage they would establish themselves firmly as part of the Amer-

[30] *New York Tribune,* December 5, 1859; James C. Malin, "The John Brown Legend in Pictures: Kissing the Negro Baby," *Kansas Historical Quarterly,* VIII (1939), 339-341; William S. Kennedy, *John G. Whittier* (New York, 1892), pp. 240-243.

[31] James H. Wilson, *The Life of Charles A. Dana* (New York, 1907), p. 142; Pike, *First Blows of the Civil War,* p. 422.

ican scene. In their joint efforts to paint war for readers whose hearts were wrapped up in events as never before, and in the hardships which they would share in the field, they were to find further touches of professionalism, towards which their efforts as chroniclers and exhorters had been leading them from the beginning.

They would, however, be working within a circumscribed framework. For war was to bring to the nation new notions of constitutional liberties. The reporters would not merely learn new ways to say things; they would meet a new class of subjects — the generals of the armies — who would have much to do with their saying anything at all. It was a contest fit for colorful coverage, and the reporters provided it and found a certain unity in playing their parts in it.

CHAPTER IV

How to Keep a Secret

ONE July day in 1861, the special American correspondent of *The Times* of London sat in a Washington hotel room writing in his diary, a document with numerous pages penned in gall. William Howard Russell, heavy, mustached, and dignified, was a veteran reporter of the Crimean War and the Indian mutiny, sent to cover the impending war in the United States. His letters suggested a certain feeling on his part that the war represented a long-awaited comeuppance for the aggressive republic, and his private comments lit stingingly on politicians and promoters of every sort whom he met daily in the crowded, hot and uncultivated capital city, as well as on his American brethren in journalism.

> A swarm of newspaper correspondents has settled down upon Washington, and great are the florifications of the high-toned paymasters, gallant doctors, and subalterns accomplished in the art of war, who furnish minute items to my American brethren and provide the yeast which overflows in many columns; but the Government experience the inconvenience of the smallest movements being chronicled for the use of the enemy, who, by putting one thing and another together, are no doubt enabled to collect much valuable information.[1]

[1] William H. Russell, *My Diary, North and South* (Boston, 1863), p. 399.

"Inconvenience" might have been regarded as too mild a word in the three-story building a short walk from the White House which housed the War Department. There, tidy military thinkers combed through regulations, looking in vain for the comfort of a precedent to guide the government in its relations with the war correspondents. They were in force in Washington, rubbing elbows in hotel lobbies and streets with soldiers, government clerks and contract hunters, or showing conspicuously in their civilian clothes among the Fourth of July finery of the embattled volunteers in the ninety-day regiments camped in the city's outskirts. They had no official status in any headquarters, but their informal prerogatives could be impressive. Most of the newly arrived units were officered by appointees of the State governors. Uniformed politicians who had gotten their commissions through influence at the State House were apt to remember the dignities and perquisites due to emissaries of the press.

The courtesies extended to some correspondents went beyond the hospitalities of the officers' mess, and included expansive statements on the prospects before the regiment. It was there that trouble began, for the telegraph and the locomotive whisked reporters' copy into composing rooms in a matter of hours, and an item confided to a correspondent after breakfast one morning could be circulating in Washington as a front-page story in a New York newspaper by the following evening.

It could also be in Richmond within a few days, and this was the understandable cause of the War Department's anxieties. There was no real bar to the passage of information between the lines. The Union army's camps, at least, always contained a sprinkling of carelessly dressed civilians — sutlers, the traveling post exchanges of the Civil War army; transient Washington officials on snooping missions; male and a few female nurses; long-faced members of the Christian and Sanitary Commissions, handing packets of writing paper and pocket Bibles among the troops; relatives with connections good enough to secure transportation and passes; escaped slaves; Southerners having business with occupying authorities; the correspondents themselves. Any of them with a smattering of adroitness could lose himself in the tangled country through which the picket lines often ran. Spies, deserters and agents of various enterprises (such as the illegal purchase and resale in the North of confiscated cotton) kept up a continued, if precarious, traffic between the sections.

It was a simple matter for a man to stuff a few folded newspapers, which rarely ran to more than four pages, into his jacket. Sometimes pickets of the two armies, in a war which had its homey touches, struck up informal truces and traded tobacco, coffee, buttons, insignia and newspapers with each other. There were planned exchanges as well. In the southern counties of Illinois, where secession feeling ran hot and strong, considerate friends of the South early in the war dropped tightly corked bottles containing copies of newspapers into the Mississippi, to drift downstream to the Confederate forces led by General Leonidas Polk, an Episcopal bishop by peacetime calling.

Early in 1862, a spy was overtaken laboring across the Mississippi in a skiff. When searched, he yielded up among other things late copies of the New York and Chicago *Times* and the *Missouri Republican.*

Such acquisitions were apparently well appreciated by Confederate staffs. Lee once revealed to President Davis that he habitually panned the Yankee press for nuggets of information, and shortly before the battle of Chickamauga, General Braxton Bragg triumphantly sent to the Adjutant General in Richmond a clipping from the *New York Times* in which a correspondent at Union headquarters had outlined a scheme for bluffing part of the "rebel" army out of its positions around Chattanooga.[2] Bragg, informed, remained unbluffed.

In their exasperated efforts to regulate the flow of military information to the public, the Union's military authorities were unsuspectingly helping to tailor constitutional theory. With each month of modern war it became clearer that the government which governed least was likely to lose most. Necessity, as the campaigns dragged on, dictated the draft, confiscations, the suspension of habeas corpus, the blockade, emancipation. By 1864 the Constitution, if not precisely buried, had at least been given local anesthetics in many of its parts — a technique to prove

[2] James G. Randall, *Constitutional Problems Under Lincoln* (New York, 1926), p. 487; James G. Randall, "The Newspaper and the Problem of Military Security in the Civil War," *American Historical Review,* XXII (1918), 303-323; *Cincinnati Commercial,* August 21, 1861; *Chicago Tribune,* March 2, 1862; *Chicago Times,* May 9, 1862; *Official Records of the Union and Confederate Armies in the War of the Rebellion* (Washington, 1880-1900) [hereafter referred to as *Official Records*], Ser. 1, XXX, Pt. 4, 599-600.

useful in later wars. There was a growing tendency to muzzle criticism. Opponents of the war continued to speak out unterrified by a later era's sweeping definitions of wartime sedition. But their tether was noticeably shorter than in the days of the War of 1812 and the Mexican War, when Federalist and Whig presses had launched their broadsides, sizzling and unrestrained, against President Madison or the Slave Power.

The generals who set out to bridle talkative reporters were not, as a rule, acting from political motives, but in approaching the privileges of the press with scissors in hand they were preparing to confront an enemy who held commanding ground. Freedom to print anything classifiable as news was of all liberties perhaps the most palpable to the public, and the editors who defended it were articulate and in possession of the clearest channel for presenting their case. In the end, the newspapermen would lose, and the correspondents would for the most part be identified, held to accountability, and blue-penciled into conformity with an established code of military manners regarding secret information. This development kept pace with the war's general trend to emphatic assertion of government power at the expense of civil liberties. The struggle to set up rules of censorship was important. But the rules had to be written and learned while the fighting went on, as almost everything else concerning modern warfare had to be learned by an army in which few regular officers had actually commanded more than companies, and in which some volunteer colonels of regiments spent their first weeks in their tents furtively learning close-order drill from copies of Hardee's *Tactics*, a then popular manual. Since the officers and the correspondents, both suddenly in the spotlight, were bulging with self-awareness, the learning process was punctuated with instances of bad faith and well-verbalized heartburning.

Opening skirmishes took place as early as June and July of 1861. Winfield Scott, the aging generalissimo of the Union forces, confided to one Washington correspondent that newsmen writing from the camps were keeping the Confederates well posted on troop movements. Scott, bred in an era of less publicized warfare, complained in fact that he would prefer a hundred spies in any camp to one reporter. His uneasiness, however, was not only that of a professional soldier rearing at novelty. At Fortress Monroe, the commanding general was newly commissioned Benjamin F. Butler. As a Massachusetts politician who was still active, he appreciated a good press, but when visited by Murat Halstead, correspondent of the *Cincinnati Commercial*, he was so far irked as to suggest that "the Government would not accomplish much until it had hanged . . . half a dozen spies, and at least one newspaper reporter." His irritation exploded into a general order, which decreed the expulsion from his department of any person who gave information of movements of troops in prospect. The immediate cause was a journalistic *gaffe* which had cost the commander a small triumph. A river steamer, the *Catiline*, during a short run up the James River, had been fired upon by a small armed tug. Before the craft's next trip, a gun had been put aboard, masked as merchandise, with the idea of luring out the Confederate vessel and capturing it by surprise. The next edition of the New York papers, however, had given away the device and spoiled the scheme.

General Butler's order was made slightly vulnerable by an addition to it which reflected the sensitive pride of an amateur at war. No reporter was to express "censure or praise of any movement." "Why, dear Major General!" snapped the *New York Tribune* when the order fell into its hands, "The newspapers have made you, epaulettes and all! Without the newspapers you would, at this moment, have been a petty attorney in a petty country town." A campaign against newspapermen was plainly not going to go uncontested.[3]

The New York papers were presumably regarded as the worst offenders. Two weeks before Bull Run their Washington staff men were summoned to a meeting at which the problem of censoring telegraphic dispatches regarding portended movements was discussed. The correspondents agreed to behave more circumspectly, but insisted that they have full leave to file unedited stories when actual fighting took place. This experiment was developed a few weeks later, after the battle, when a shake-up in the high command brought to the head of the army Major General George Brinton McClellan. Handsome, popular, thirty-five

[3] *Cincinnati Enquirer*, July 3, 1861; *Cincinnati Commercial*, June 20, July 13, 1861; *New York Tribune*, July 13, 1861.

and reputedly gifted, McClellan had stepped out of army retirement and a superintendent's job with the Illinois Central Railroad to save the Union and assume the title of Young Napoleon. On the 2nd of August he collected the correspondents of the Washington, Philadelphia, New York, Boston and Cincinnati papers and reached a gentleman's agreement with them. They were not to publish information that would "furnish aid and comfort to the enemy," while the general would guarantee the army's assistance in getting the reporters facilities for transmitting their stories, if "suitable for publication." This would become increasingly important when the army moved from Washington to less civilized seats of war, for the correspondents would often have to depend on military assistance in feeding, housing and mounting themselves. The agreement, however, was rapidly shredded away. The Baltimore newspapers, which were not in on it, continued to enlighten readers with descriptions of troop movements in the capital area. The reporters, too, had a more generous estimate than the generals of what was "suitable for publication," and newsmen who trudged the streets of Washington in ninety-degree heat, tracking down items, were understandably slow to see suspected dangers in them.

The result was a sharpening of the official tone. McClellan had left an operation against Confederate forces in West Virginia to be mopped up by another retired West Pointer, William S. Rosecrans. In mid-August, Rosecrans called into his tent correspondents covering the campaign through the isolated and mountainous backwoods region, and tongue-lashed them for indiscretion. By the beginning of September, the War Department had emerged with the one Article of War that *did* bear on the subject, the Fifty-seventh. It provided that the communication of information to the enemy *by any means whatever* should be punishable by sentences up to death. This was circulated in the journalistic camp, confronting its members, as one of them put it, with "the prospect of a noose, and a war correspondent dangling to it." Soon thereafter, the rules regarding passage from Washington across the Potomac were tightened, and newspapermen, unless they could manipulate their army connections to get a pass, found themselves barred, along with those on less public business, from crossing the Chain Bridge to Virginia.[4]

There was reason for the asperity of the generals, for the press showed a strange density about understanding the importance of leaks in military news. The New York press had almost weekly summaries of the location of regiments around Washington. Despite General Butler's fury, his picket lines, regimental headquarters and supporting naval forces were spotted in the papers which found their way so easily into enemy hands. Columns filed from West Virginia sketched the composition of Federal forces, man for man and gun for gun, at every key point in the region, and added informed guesses as to the uses to be made of them. The same thing was happening in the West; a

[4] *Cincinnati Commercial*, August 9, 1861; *New York Herald*, August 15, 1861; *Boston Journal*, August 8, 1861; James M. Lee, *History of American Journalism* (Boston, 1917), p. 288; *Cincinnati Commercial*, September 5, 1861; *Missouri Republican*, September 14, 1861.

typical story from Cairo, Illinois, a mud-sodden small town at the lowest tip of the State, catapulted suddenly into fame as an assembly area and base camp for the Western army, ran:

> Our forces at Bird's Point now consist of the following regiments: Colonel Wallace's Eleventh Illinois Regiment, Colonel MacArthur's Twelfth Illinois Regiment, Colonel Lawler's Eighteenth Illinois Regiment, and Colonel Dougherty's Twenty-second Illinois Regiment; also, 17 pieces of artillery, consisting of six 24 pound siege guns, three 24 pound howitzers, two 12 pound howitzers and six 6 pound brass pieces.

Some of the newspapermen themselves were surprised at the simplicity of their colleagues. On a trip to Baltimore, in June, Murat Halstead learned of the passage of two Pennsylvania regiments through the city on the way to Chambersburg. It seemed to him a clear giveaway of an intended movement on Harpers Ferry, which sharpened his surprise when "the Western press" — west of the Alleghenies, that was — published the news the next morning, spoiling any notion of a secret concentration. When he went on to Washington, he affected a certain civic-minded horror on learning that correspondents of New York papers visited the offices of the War and Navy Departments and intercepted official reports from friendly government workers in order to publish them. Sometimes they got them into print before the Secretaries had seen them.[5]

[5] *New York World,* July 9, 1861; *New York Herald,* May 31, July 4, 1861; *New York World,* August 28, 1861; *Chicago Tribune,* June 24, 1861; *Cincinnati Commercial,* July 1, 1861; *New York Tribune,* July 16, 1861;

Part of the reason for the reporters' carelessness lay in the homespun facts of Civil War recruitment. Companies and regiments were raised locally and mustered into State and then Federal service. Keeping readers informed of the whereabouts of these units was a folksy bid for circulation; as the *New York Tribune* put it, during a passage at arms with the commanding general at Fortress Monroe:

> Millions of men and women, fathers, mothers, children, wives, sweethearts, who have sent those dearer than life to these wars, look every day at this journal, and at other journals, with eyes brimful of anxious tears, and turn these pages with hands made unsteady by emotion. It is quite as important that this love should be respected, that these apprehensions should be allayed, that these tortures of suspense should be averted, as that Gen. Benjamin F. Butler should keep secret any expedition which he is likely to undertake.[6]

The army, however, could hardly feel the force of this argument, even in such throbbing prose. It was clear within a month that "voluntary agreement" as a technique of preserving security had failed.

Actually, the government had, for several months, been experimenting with one kind of direct censorship. In April, 1861, there had been considerable official fear of a secessionist *coup* in the capital city, and the authorities — acting,

---

Cincinnati Commercial, July 4, August 16, 21, 1861; *Cincinnati Enquirer*, August 20, 25, 1861; *Chicago Tribune*, May 21, 1861; *Cincinnati Commercial*, June 8, 10, 1861.

[6] *New York Tribune*, July 13, 1861.

oddly, through the Treasury Department — had taken control of the telegraph lines from the city. The responsibility for them was passed briefly to the War Department and then to the office of the Secretary of State. For the balance of the year the task of pruning outgoing telegrams of anything supposedly helpful to rebellion fell to William H. Seward. The short, hawk-nosed, brilliant Secretary promptly brought the matter of security into the political warfare at which he was an expert.

In April, the 6th Massachusetts Regiment, marching through Baltimore towards the capital, was stoned by an angry secessionist mob. When the Washington correspondents went to the telegraph office to file stories of the event, they learned that an order was out to "kill" the lists of wounded and dead. A deputation proceeded to see Secretary Seward, who explained, in a "semi-jocular way," that the release of such inflammatory details would be "an obstacle in the path of reconciliation." [7] Seward had been laboring for a peaceful restoration of the Union for some months, presumably expecting that the credit for managing it would restore him to what he thought was his rightful position as leader of the Republican party. Balked in his effort to win the nomination in 1860, he was, in these early days, thinking of converting his State Department role into that of a prime minister, and the use of the censorship to keep interfering hands off his plans evidently gave him no constitutional uneasiness.

[7] Benjamin Perley Poore, *Reminiscences of Sixty Years in the National Capital* (Boston, 1886), II, 78-79.

In October, however, when the chances of peace were beyond resurrection, and Seward was better reconciled to the leadership of Lincoln, a new and startling order appeared. The censor was to forbid "all telegraphic despatches from Washington" which related to "the *civil* or military operations of the government." This was a considerable expansion of any agreement then existing with capital reporters; the motive for it was in a new political battle whose lines were forming. In Congress, a group of "Radical" Republicans — eager to go far beyond Lincoln on questions of emancipation and all-out war against the South — was organizing to dictate wartime policy, if possible. Seward was not a member of the group, and, as a "conservative influence" on the President, was a target of its attack.

Where the October gag rule fitted into this picture was made clear when Congress, after it convened in December, inaugurated an investigation of the censorship. It was carried on by the House Committee on the Judiciary, whose chairman was a belligerent Radical, Representative John Hickman of Pennsylvania. A parade of Washington newsmen filed to the committee's witness chair; when their testimony was finally embedded in the fine print of a fourteen-page report, no one connected with the entire enterprise had any particular cause to feel flattered.

To begin with, the October decree against wiring discussions of "*civil* or military operations" was not universal. It exempted the stories of Mr. L. A. Cobright, who was the Washington agent of the Associated Press. Mr.

Gobright, under questioning, said that he could not understand the reason for this useful honor, unless — and here he seemed to be jabbing an elbow into the ribs of his colleagues and winking slyly — it was because he recorded only "dry matters of fact and detail," while others wrote "to suit the temper of their own organs," a provocative and universal journalistic practice.

The committee was not satisfied, however, with a censorship which muzzled everything but "dry matters of fact." It called, for further light, on Mr. Samuel Wilkeson, a native of Buffalo, New York, and a kind of prototype public relations expert specializing in political clients. Wilkeson was a close friend and associate of Simon Cameron, the Pennsylvania manufacturer and political boss who was Secretary of War. Cameron had taken him along on a public-expense trip to Missouri in the autumn of 1861, when he was having a look into army purchases and enjoying a politician's tailored view of a war theater. Through Cameron, in fact, Wilkeson was later introduced to Jay Cooke and put in charge of the advertising campaign to promote the Philadelphia banker's bond issues.

However profitable his friendships, Wilkeson was, at the time of the investigation, ostensibly nothing more than the Washington correspondent of the *New York Tribune*. In this role, he told Hickman's investigators, he had been forbidden to wire out anything "damaging to the character of the administration, or any individual member of the cabinet, or . . . the reputation of the officers charged with the prosecution of the war, and particularly those of the regular army." To the initiated, this needed no translation. Cameron was then in alliance with the Radicals. One of the articles in their faith was that the regular army was not sufficiently indoctrinated in the high aims of the war. Many of its officers who were Southern by birth had left; many of those remaining were allegedly sympathetic to slavery as the kind of solid and well-regulated institution which would appeal to hidebound martial thinkers. There were rumors that McClellan, the very model of a regular major general, opposed fighting for anything other than the restoration of the Union without emancipation. He was thus marked by the Radicals as an enemy to watch. Seward had openly shown his friendship for McClellan.

Mr. Wilkeson was saying, therefore, that Seward was using the censor's role to seal the lips of any newspapermen patriotically anxious to criticize the conservative Secretary of State or the regular army so evidently infiltrated with Democrats. Mr. Wilkeson's testimony did not dwell on his relations with Secretary Cameron, another "individual member of the cabinet," nor did the committee see fit to print a letter sent by Cameron to the censor, asking as a personal favor that he "neither suppress nor alter the telegrams of Mr. Samuel Wilkeson." The proadministration *Cincinnati Commercial* somehow acquired that story and ran it in its issue of March 27, 1862.

The committee, in fact, like others which came after it, was interested in witnesses whose answers were certain to be acceptable to its chairman. Such a one was forty-year-old Massachusetts editor, diplomat, archivist, biographer and traveler Benjamin Perley Poore, who was the *Boston Journal's* Washington correspondent. He and the questioners went through an exchange like a well-timed minstrel routine:

> Q: Suppose you had received information from a reliable quarter which clearly indicated the impolicy of trusting a command to General McClellan or any other officer in the army, would you have tried to transmit it by telegraph?
>
> A: I would not have tried, because I understood that it was the request of the army that it should not be embarrassed by any remarks of the telegraph.
>
> . . . .
>
> Q: Did you understand that you would be restrained from any criticism upon the general conduct or particular conduct of army officers?
>
> A: Yes, sir; distinctly. I would think it useless to write anything of the kind.
>
> . . . .
>
> Q: Did you understand that you could not criticise the everyday conduct of a cabinet officer? [This was likely to mean Seward, but not Cameron]
>
> A: I did.

To Hickman, such testimony was manna, especially when followed by an appendix of killed dispatches prominently featuring those which praised prominent Radicals or criticized regular army leaders. The effect of the report was to paint the slightly built, eloquent Secretary of State as an autocrat, playing Richelieu to the President and throttling into silence a press which was critical of proslavery cliques in uniform. It was high political craftsmanship on the part of Hickman. Since all the newspapers resented the censorship, Seward was left temporarily almost friendless among the editors. The Radical journals hoisted the Bill of Rights to the masthead and spread all sails, and even to a Democratic — and therefore thoroughly anti-Radical — paper such as the *Chicago Times* the Secretary was guilty of a "most odious tyranny" with "No parallel in the annals of free nations."

Politics aside, the matter had been badly handled. The censor chosen by the State Department had experience in telegraphy — he had been a maker of mathematical instruments, of all things — but little discrimination. He had buried numerous innocent stories relating to the "civil" operations of the government, but at the same time made some capricious omissions. A *New York Herald* correspondent had been allowed to wire to Bennett portions of the President's annual message to Congress for 1861 before Lincoln himself had delivered it. A particularly galling slip had allowed London *Times* correspondent Russell to telegraph a New York friend a hint that the United States and Great Britain would not go to war over the American seizure from the British packet *Trent*, at sea, of two Confederate emissaries. This was at a time when a blackout on news of the negotiations on the affair was supposed to exist. Russell was disliked throughout the North for a spectacularly unflattering description of the Union army at Bull Run, and the censor's error not only meant a scoop for him but a possible speculative killing on the stock market, which was sure to rise when the news of peace broke.

Above all, however, information suppressed in Washington could be and was wired from Baltimore or Philadelphia, and in any case was passed by letter to New York and the country at large within a few hours. Among its other deficiencies, Seward's control of the wires had little real effect. It was, therefore, probably without regret that on February 25, 1862, he yielded it to the War Department, under a new and coldly efficient Secretary of War, Edwin M. Stanton. (Some political legerdemain had removed Cameron and sent him, in January, to Russia as minister.) Stanton acted briskly; the Department assumed supervision of *all* telegraphic lines in the country, and announced that newspapers would be banned from publishing anything which would support inferences as to "the number, position, or strength of the military force of the United States." With that businesslike beginning, a new period of telegraph censorship began. The first had ended with a whimper.[8]

[8] The whole story, with a few exceptions not altogether helpful to the Radicals, is in "Report of the Judiciary Committee on the Telegraph Censorship," *House Reports*, 37th Congress, 2nd Session, Vol. 3, No. 64. Something of reporter Wilkeson's connections is revealed in E. P. Oberholtzer, *Jay Cooke, Financier of the Civil War* (Philadelphia, 1907), I, 232-234, 480, 577-582, 653. The Seward-Cameron feud and its connection with McClellan and the regular army is covered in Burton J. Hendrick, *Lincoln's War Cabinet* (Boston, 1946), pp. 224-227. A typical Radical comment on the committee report is in the *New York Tribune*, March 22, 1862, and the comment of the *Chicago Times* was in the issue of March 26, 1862.

Through the early months of the year, the situation in the camps grew worse, as reporters took advantage of a general lack of control or of the calculated tolerance of certain officers, grateful for a flattering paragraph now and then, to consolidate their positions. Many of them wrote with what seemed to be a stag-party exhibitionism, determined to conceal nothing.

> Within the last few days not less than half a dozen vessels belonging to the blockading fleet have left . . . under orders to rendezvous in the neighborhood of one of the principal Southern ports . . . in range of the original seats of rebellion. . . .
>
> In view of the anticipated early opening of the campaign by General Buell's army, the subjoined exhibition of the number of regiments composing it, their agglomeration into divisions, their present position, . . . &c., will doubtlessly be welcome . . .
>
> I presume I shall violate no confidence if I state on common rumor and belief that the expedition will rendezvous at Hatteras inlet, and that Pamlico and Albemarle Sounds will be the immediate field of operations. . . .
>
> I learn from Huntsville, that two brigades were detached early this week by General Buell for the relief of Nashville, and that one of his divisions was advancing in the direction of McMinnville, for the purpose of cutting off the retreat of the rebels . . .[9]

[9] *New York Tribune,* September 20, 1861, January 13, 14, 1862; *Cincinnati Commercial,* July 25, 1862.

It did not matter where operations were taking place; the reporters were ubiquitous. In Missouri, in October of 1861, a *New York Tribune* writer described a concentration of fifteen thousand troops sixty miles west of Jefferson City, "waiting for the remainder of the army to join them." It was an engraved invitation to an attack. In Kentucky, during the same month, another of Greeley's correspondents gave the number of troops posted in one region by General William T. Sherman as twenty thousand. Sherman was at the time tormented by nightmares of being outnumbered and desperate lest the enemy suspect his inadequacies. Furious at such slips, when a reporter approached him for information as to his forces, he ordered the man to leave camp in fifteen minutes or be hanged as a spy.[10]

At Cairo, where General Grant took command at the beginning of the year, newspapermen daily listed the arrival of fresh troops and publicly "guessed" that the chunky Illinois soldier's first move would be up the Tennessee River to attack Fort Henry. Cairo was for the reporters a place of mixed good and evil. They hated the town, with its unpaved streets, littered by sheds, shanties, pigsties, woodpiles and barrels, and its jam-packed hotel which fed them stringy chickens, spongy beef and bitter coffee. On the other hand, Grant was courteous to the press and his arrival mysteriously coincided with a rise in the availability of whiskey at headquarters. Moreover the naval

[10] *New York Tribune*, October 8, 17, 1861; William T. Sherman Papers, Library of Congress, Sherman to —— L'Hommedieu, July 7, 1862.

forces, in February, were commanded by Commodore Andrew Foote, a religious, soft-voiced officer, gentle and simple, and so cordial to friends who were newspapermen that he once visited a Boston correspondent in his room after midnight to give a personal account of the battle of Fort Henry. The town became an even drearier place in April, when Grant and Foote had left, and censorship was drastically tightened.[11]

Above Memphis, near Island Number Ten, Union forces were stopped at a horseshoe bend in the Mississippi. General John Pope, bombastic commander, masterminded a plan to cut a canal between the prongs of the horseshoe and bypass Confederate positions with his transports. But while his engineers worked waist-high in the river in the dead of night, correspondents of a Cincinnati paper described the operation, placing its whole success in danger. Almost at the same time, a Union force was moving on Corinth, a railroad junction in northern Mississippi, under the command of General Henry Wager Halleck; daily reports from correspondents listed strength reports, dispositions, and combat assignments of every unit in his command.[12]

[11] *Missouri Republican*, January 2, 1862; *New York World*, January 15, 1862; *New York Herald*, January 18, 21, 1862; *Chicago Times*, February 8, 11, 1862; Charles C. Coffin, *The Boys of '61* (Boston, 1881), pp. 52, 76; Franc B. Wilkie, *Pen and Powder* (Boston, 1888), pp. 81-86, 98-99; *Boston Journal*, April 3, 1862; *Missouri Democrat*, April 3, 1862; *New York Tribune*, January 19, May 16, 1862.

[12] *Cincinnati Commercial*, April 12, 1862; *Chicago Tribune*, May 4, 7, 1862; *Cincinnati Commercial*, May 7, 15, 1862; *New York World*, May 15, 1862.

In the East, McClellan had brought the army to the swampy peninsula between the York and the James and was edging towards Richmond by a side door. He had consistent trouble with newspapers, which threatened to kill him with kindness publicity-wise. He issued general orders forbidding the camps to reporters without passes from his chief of staff, and preventing his subordinates from circulating their official reports publicly, apparently a frequent vice with certain preening or disgruntled officers. He wrote to Stanton, asking his assistance in preventing journalistic indiscretions, and in Washington Stanton himself had already commissioned the president of the American Telegraph Company a colonel and given him wide powers of censorship. The reporters joked nervously, and chaffed each other about shouldering guns or helping to dig entrenchments in order to remain legitimately at the front. When *Harper's Weekly* lost its right to circulate in the camps, for printing sketches of some of McClellan's seige works, the *New York Herald* suggested sarcastically that if the Secretary of War hanged the publishers it would make an excellent subject for a drawing in the magazine.[13] Fundamentally, however, the question of control of military information was getting beyond the province of humor. Matters were brought to a head for the first time by an incident in Mississippi in May. General

[13] *Official Records*, Ser. 1, XI, Pt. 1, 167, 181, 194, 214; *Cincinnati Commercial*, April 14, 1862; *Cincinnati Enquirer*, May 13, 1862; *Philadelphia Press*, June 20, July 31, 1862; *New York Herald*, April 22, 1862.

Halleck, in one sweeping order, ran more than thirty correspondents out of his camp.

Halleck was an officer with a large, tabular face and a scholarly mind. He had, in fact, written a textbook on strategy, and was, in addition, an expert on mining law. Accordingly, the country looked for great things from him, and one reporter (of the *New York World*) claimed the credit of devising the label "Old Brains" by which he became known to a good part of the press. In the early stage of his campaign in northern Mississippi he got on well with the correspondents; he even once released Warren P. Isham, a writer for the *Chicago Times*, after another general — with a roar of "What in hell brought you here?" — had arrested the newspaperman upon finding him riding in an area to which he did not have a pass. But as the weeks of April and May dragged by with Corinth untaken, transport hopelessly bogged, the weather subtropical, sickness hollowing the regiments, and daily disclosures in the newspapers of what was afoot in headquarters, Halleck's staff, at least, grew liverish towards the reporters. His provost marshal general turned down the application of a *New York World* correspondent for a renewed pass, citing a common rumor that certain newspaper representatives had been paid by some officers for complimentary reports. Pressed for names, however, he backed down. The assistant provost marshal general, a youthful captain who amused the press by wearing, as part of his uniform, a hat flanked by an oriental bird's tail, was equally grudging with passes. A *New York Herald* writer was briefly arrested for circulating a rumor that Grant had been drunk at the battle of Fort Donelson.[14]

Finally, Halleck himself issued a field order which demanded the removal of "unauthorized persons" from the camps. The correspondents could, if they liked, remain at the old battlefield of Pittsburg Landing, nearly twenty miles in the rear. A bulletin board would be available there, containing digests of Associated Press dispatches, antiseptically prepared at headquarters by a member of the general's staff. A deputation of reporters representing such topflight papers as the *New York Times* and *Tribune* and the *Boston Journal* called on the commander to remonstrate. They offered affidavits of their loyalty, promised to keep headquarters posted continuously on their whereabouts, and pledged obedience to any regulations. Halleck did not relent, however, and when Wilkie of the *Times* remonstrated too enthusiastically, he was cooled off with a four-hour detention in a guard tent. The newspaper representatives then announced that they would accept no precooked releases, signed a declaration which accused the general of conspiring to keep from the country "the condition of the army, the treatment . . . of its soldiers, or the management of battles," and left for more rewarding beats.

From the safety of Cairo and other points, they retaliated as well as they could. The ousted *New York World* correspondent called Halleck "an irritated old maid, a

[14] *New York World,* May 15, 16, June 13, 1862; *Chicago Times,* May 20, 1862; *Cincinnati Commercial,* May 24, 1862.

silly school girl, a vacillating coquette," and a fellow exile from the *New York Herald* said that the frustrated strategist had been anxious to get rid of outside witnesses to a campaign which had been thoroughly fumbled. A Philadelphia reporter claimed another inside story. One clique of political officers had secured the promise of some of the correspondents to tout them for promotion; jealous regular army members of Halleck's staff had gotten wind of it and worked upon the commander to exclude newspaper writers from the camps in order to forestall such favoritism.[15]

The next month, "Old Brains" was transferred to Washington to supervise the entire Union war effort from a War Department desk. Ineffective at his job, and unloved by enemies of the administration both in Congress and the army, he was in no position to afford the almost unanimous hostility of the press, and he rapidly became one of the war's forgotten men. But if, in the long run, the newsmen had their revenge, Halleck had won an important battle. His order stood unchanged; all the fury of the editors broke vainly against his assertion of the army's right, in its own interests, to regulate or exclude reporters as it chose. It was the largest and best publicized crackdown effected by field authorities up to that time, and Halleck had, while losing his reputation, gained ground for his viewpoint.

[15] *Cincinnati Commercial*, May 24, 1862; Wilkie, *Pen and Powder*, pp. 179-180; *New York World*, June 13, 1862; Thomas W. Knox, *Campfire and Cotton-Field* (New York, 1865), p. 166; *Philadelphia Press*, May 27, 1862; *Missouri Democrat*, May 23, 24, 1862. For typical editorial outbursts see *Chicago Tribune*, May 29, 1862; *Chicago Times*, May 23, 24, 1862; *Missouri Republican*, May 24, 1862.

Halleck's gesture brought to boiling a deep kettle of editorial resentment. The fundamental issue was between a traditional freedom and the power requirements of a government managing a modern war. The scissoring of miltary intelligence tidbits from press dispatches was only one reflection of that struggle between emergency need and historical practice. Some of the angry editors and reporters dug down to the root question. Others shot it out in print with the authorities over side issues.

One favored argument early in the war rested on a curious proposition that the censorship was an imposition largely because it was not one hundred per cent effective. Spies got the secrets through to the Confederates anyway; therefore, what was the use of harrying newspapermen with regulations? "Any rebel spy . . . may count each regiment, battalion, squadron and battery in Missouri," said the petulant *Chicago Tribune* in 1861, and enforced secrecy was thus "the merest pantomime." A Cincinnati paper's correspondent attending the siege of Vicksburg wrote that it was difficult for his letters to convey to the rebels "any information relating to army movements until it has become 'old' in the Confederacy." If secret agents did not puncture the security curtain, high-ranking staff officers let their tongues wag freely. Indeed, many a Civil War general, behind his impressive knee-length blue coat with its double row of gilt buttons and enormous sash, hid the tender heart of a prima donna. If he felt that headquarters had slighted him, he was apt to carry his troubles to a sympathetic correspondent. And there were staff warriors who, according to one correspondent in Nashville, became "inebriated" and in "coffee houses and beer saloons" let slip more information than any amount of newspaper leg work could gather.[16] According to this logic, a censor would be something like a high-wire artist. One slip and his act went off the program.

An argument held by the editors in close support behind this one was that inconsistency and favoritism tangled the rules of the censorship so badly that they could not be followed intelligently. The *New York Tribune* objected that news cut from its dispatches appeared in Baltimore papers. The Washington correspondent of the *Boston Journal* complained that items which the censor kept him from sending to the Hub of the Universe appeared in New York newspapers. In fact, the metropolis on the Hudson paid the usual price of greatness; for there were many editors in less gilded cities who agreed with the *Cincinnati Enquirer* that most of the slips which provoked controls were made by the "sensation papers" and "tattling" press of New York. A New York correspondent covering operations on the sandy islands off the South Carolina coast in 1863 bemoaned the lack of uniform and explicit rules as to what stories would pass inspection; a Chicago observer in Washington found the regulations ironclad one day and rubbery the next; a Cincinnati editor during a campaign in 1862 pointed

[16] *Chicago Tribune*, October 8, 1862; *Cincinnati Commercial*, March 4, 1863; *Chicago Tribune*, February 11, 1865. See also *New York Herald*, July 30, 1861; *Chicago Tribune*, April 7, 1862, March 7, 1863; *Cincinnati Commercial*, May 31, 1862; *Chicago Times*, April 18, 1862; *Missouri Republican*, April 18, 1862; *New York Tribune*, October 29, 1861.

with vexation to contradictory orders issued by the general in charge and the Secretary of War; a Philadelphia journal summed it up by asking for deliverance from the "ignorant, political fops" entrusted with censors' jobs. The *New York Tribune* charged that General Grant gave reports on the battle of Shiloh, which were withheld from other correspondents, to a pet reporter of the *New York Herald*; the *Herald* accused the *Tribune* of printing secret information from McClellan's army in order to hasten the downfall of the young commander and his replacement with a general more hospitable to Greeley's abolitionism.[17]

A legitimate editorial complaint was that the censorship did not apply to the soldiers and the perennial camp visitors whose letters to local gazettes furnished the real bulk of war correspondence. Generals, privates, chaplains, doctors and contractors, all yearning for self-expression, wrote to home-town publishers, criticizing the government, the high command, the War Department, and bubbling over enthusiastically with any military plans they knew. Every headquarters — like headquarters from the beginning of time — buzzed with rumors. Washington buzzed loudest of all, and in Washington the rumors were likely to be snapped up and sent out to the country at large. Regular paid correspondents objected to suffering for the sins of "itinerant scribblers and irresponsible penny-a-

[17] *New York Tribune*, July 22, 1861, May 26, 1862; *Boston Journal*, March 4, 1862; *Cincinnati Enquirer*, October 18, 1861; *New York World*, March 17, 1863; *Chicago Times*, November 19, 1862; *Cincinnati Commercial*, April 12, 1862; *Philadelphia Press*, June 2, 1862; *New York Herald*, August 25, 1862.

liners," writing for papers "which would be compelled to seek refuge in the Court of Insolvency if charged with the expense of a special correspondent for a single month." If the government insisted that bulletins which it cleared were the only fountains of truth, it had an obligation to filter the waters free of rumors, a job which only trained newspapermen could undertake. With experienced reporters gagged, the public was "at the mercy of every rogue, or coward, or ignoramus . . . with a batch of rumors." Thumbing their copies of *Areopagitica*, the editors insisted that the only way to defeat error was by giving a free rein to truth.[18]

One weapon in the editors' arsenal often sent shots close to the target. This was ridicule of censorship as a shield for the vanity of volunteer officers whose sudden honors had made them dizzy with self-importance. It was, according to some papers, only political generals, accustomed to "bought" party sheets, who bridled under the whips and scorns of correspondents. Or pettifogging commanders who thought that the war hinged upon their assignments. As a Western correspondent for the irreverent *Chicago Times* explained, after weeks of inactivity

> Toodlesville is attacked. . . . The loyal Rangers and the Sappington Guards are ordered out. . . . Suddenly a little great man approaches and addresses himself to the quill corps: "This affair must be kept quiet; the good of

[18] *New York Herald*, January 19, 1862, February 5, 1863; *Boston Journal*, October 25, November 15, 1861; *Cincinnati Commercial*, September 2, 1861, April 15, 1862, May 19, 1864; *New York Post*, quoted in *Cincinnati Commercial*, September 5, 1862; *Missouri Democrat*, February 28, 1862.

> the service requires it." The corps expostulates, reasons the thing, begs, entreats. It's all of no use. "Suppose," says the little great man, "suppose Toodlesville should fall; what a damper it would be to enlistments to let it be known. Mum's the word." And no dispatch.

Truthful reporting, said some correspondents, irked only "ex-butcher boys, country pedagogues, and counter-jumpers, elevated into positions of small trust." Also, as William D. Bickham, a battle-seasoned observer for the *Cincinnati Commercial*, pointed out, no complaint was ever made about correspondents who *flattered* commanders. It was the general who was all "sword, plume and buttons," the thieving supply officer, the military man used only to the reports of "parasites and toadies" who found the fierce white light of criticism unbearable.[19]

Lastly, there *was* the question of freedom of the press. It was not presented in an entirely nonpartisan manner. Democratic papers supporting the war suffered the embarrassment of a loyal opposition in a national emergency. They had no way to avoid what would later be called a "me too" position on major issues. In prospecting for lesser issues on which to challenge the administration, they struck a rich vein in the censorship. The *New York World*, choking in anger at the War Department's announcement that telegraphic dispatches would be supervised, said that it was a "people's war." It is their institutions which are

[19] *New York Herald*, July 18, 1861; *Chicago Tribune*, April 21, 1862; *Chicago Times*, April 17, September 10, 1862, February 16, 1863; *Cincinnati Commercial*, September 23, 1861, March 29, 1862; *New York Tribune*, July 13, 1861, May 26, 1862.

at stake," cried an editorial. "They have a right to know how their war is conducted." The *Chicago Times* groped for adjectives to convey the "enormity of the hideousness of this censorship"; the *New York Herald* declaimed on the government's moral obligation to relieve the public's anxieties. But even the purebred Republican *Chicago Tribune* used the *World's* very phrase, a people's war, in attacks on the government's control of information, and argued that the home front was entitled to a relief from the tedious waiting for official bulletins. One correspondent planted a seed out of which, in time, press relations bureaus would flower rewardingly in headquarters:

> When a government is loudly calling for more men and money should it not at least be willing to entrust that people with a knowledge of what is going on?

It should have been, but in May, 1862, it was not, and the pessimism of a Cincinnati paper which saw "no compensation . . . in any quarter" for the grievances of the curious rested solidly on the facts of life. The editors had the eloquence and the shibboleths, but, as usual in wartime, the government had what was more important, the last word.[20]

As the war moved into its second year, the restrictions rained down thick and fast on the reporters. McClellan

[20] *New York World*, February 27, 1862; *Chicago Times*, March 28, 1862; *Chicago Tribune*, May 21, 1862; *Cincinnati Commercial*, May 22, 1862; *New York Herald*, August 27, 1862, July 13, 1864.

went to the Peninsula in the spring, and correspondents trailed after him in droves, with every big-city paper ready to throw open its front page to "exclusive eyewitness" write-ups of the Confederacy's fall. A security crackdown was imposed, and one of the first victims of the tightened rules was George Alfred Townsend, a witty sprig of a correspondent for the *New York Herald*. Townsend, who had just turned twenty-one, went scouting with a cavalry patrol, a nonregulation procedure to begin with. At an abandoned tavern he picked up several Richmond newspapers, and on his return to the base camp at White House, on the Pamunkey River, gave them over to the *Herald's* agent there. Someone let the story out, and Townsend was arrested and taken to the tent of General Marcy, chief of staff, who received him at a desk littered with books, maps, and empty bottles, under which the reporter's eye caught a bucket half full of water and ice. He spent a night under arrest before his plea of ignorance of the order was accepted. Meantime, soldiers on duty at headquarters spread rumors that the slender youngster was the captured nephew of General Lee. When a teamster brought him a log to sit on, Townsend announced to him gravely, "If you ever get to Richmond, you shall be considerately treated." [21]

Other newspapermen had their troubles. In northern Virginia, in August, 1862, a shift in command brought General John Pope to the head of the army. Pope, on or-

[21] *Official Records*, Ser. 1, XI, Pt. 1, 167, 181, 194, 214; George Alfred Townsend, *Campaigns of a Non-Combatant* (New York, 1866), pp. 91-102.

ders from Halleck, who was now exercising over-all command from Washington, ordered all newspapermen to leave the camps. There was a great scurrying for appointments as "volunteer aides-de-camp" on the part of correspondents who were friendly with politically appointed officers, always willing to recollect that publicity was the key to Congressional seats, governorships, and other lawful spoils of war. It was just as well for Pope, a man of marvelous conceit, that his forces did operate in virtual secrecy for the next few weeks. He was thoroughly defeated at the second battle of Bull Run on August 29th, and one of the results was to throw the censors into a spasm of bureaucratic fear, so that in New York the provost marshal sent squads through the city to tear down information from the bulletin boards which, in the days before radio, hung in front of newspaper offices.[22]

When the Confederates pushed northward into Maryland, heading toward the showdown battle at Antietam, the blackout grew in density. The *New York Herald's* Washington bureau chief wrote to Bennett that he was obliged to back up dispatches sent to the telegraph office with duplicates in the slower-moving mails, having no assurances of what would pass the wire censorship. Even five weeks after the battle, the censor's office at Pennsylvania and Four-and-a-Half Streets was operating so efficiently that the *Herald's* capital agent, whose force of reporters

[22] *Official Records*, Ser. 1, XII, Pt. 3, 602, 608; Albert D. Richardson, *The Secret Service, The Field, The Dungeon and The Escape* (Hartford, 1866), p. 278; George W. Smalley, *Anglo-American Memories* (New York, 1911), pp. 95-140; *New York World*, August 30, 1862.

was the largest of any paper's, spoke of being "dissevered" from the army.[23]

In southern Tennessee, meanwhile, the situation for correspondents was made bleak by the presence in command of Major General Don Carlos Buell, a high-foreheaded professional soldier trained to a meticulous observance of regulations by long years of service in the office of the Adjutant General. The Radical Republican press had it in for Buell in any case as a close intimate of the conservative McClellan, and he quickly depressed his standing to new lows by a uniformly frigid attitude towards all reporters, so intense that he once turned down the request of a practical staff officer merely to admit a correspondent as a shorthand reporter at a court-martial. When, in September, a Confederate force dodged past Buell and reached the Ohio River at a point only a few hours from Cincinnati, the bustling river port was put under martial law, and its mayor and chief of police, under direct orders from Washington, spent several nights scanning the first issues of the six local papers (two of them printed in German) which rolled off the presses. They had the power to suppress any which were indiscreet in divulging military news.[24]

But it was in Mississippi, where Union troops moving down the river had halted before the immovable obstacle

[23] *Boston Journal,* Washington correspondence, November 11, 1862; James Gordon Bennett Papers, Library of Congress, L.A. Whitely to Bennett, September 10, 1862, penciled appendix to letter of S. M. Carpenter to Frederic Hudson, October 27, 1862.

[24] *Official Records,* Ser. 1, XVI, Pt. 2, 164, 354; "Prominent Early Citizens of Brighton," by "Conteur" [Alfred Henderson], *Cincinnati Enquirer,* December 24, 1922.

of Vicksburg, that a second clash between reporters and generals, which exploded in print as loudly as the Halleck incident, underscored once more the intention of the army to have security regulations taken seriously. Into the picture stepped Major General William Tecumseh Sherman, a man whose fierce red-headed features, often puckered with concentration, gave every evidence that he meant business. He did. In February, 1863, he made a serious effort to hang Thomas W. Knox, ace correspondent for one of the country's most powerful papers, the *New York Herald.*

To the reporters, Sherman was cast in the role of nemesis wherever they met him. He wrote to his brother, then a Republican Senator from Ohio, that he would prefer to be governed by Jeff Davis than to be

> abused by a set of dirty newspaper scribblers who have the impudence of Satan. They come into camp, poke about among the lazy shirks and pick up their camp rumors and publish them as facts, and the avidity with which these rumors are swallowed by the public makes even some of our officers bow to them. I will not. They are a pest and shall not approach me and I will treat them as spies which in truth they are.

In other letters he raged that the newspapers had foiled every Union move of any importance by untimely tip-offs, that lying was a reporter's trade, that Napoleon would have been beaten with a free press. Being a man given to acting on his words, he had ousted several correspondents from his camps.[25] The newsmen, a testy lot in their own right, chose their own ways to retaliate. Newspaper stories from Kentucky, where Sherman commanded in the autumn of 1861, insisted that the army there was entirely unready for action. When Sherman, nervous and irritable, made extravagantly gloomy guesses about enemy prospects, they whispered that he was insane. Some accounts of the battle of Shiloh said that his troops had been completely caught by surprise by the Confederate early morning attack. Sherman, possessing to a morbid degree a regular-army phobia of encirclement by "politicians," nursed his bile and waited.[26]

The Christmas holidays of 1862 found Sherman commanding the 15th Army Corps in the Army of the Mississippi and about to use it to outflank the defenders of Vicksburg. A few miles above the city, the tributary Yazoo River curled into the Mississippi. The plan was to take the corps up the Yazoo with an escort of gunboats, land it, and drive around the Confederate right wing into the key town. The troops went ashore on the day after Christmas, and on Monday, the 29th of December, charged the enemy works in waves. But the Confederates were posted on heavily wooded bluffs, and within a few hours the attack, whose co-ordination became badly scrambled, was shot to bits.

[25] Sherman Papers, Sherman to John Sherman, May 12, 1862, to Lieutenant Governor Stanton, Ohio, N.D., 1862, to —— L'Hommedieu, July 7, 1862; Rachel S. Thorndike (ed.), *The Sherman Letters* (New York, 1894), Sherman to John Sherman, February 18, 1863, pp. 191-192; Lloyd Lewis, *Sherman, Fighting Prophet* (New York, 1932), pp. 190-193.

[26] *Chicago Tribune*, November 24, 1861, April 14, 1862; *New York Tribune*, January 13, 1862; Sherman Papers, Ellen Sherman to Abraham Lincoln, January 10, 1862.

The next day a chilly rain soaked the ground and the miserable wounded. Then a heavy fog blanketed a plan to move the troops further upstream for another effort, and the river began to rise dangerously. On the day after the new year had begun, steamboats splashed downstream, carrying an army which had left the field, as one correspondent put it, with its tail drooping between its legs.

It was a bad time for a defeat. Only three weeks before, the Army of the Potomac had suffered its bloody setback at Fredericksburg, in Virginia. Besides, Sherman was about to be superseded in command by General John A. McClernand, a long-bearded ex-Congressman from Illinois, of limitless conceit, who had talked Lincoln into giving him a special, separate command for an attack on Vicksburg. (The President, in offering to McClernand an amorphous task force of Western regiments, had hopes that a famous victory won by a Democrat such as McClernand would go far to dissolve the hostility which too many of the farmers of southern Illinois felt towards a Republican-managed war.) The new commander was on his way down the river when the battle was fought, and Sherman was wide open to the charge that he had rushed into a hopeless operation in a last-minute effort to win credit for capturing Vicksburg. Some papers were saying as much the moment the story was broken.[27]

Figuratively feeling the edge of the skinning knife along his scalp, the corps commander decided on a counter-

[27] *Chicago Tribune*, January 14, 1863; *Cincinnati Commercial*, January 15, 1863; *Boston Journal*, January 20, 1863.

attack. He ordered his chief of staff and mail agents to impound and open any bulky letters addressed to Cairo, and, hurdling legal objections, pounced on a fat manuscript, accompanied by two maps, carrying the signature of the *Herald's* Thomas Wallace Knox. The choice of Knox was especially satisfying. The *Herald* observer was a twenty-eight-year-old New Hampshireman who had kept school for a time before striking westward to Denver and newspaper work. He still could scold like a Yankee pedagogue, and his drawled sarcastic remarks in public probably did little to disguise his private opinion that Sherman was "making an ass of himself." In addition, as a representative of Bennett's influential paper, he would presumably be an especially educational example to other sinners. Lastly, the ungainly reporter had come down the river as a guest aboard the headquarters steamboat of General Frank P. Blair. Blair, a Congressman, the brother of the Postmaster General, and member of a family which had enjoyed fairly regular access to the White House for thirty years, was classed by Sherman with the political officers. This was not entirely fair, for Blair was a hard fighter, but Sherman, obsessed with the idea of a plot between a reporter and a politician to do him in, was not a reasonable man. He cross-examined Blair by mail, asking if he had any complaints to voice about the conduct of the engagement, and hinting strongly that he disapproved of officers who made newspapermen familiar with their discontents. Blair, unintimidated, replied tartly. Yes, he had shown his official report to Knox; no, he had not criticized the operation, and plainly, he did not like his commander's tone. Sherman replied with contentment that he had only wanted to straighten the facts before putting Knox where he belonged.[28]

Knox himself had been expecting trouble, for after confiding his first story of the battle to the official mail boat (where it was intercepted) he had gone personally to Cairo and filed a second account. This one got through to the *Herald* and reflected, among other things, the bitterness of a man who had spent a hungry night sleeping in the open in order to get a story which he suspected would be snatched from the mail pouch by the censor. Sherman, the account ran, had made such faulty dispositions that two days were given to the "rebels" to fortify while the units were reshuffled. Sherman's instructions concerning support assignments for the divisions were so erratic that "discussion . . . with respect to his sanity was revived with great earnestness." Sherman had delayed sending out a flag of truce for two days for fear of exposing the extent of his losses. For days after the fight he kept hospital boats from proceeding up the Mississippi, where observers in the rear areas could count the cost. Sherman had left tons of salvagable bread, pork, powder and stores to be destroyed when pulling out of the position. A sane mind was now needed to conduct operations.[29]

[28] *Official Records*, Ser. 1, XVII, Pt. 2, 581-588, 890-892; Wilkie, *Pen and Powder*, pp. 23-24; Bennett Papers, Knox to Bennett or Frederic Hudson, July 25, 1862.
[29] *New York Herald*, January 18, 1863; Knox, *Campfire and Cotton-Field*, pp. 245-250.

When Knox, apparently confident of his paper's protection, returned from Cairo, he found himself under arrest and slated to face a board consisting of one brigadier general, four colonels and two majors, on charges of spying, conveying information to the enemy, and willful disobedience of orders. He had incurred the last by the simple act of filing any story at all, because a general order, buried since 1861 in War Department folders, forbade the publication of any account of military movements without the imprimatur of the commanding general. Knox was kept in confinement aboard a river steamer during the trial, and in the book which he hastened to commit to the postwar market for memoirs in 1865, he claimed to have spent the time leafing through novels and calmly drinking a dozen bottles of ale sent aboard by a friend. Like many correspondents, his bravery improved in retrospect. He actually had been frightened badly enough to write Sherman a letter of recantation, pleading ignorance of orders, offering to send a correct account to the *Herald*, praising the admirably "full and complete" plans for the operation, and apologizing for ungentle remarks about subordinate commanders seriatim.[30]

Knox had yielded unnecessarily to panic. Even to please the commanding general, the court-martial could hardly have hanged him for conveying information to the enemy in a letter printed nearly three weeks after the engagement. He was judged only to have flouted orders "without

[30] Knox, *Campfire and Cotton-Field*, pp. 250-253; *Official Records*, Ser. 1, XVII, Pt. 2, 580-581; Sherman Papers, Knox to Sherman, February 1, 1863.

criminality" and was sent out of the zone of operations. Scarcely had he left when the *Herald's* influence was set to work. A Colorado Congressman, flanked by a brace of newspaper reporters, called at the White House to ask that the ban be lifted. Lincoln's reply was characteristically canny. He said that Knox might return, depurged, if Grant gave his consent, expecting accurately that Grant would not thus repudiate his friend and subordinate. It was just as well for the correspondent, for Sherman had made up his mind that Knox would go "down the Mississippi floating on a log" the next time he was caught in camp.

By the time the affair finally ended, Sherman could feel satisfied. McClernand, who had optimistically brought his wife and her baggage down the river with him, was getting nowhere. Knox gave up war correspondence altogether, and even though he had not dangled from a gibbet his banishment had a sobering effect on his colleagues. Near the beginning of March, the *Herald's* agent at Memphis wrote to his managing editor that the correspondents of the *New York World* and *Times* had left the Vicksburg area, and that "many of the letters published in the St. Louis and New York papers, are written, not from the fleet, as they purport, but from Memphis."

It was safer to criticize William T. Sherman from a distance. Thereafter, letters from his camps were wholesomely impersonal. Another clear-cut round had gone to the army.[31]

[31] *Official Records,* Ser. 1, XVII, Pt. 2, 889-897; Sherman Papers, Sherman to John Sherman, April 3, 1863; Richardson, *Secret Service Field, Dungeon and Escape,* p. 320; Bennett Papers, Bingham to Frederic Hudson,

After that, matters became more serious for the reporters. Not the least of their troubles was the gradual elimination of most of the straight-out political appointees from influential positions. There were few leaks in the headquarters of tough professionals such as Sheridan, Thomas, Meade, Hancock, Gillmore, Weitzel or McPherson. Correspondents not only lost their opportunities to preview official reports, but had all they could do to extort mess privileges, food for their mounts, and travel passes from supply officers. A paper the size of the *Herald* even took to furnishing logistical support for its own large detachment of reporters. They were provided with horses, and a wagon painted with the paper's name in eminently readable letters rolled with each corps headquarters, carrying extra necessities for them.

The stockade of regulations around the news-gatherers continued to grow. In January of 1863, the Army of the Potomac changed hands once more, going this time to the handsome General Joseph Hooker. And Hooker issued an order clever enough for a diplomat. Reporters were to be allowed to criticize as freely as they pleased after any engagement, but they would have to sign their letters, a requirement which made it certain that a good many second thoughts would be given to any hasty judgments.[32] At

---

February 23, 1863. The correspondents took it out on Sherman at a prudent range; see, for example, *Cincinnati Commercial*, February 14, 27, 1863; *New York World*, February 17, 1863; *Chicago Times*, January 13, February 13, 17, 1863; *Boston Journal*, March 3, 1863; *New York Tribune*, February 18, 1863.

[32] *Official Records*, Ser. 1, XXVII, Pt. 3, 192.

least two correspondents who were not slowed down were under arrest in March. The next month, the army had an opportunity to control the press gallery almost en masse at an operation for the first time in the war.

What made it possible was the fact that it was a naval expedition. On the 6th of April, 1863, part of the Atlantic blockading fleet tried to shoot its way into Charleston harbor, which was thoroughly guarded by forts. During the planning of the attack, arrangements were made for ten correspondents to witness the fighting from the small steamer *Nantasket.* They were under the stewardship of a General Seymour, a regular army officer from Connecticut, who was chief of staff of the accompanying land expedition which was to follow up the victory by taking Charleston.

But at that point the "rebels" were still prospering, and the shore batteries successfully pounded the attacking fleet until it limped away. This was witnessed by the ten correspondents on the *Nantasket*, by three others (representing the *New York Times*, *Herald*, and *Baltimore American*) who had gone aboard a small scouting craft, and, most satisfactorily of all, by the correspondent of the *New York Tribune*, the enterprising Henry Villard, who had declined the army's hospitality, having something better in hand, the personal invitation of Admiral Samuel DuPont to come aboard his flagship, the *New Ironsides*. From the ship's stripped-down decks, piled high with splinter-catching hides and wet sandbags, Villard had a front-row seat at the operations. What was even better, he sailed northward the next evening on the admiral's dispatch boat.

The ten observers on the *Nantasket* found official recognition to be a boomerang. Unable to scatter individually to the telegraph offices, they stayed afloat with the *Nantasket*, which was under military control, or, more specifically, the control of General Seymour. The general apparently felt that the North was in no hurry to absorb new disappointments; he kept the frustrated "specials" at sea until two days after the fighting (and well after they had been scooped by Villard), and finally permitted them to return morosely to base at Port Royal, further down the coast, where they caught a mail steamer for New York.[33]

In the West, things were no better. Correspondents at besieged Vicksburg in the spring sifted asterisks through their letters, occasionally making tongue-in-cheek absurdities of stories:

> An expedition is destined to the neighborhood of **, there to disembark and go across the country to **, on the ** with a view of capturing ** which interposes an obstruction to the descent of our forces from ** to **.

At Murfreesboro, Tennessee, in July, an order from the chief of staff to the commanding general, William S. Rosecrans, denied the telegraph wires to correspondents altogether during any movements. What made this particularly significant and melancholy was that the chief was General James A. Garfield, a politician only seventeen years from the White House in that summer, and slated to occupy a Congressional seat before the year was out. There was no

[33] *Boston Journal,* April 15, 1863; *New York Tribune,* April 14, 1863.

telling what might happen if officers with *that* kind of aim in life became security-conscious. The unkindest cut of all, however, was experienced at Chattanooga, in October, by Albert H. Bodman, a representative of the *Chicago Tribune*. Standing in a group near the headquarters of Rosecrans, Bodman overheard a question concerning the make-up of several units in the city's garrison. Preening himself slightly on his industry, the correspondent produced from a pocket a privately compiled order of battle of the Union forces. Included among the bystanders was Charles A. Dana, late managing editor of the *New York Tribune*, then serving the country as a special observer for the War Department, with the title of Assistant Secretary. (In practice, he was keeping an eye on the commanding officer for Stanton, a war minister whose faith in his generals thinned rapidly with their distance from Washington.) The next day the reporter learned, by being called to the office of the provost marshal general and relieved of his list, that Dana had reported the incident. His chagrin was considerably enlarged by Dana's complicity; he had expected much better treatment from a fellow initiate in journalism.

Within a few weeks, Chattanooga was made forbidden territory to another correspondent, Joseph B. McCullagh, of the *Cincinnati Commercial*. "Mack," as he signed his letters, was a baby-faced, thin Irishman, capable of laying a tongue as briny as a herring barrel on anything military. "Mack" had reported the movement of a corps across the Tennessee River, a maneuver clearly visible to the dozens of rebel lookouts posted in the high mountains to the southward overlooking the entire city and its environs. An order from higher echelons nevertheless enjoined dismissal of the correspondent, who reported before the provost marshal general with a copy of the paper containing the story. The officer could not find the incriminating paragraph, wrote "Mack":

> He . . . wandered through the advertising columns, perused "correspondence wanted," and glanced carefully at the river column without finding what he was after, until I gave him the hint, when my character as a spy loomed up before him in vivid proportions; and he forthwith executed a long order full of good intentions and bad grammar, declaring me hereafter banished the department.[34]

In 1864, the press had come a long distance from voluntary agreement. Grant fought the battle of the Wilderness under the observation of a press section so well educated that, on the day the campaign began, a *New York Herald* man could decorously declare that there was

> news enough to write to fill the *Herald;* but, knowing how essential is prudence in such a time as this, I shall not in any manner thwart the designs of the great planner of the campaign, General Grant, by making public any matter pertaining to the same until we have met the enemy.

The adventurous virtues of the early days, however, lingered on among some correspondents. Early in the fighting,

[34] *Cincinnati Commercial,* April 10, 1863; *Chicago Tribune,* July 2, October 20, 1863; *Cincinnati Commercial,* November 4, 1863; Wilkie, *Pen and Powder,* pp. 54-55.

Congressman E. B. Washburne, of Illinois, visited Grant's headquarters and introduced to him a "literary gentleman" who wished to accompany the army. This was William Swinton, whose literature at the time consisted of war correspondence for the *New York Times*, a fact with which he did not burden Grant as he joined the headquarters group, under the protection of his Congressional introduction. One night, when the general was setting up the next day's operations at a secret firelight conference, one of his staff, noticing a peculiar shadow at the base of a stump, pulled Swinton to his feet. The correspondent, who was after a story that came straight from the top by the most direct route, got off with no more than a reprimand. Swinton's *élan* was not in the least reduced. In a short period of time he had managed to write something so irritating to General Ambrose E. Burnside, then commanding a corps, that the side-whiskered soldier ordered him to be shot, upon which Grant stepped in and had the *Times* eyewitness sent out of the lines, Congressman or no Congressman. Soon afterwards, tighter orders were issued, requiring the newspapermen to keep commanders of units with which they worked fully informed of their whereabouts, a practice which ended convenient disappearances into the anonymous confusion of a moving army during periods when pressure was on the correspondents.[35]

As for Sherman's march through Georgia, at its beginning, in May, he took care to recall the ground rules to

[35] *New York Herald,* May 5, 1864; Ulysses S. Grant, *Personal Memoirs* (New York, 1886), II, 143-145; *New York Tribune,* September 10, 1864.

any of the reporters who might possibly have forgotten Knox. An order to the officers of the army advised them paternally of what their relationships should be with correspondents — men who, it was explained in the tones of a lecture to young men on life in the city, would not take muskets and fight, but followed armies, picking up "news for sale" and bolstering "idle and worthless officers" while those who virtuously spurned flattery by the press were ignored and left in the shadows with only the consciousness of duty well done. Most of the audience apparently took the advice seriously. At least one correspondent — a *New York Tribune* man — was pounced on and asked for his pass by an officer whom he had been questioning amiably while they stood on a hilltop watching the shelling of Confederate positions on one side of the gorge through which the railroad to Atlanta threaded. He was kept under guard at headquarters until he had it fetched from his tent. A staff officer hotly rebuked an inquisitive reporter and told him to go to Washington, where the news would filter from official channels suitably purified. Told that the country was eager for information, the officer bellowed: "What the hell do we care about the country?" The remark was reported by the chastised interviewer — who might, however, have added that touch to make sure of directing public sympathy in the right way. The first month of the campaign saw a press representative, Benjamin F. Taylor, of a Chicago paper, given a notice of eviction from the camps. The reporters took what small comfort they could in such petulant ways as signing letters "Stone-Blind." All the same, their stories — which usually did not appear until two weeks after any action — held narrowly to facts.[36]

Even that was not always safe. Among the writers for the *New York Herald* following the army was one DeBow Randolph Keim, a journalist of singular immodesty, who left three scrapbooks of his writings to the Library of Congress, on his death, and once confided to a group of his fellow correspondents that he never read Shakespeare for fear of its interfering with his own style. Keim made an interesting discovery, namely, that Union cryptanalysts had unraveled the code in which Confederate units were signaling to each other by flags waved from high platforms in the wooded mountains towering over the route of advance. This news appeared in the *Herald* of June 23rd, causing an apoplectic reaction in headquarters, for if the news got to the "rebels" it would mean a change in the system and the slamming of a shutter over a helpful window into enemy plans. Sherman sent a scorching note down through channels, and conceivably thought once more about gibbets, but the actual handling of the case rested with the less inflammable General George H. Thomas, who sent Keim on the reporters' road to exile northward.[37] Both in the East and the West during 1864, there was more than enough for newspapermen to cover, but in order to get

[36] David P. Conyngham, *Sherman's March Through the South* (New York, 1865), pp. 51, 74; *New York Tribune*, May 20, June 10, 1864; *Cincinnati Commercial*, May 16, November 4, 1864.
[37] *Official Records*, Ser. 1, XXXVIII, Pt. 4, 637, 642; Wilkie, *Pen and Powder*, pp. 201-202.

a truly free hand in filing copy a reporter had to be ready to die game.

One of the *New York Tribune's* correspondents following Sherman to Atlanta wrote that what was needed was "the establishment of certain military rules governing the representatives of the press accompanying the various armies." By the war's end, a number of principles had been established but there was a long road to travel before they were made uniform and enforcement machinery provided. The correspondents had not yet even gotten the *quid pro quo* for their loss of complete independence — the authorization of someone to see that they were provided for in the rough and tumble of cross-country campaigning, when eating and sleeping were apt to be haphazard unless officially arranged. There was a step that way toward the end, when quartermasters were allowed to sell forage to correspondents, which meant that the horses which carried the eyes of the nation had at least an equal chance at government mangers with teamsters' donkeys.[38]

Still, not all the troubles of the correspondents had been useless. The army authorities, in all their harrying and pursuit of newspapermen, had thought of them as a group, and had acted towards them in their collective character as members of a particular (and, to the military, exasperating) calling. They had managed to confer upon them that curiously elusive and significant possession in the

[38] *New York Tribune,* June 10, August 31, 1864.

modern world, status. The reporters, joining together in manifestoes to Halleck, or writing separately to their papers defending their own missions and importance, were arguing their case not as fringe observers of a war, without rights or recognition, but as professionals. In the long run, that was the first important issue of their struggle with the powers and princedoms of the army.

Besides, they were involved in a story as far-reaching in its own way as any they covered. Freedom of the press, in new-style war, was an early sacrifice. It was not killed. It went into pawn, and after the armistice the claim checks were presented and the safe opened. The system would be used again, and would work again, though not without raising nervous disturbances. In their own enforced tongue-biting and lip-pressing, the correspondents were recording the gamble which a democracy took with the political fates when it rolled up its sleeves for war.

CHAPTER V

Mr. Bennett's War

LATE in November, 1861, Thomas W. Knox handed a bulky envelope to a soldier in Springfield, Missouri. It contained Knox's most recent stories of Union operations in the southwestern corner of the State, and he wanted it to be slipped into the mails somewhere in the rear of the army, where things were less unsettled. The messenger, however, muffed his instructions, and dropped the copy off at a telegraph office from which it was sent to New York at a cost of $255.62. A St. Louis editor who got wind of this through newspapermen's channels thought it hugely funny; it was "a pretty severe jolter" for James Gordon Bennett, but the old man would cover the mistake by calling it "enterprise."[1] Undoubtedly Bennett did pay the bill without flinching; unlike the Scotsman of the joke-books, he was prodigal with the dollars he spent on his paper, knowing perfectly well that in the long run the jokes, if any, would be on his far outdistanced competitors.

From the start, the *Herald's* correspondents operated like a well-drilled team amply backed up by reserves. A Midwestern editor visiting the capital in June of 1861 watched the Washington squad in action with helpless pro-

[1] *Missouri Republican,* November 25, 1861, quoting St. Louis correspondence of *Chicago Tribune.*

fessional admiration. There were then four of them, combing camps, office buildings and "public resorts" daily, with incidental expenses guaranteed and orders to send any copy, even "in wads," by wire. Once, when a small naval force dropped down to the mouth of the Potomac and fought a brief action, a *Herald* man was aboard one of the vessels, another camped at the Navy Department to have the first look at the official report when it came in, and a third made his way to the navy yard to await the return of the group and round up any missing details from the officers. A little over a year later, the paper's Washington superintendent was posting half a dozen reporters to the various corps headquarters of the Army of the Potomac alone. By December of 1862 Bennett, never reluctant to let his light shine before men, was proudly telling readers that the *Herald* had over thirty reporters with the armies, and that the cost of keeping them ran to more than two thousand dollars weekly, not counting tolls for Associated Press wire dispatches.[2]

As a result, *Herald* men were in plentiful supply whenever there was action. They covered all operations worth reporting, and in slow periods were capable of finding stories in unlikely ways. One enterprising reporter in a quiet zone in North Carolina in 1862, for example, put on a slouch hat with the top gone, a pair of battered shoes and a ragged jacket, and wandered undisturbed behind Confederate lines for four days collecting copy. Others

[2] *Cincinnati Commercial*, June 6, 1861; James Gordon Bennett Papers, Library of Congress. L. A. Hendricks to Bennett, September 10, 1862; *New York Herald*, December 6, 1862.

turned routine hazards of war to advantage. In February of 1863, the Union gunboat *Queen of the West* ran aground in a Louisiana river and was captured. The spoils included a *Herald* correspondent, Finley Anderson, who had remained indecisively standing on the hurricane deck while the officers and crew scrambled over the side to escape to a rescue craft. He was waiting, as he later put it with dignity, for the captain to return and destroy the ship. It was a mistake which cost him a year in prison camps, but got him a four-column story over his signature after he was exchanged. When Jeb Stuart raided the headquarters of the Army of the Potomac in the summer of 1862, a nameless *Herald* reporter lost his spare clothes, blankets, notebooks and camp bed, but was compensated by having a sheaf of sprightly copy to turn in. During the battle of the Wilderness, two of the paper's men heading rearward to file stories were pounced upon by Confederate guerrillas. They were stripped of everything but shirts and pants, driven several miles through the woods on foot, and released. From there they found their way to the Potomac, floundered to midstream on a raft and were picked up by a gunboat. They were blistered, burned and half-starved. But the story filled part of the May 11th front page. The *Herald's* men always had a story to bring back, to claim attention along with the shipping columns, Bennett's strident editorials, and the advertisements for Dr. Tobias's Pulmonic Life Syrup, Wood's Minstrels, or Hostetter's Bitters.[3]

[3] *New York Herald,* November 17, 1862, March 6, 1863, March 6, 1864, August 29, 1862, May 11, 1864.

Three *Herald* correspondents did not come back. Phineas Homans fell from the deck of a steamer in a South Carolina inlet and died of concussion of the brain. Another, J. P. Dunn, was found dead of illness in the stateroom of a river boat on the way home from covering Vicksburg. A certain Mr. Buckingham came closest to death in combat; in an unexpected brush with guerrillas in Virginia, his frightened horse pitched him to the ground, fracturing his skull. Alec Waud, an artist for *Harper's Weekly*, dug a temporary grave with his own hands; the body was later shipped North.[4]

That was a human cost to add to the half million which the managing editor later guessed to be the total expense of covering the war. The results of the outlay were, however, significantly rewarding. According to Bennett himself, the paper, which was selling 60,000 copies a day at the outbreak of the war, had doubled that total by July, 1862, and in the early part of 1863 was on some days reaching a circulation of 135,000.[5] Those were bonanza figures for the sixties. They were the seals on a diploma certifying big-city journalism's graduation from the class of small business; they were also impressive vindication of the strenuous methods which Bennett had brought to the newspaper profession.

A satisfying chain reaction was kept in motion. The superiority of the eight-page daily in readability and thoroughness kept its readership high; because of the size

[4] *New York Herald*, June 17, 1862, June 25, July 23, 1863.
[5] *New York Herald*, July 23, 1862, February 14, 1863; Frederic Hudson, *Journalism in the United States., 1690-1872* (New York, 1873), p. 482.

of its audience it was a political power; because it was a political power, its reporters enjoyed entrees for which colleagues would have traded months of pay, and they exploited the *Herald's* head start to keep it well ahead of the pack in the hunt for news. The paper's editorial course was erratic, since Bennett's restless enthusiasms could not be confined for long in one place, but it was uniformly inhospitable to the administration, and as often as not downright venomous about what it regarded as abolitionist influence in the White House. All the same, Republican major-domos swallowed hard and opened doors for the *Herald* as a matter of precaution.

Lincoln himself was as gingerly with the paper's owner as a housewife with a distasteful dead mouse to dispose of. During the secession crisis he sent Thurlow Weed, boss of the New York Republican machine, to ask Bennett if the *Herald* would take a firmer antisecession tone for the benefit of impressionable European readers. Over the fruit course in the editor's Washington Heights home, Weed put the question, and, much as expected, got a ten-minute tirade against the abolitionists and the war which they had brought on themselves. Still, Lincoln did not express any open disappointment over Weed's failure to get results and in the autumn of 1861 he wrote personally to Bennett to apologize when the Navy Department held up a pass for a *Herald* reporter to go aboard one of its ships. The following spring he again took trouble to smooth the paper's feathers, explaining in his own hand to Bennett that the proclamation of an overzealous Union commander,

General David P. Hunter, freeing the slaves in his command in coastal South Carolina, had not been gotten up with Secretary Stanton's connivance. Almost at the end of the war, he offered Bennett the ambassadorship to France, in circumstances that later led to suspicions of a payment for services rendered in the 1864 campaign. If so, it was a curious decision, since the journal's Election Day comment had been that the voters were offered "rather a choice of evils than a choice of excellencies." Still, the *Herald* had never traveled with the peace-at-any-price faction, and even its neutrality might have been considered worth something. Whatever the reasons, Bennett declined the invitation, gratifying as the tender of the post may have been.[6]

In the War and Navy Department offices there were profitable good feelings shown to *Herald* correspondents. Malcolm Ives, a Washington operative, wrote privately to his employer and claimed, perhaps untruthfully, that Assistant Secretary of the Navy Gustavus V. Fox had personally given him, at the start of 1862, a private list of all vessels then in service, and had promised darkly to "have *every thing* given to the *Herald*" exclusively. Fox, a retired naval officer from Massachusetts, was apparently regarded as a special channel by *Herald* men, for just prior to the 1864 election, Thomas M. Cook, a correspondent assigned to cover a naval expedition against the North Carolina coast, approached him with a demand to be sent

[6] Don C. Seitz, *The James Gordon Bennetts, Father and Son* (Indianapolis, 1928), pp. 173-177, 187, 193; Oliver G. Carlson, *James Gordon Bennett, The Man Who Made News* (New York, 1942), pp. 336, 369-371; *New York Herald*, November 7, 1864.

aboard Admiral David Porter's flagship and given special facilities for returning with his story ahead of other newsmen. If the arrangements were satisfactory, said Cook, he would make a report "acceptable both to the Admiral and the Department." Fox, according to the correspondent's letter to Frederic Hudson, the *Herald's* managing editor, offered to see what he could do, which was evidently not quite sufficient a guarantee for Cook, who wrote the home office:

> I yet think the Navy Department could be induced to procure for us an outside vessel which we might call our own were Ashley or some other person who is on confidential terms there authorized to promise Fox that thereafter he and the Department would be exempt from attacks in the columns of the Herald. This hint is, of course, *sub rosa.*[7]

In the military preserves of the war office, too, *Herald* men carried a big stick. Malcolm Ives spun lengthy, but suspect, tales of kindnesses received from Secretary Stanton. S. P. Hanscom, another member of the Washington bureau, had a pipe line in the Department through which, in the autumn of 1861, he was receiving information on the military situation in Missouri supposedly known only to General Scott and two others. L. A. Whitely, at the head of the paper's Washington staff, wrote in 1863 that every effort would be made to get advance copies of official reports, "even if it should be necessary to *pay*" — suggesting that

[7] Bennett Papers, Ives to Bennett, January 27, 1862, Cook to Hudson, November 3, 1864.

some of the *Herald's* money went into the pockets of co-operative departmental clerks.[8]

In the headquarters tents of commanding generals, *Herald* men were frequent confidential visitors. The most striking rapport between a military chief and a reporter was that which bound the normally undemonstrative Grant to one of Bennett's correspondents, known merely as S. Cadwallader. A swarthy, wrinkled man with a nervous manner, Cadwallader was always allowed to remain at Grant's headquarters. The stocky future President not only wrote a letter, embalmed in the official records, in which he declared the reporter to be a model of his calling, but he also got General Benjamin Butler to commission Cadwallader as a lieutenant in his headquarters when he was evidently threatened by the draft in 1864. (Cadwallader responded with what Butler regarded as base ingratitude. When the Massachusetts politician, thoroughly inept as a soldier, was removed from command after the election victory had neutralized his capacity for damage, Cadwallader learned of the fact privately and broke the story before it had gotten back to the deposed general himself.) A spicy tale was whispered concerning the strange alliance, namely that Cadwallader had spirited Grant quietly and anonymously back to headquarters after the hero of Vicksburg had gotten resoundingly drunk on an inspection trip during the siege.[9]

[8] Bennett Papers, Hanscom to Bennett, October 6, 1861, Whitely to Hudson, November 29, 1863.

[9] William T. Sherman Papers, Library of Congress, copy of Letter from Grant to Cadwallader on the occasion of his commission, September 23,

Other *Herald* men contrived to occupy commanding ground for covering a war. William F. G. Shanks, a Kentuckian in his twenties, was a volunteer aide to General Lovell H. Rousseau — by happy coincidence also a Kentuckian — and was gratefully mentioned in dispatches. Winfield Scott Hancock, a corps commander in the Army of the Potomac, was sufficiently impressed with the talents of Finley Anderson, assigned to his headquarters after returning from his year in Confederate prisons, to get him a commission. (Anderson's first official act in his new role was to quit the paper, but by then it was already November of 1864.) Thomas M. Cash, a *Herald* observer in New Orleans, was offered a furnished house and office "for a mere nominal rent" by General Nathaniel P. Banks; his persuasive ways seemed to act upon naval officers as well, for he claimed that Admiral Farragut promised him a berth for an assistant on any ship he chose to name. When T. M. Cook was sent to Chattanooga in May, 1864, he was brought up short of his destination by a ban on correspondents. But providentially one of the generals in the Union force there was Daniel E. Sickles, a whilom Democratic Congressman from New York, and in that role an old *Herald* crony. A few notes were exchanged, and Cook was on his way to Chattanooga, pass in hand, to join the camp as General Sickles's private secretary. When the navy forced its way

---

1864; *Official Records,* Ser. 1, XLVI, Pt. 2, 120-121, Butler to J. Rawlins, January 13, 1865; Franc B. Wilkie, *Pen and Powder* (Boston, 1888), pp. 205-209. Wilkie's story of Cadwallader's hushing up of Grant's binge was given on hearsay evidence, but a letter of Lloyd Lewis to his publishers confirms the story by documents which he found in the Grant papers. See the *New York Times Book Review,* April 2, 1950, p. 3.

past the defenses of New Orleans, the chief communications officer aboard the flagship, Bradley Sillick Osbon, reserved part of his heavily taxed attention for observations for the *Herald*, for which he corresponded on the side. Everywhere, Bennett's men were planted in sensitive locations, like the spies of a superefficient policy agency.[10]

To rival editors, Bennett's pre-eminence was a continuing gloomy reminder that the rain fell alike upon the unjust and the just. Republican editors, especially, lamented over the favors granted to the hypercritical *Herald* when their own loyalty went unrewarded. Occasionally, however, they had a rare chance for laughter, and in February of 1862 they were able to rejoice immoderately in the chastising of two *Herald* Washington correspondents, though in the end it was difficult, as always, to say whether the publicity had done the paper more harm than good.

Malcolm Ives had enjoyed a checkered past before coming to Washington in the first winter of the war. According to the *New York Tribune* — by no means an infallible source where one of Bennett's men was concerned — he had worked in a Philadelphia bank, gone to Rome on a trip, become a convert to Catholicism and returned home a priest. After a time the life ecclesiastical became too taxing, and he defrocked himself in order to marry, came to New York, and (so the *Tribune* said) involved himself in Democratic

[10] *Official Records*, Ser. 1, XVI, Pt. 1, 1048; Bennett Papers, Anderson to Bennett, November 7, 1864, Cash to Hudson, March 5, 1863, Cook to Hudson, May 3, 1864; F. Lauriston Bullard, *Famous War Correspondents* (Boston, 1914), pp. 401-434.

politics, with the happy result of landing a position in the customs house through the influence of Mayor Fernando Wood. He was also supposed to have a brother, a West Point graduate, who had gone over to the Confederacy.

Whether or not the *Herald* had sent him to Washington, Ives considered himself one of the paper's employees, and in January of 1862 wrote a series of amazing letters to Bennett, claiming to be a tender intimate of Stanton, McClellan and other high officials, and relating excited stories of items given to him in sacred confidence for Bennett's use only. On the 8th of February he bounded into the War Department office, cornered an Assistant Secretary, Peter Watson, and hinted that the *Herald* would have unkind things to say about the management of the war if an exclusive story was not forthcoming. At that point Secretary Stanton, a man mirthless about mental aberrations, decided to demonstrate publicly that the *Herald*, too, could be touched. He had Ives clapped into Federal confinement at Fort McHenry, in Baltimore, charged with espionage.

The dark-eyed, imaginative correspondent got no support from Bennett. The *Herald* editorially doubted that Ives was a spy, but denied that he was a staff regular and sanctimoniously applauded Stanton's "fidelity to his trust." Either Ives, plainly of shaky mental stability, had dreamed up his entire *Herald* connection, or the paper was unwilling to lose its other War Department contacts by battling it out over one correspondent. Ives was released in a few months, apparently unimpaired, since he was able to write to Bennett and express his "unabated interest" in the *Herald's* welfare. Meanwhile, other papers capered with delight over the rebuke to the "frightful old snob" and even the venerable *National Intelligencer* ran a coltish pseudo letter from Ives to the managing editor, full of labored jokes about being the *first* reporter to reach Fort McHenry, and having prospects of being *elevated* for his pains.[11]

Almost at the same time, one of the more picturesque of the capital's wartime residents, temporarily enlisted as a *Herald* scribe, was making news. The House Judiciary Committee was conducting its politically loaded inquiry into the government's censorship of telegraph facilities. Investigation revealed that portions of Lincoln's December message to Congress had gotten to the *Herald* in advance of the speech's delivery. Evidence pointed to Henry Wykoff, one of Bennett's correspondents in the city, as the culprit.

Wykoff, a debonair type sometimes known as "the Chevalier," was a colorful person whose métier seemed to be that of a contact man in various capitals. There were rumors of an embroilment in England involving no less a person than Lord Palmerston, and it was known that in Italy he had been smitten with an English heiress, tried to kidnap her, and spent a year in a Genoese jail on being caught. In Washington he mixed whatever business he had

[11] *New York Tribune*, February 12, 1862; Bennett Papers, Ives to Bennett, January 27, 29, July 3, 1862; *New York Herald*, February 11, 1862; *Missouri Republican*, February 17, 1862; *Chicago Tribune*, February 14, 15, 1862; *Chicago Times*, February 15, 1862; *New York World*, February 11, 1862; *Triweekly National Intelligencer*, quoted in *Chicago Times*, February 22, 1862.

for the *Herald* with unrestricted private enterprise. Once he approached Whitely and asked that Bennett's name be used to improve the War Department's opinion of a bid made by a revolver company with which he was connected. He was apparently unperturbed by a refusal, as well as by the ungenerous attitude of colleagues such as the Cincinnati correspondent who described him as a "political pimp."

Wykoff was brought before the committee and asked for the source of his information about Lincoln's message. He refused to speak under numerous threats, and was finally imprisoned by the sergeant at arms in the basement of the Old Capitol prison, a penalty which, as a veteran of a European jail, he took with considerable urbanity. At that point the committee was presented with a piece of evidence that set some kind of record for ludicrousness; it was told that the White House gardener, a man named Watt, had seen the message on the President's study table, *memorized* entire portions of it, and given them to Wykoff. Watt, when summoned, added to the confusion by obligingly swearing to the truth of this. But before the Radicals on the committee could pounce on this story, the matter was suddenly dropped completely.

The rumored reason was disclosed years later by Benjamin Perley Poore, Washington correspondent of the *Boston Journal*, and an indefatigable dragnet of capital gossip. Wykoff had, it was said, paid the most flattering notice to Mary Lincoln; the ex-Kentucky belle, flustered by these Continental attentions, had rewarded him with confidential White House data. When the trail led to the gardener,

Lincoln supposedly visited the Republicans in the Capitol and urged them to drop the affair before it exploded into a public scandal. Wykoff was then released.

Properly tested, the story might have assayed a small yield of truth. The *Herald's* columns had been notably kind to the plump First Lady, who was not popular in the capital. During Wykoff's imprisonment the *Herald* sniffed that only Radicals would sink low enough to rake over back-fence scandal in order to attack the President and his conservative circle of advisers. But, truthful or not, rival editors had had their second spasm of public glee within the month at the expense of Bennett. Still, the Washington correspondent of the *Cincinnati Commercial*, at least, tempered the general gaiety with a note of pained realism:

> The upshot of the whole disgraceful business will, of course, be to advertise the New York Herald — already sufficiently notorious — and no advantage will accrue to the cause of truth and fair dealing.[12]

In his brief and breathless correspondence with the *Herald's* editor, the most singular statements made by Malcolm Ives were those concerning his alleged relationship with General McClellan. The whole attitude of the *Herald* to McClellan was a strange one, composed in varying parts of hero worship, gratitude to a rarely failing source of copy, and affection for a soldier whose political pursuers were

[12] Bennett Papers, Whitely to Bennett, June 29, 1862; *New York Herald*, February 5, 14, 17, March 3, 1862; *New York World*, February 12, 14, 1862; Margaret Leech, *Reveille in Washington* (New York, 1941), pp. 290-299; *Cincinnati Commercial*, February 17, 1862.

favorite targets of the paper. McClellan was loved, among other things, for the enemies he made. The coverage of McClellan's campaigns showed up plainly the influence of Bennett over his corps of correspondents. Either they were hand-picked or uncommonly knowing about the short cuts to a place in their employer's heart, but they marched in step with the New York office — always provided that they did not cut off any potential sources of news in the process.

The whole period of McClellan's command, in fact, was one of education for certain editors in the art of creating a military hero in response to an obvious popular hunger for one — a sort of apprenticeship in public relations on a modern scale. The dapper general himself was made for the spotlight. Cultivated, multilingual and flamboyant, he *looked* the part of a "young Napoleon."

When he was lifted from command after slightly over a year, in November of 1862, it was impossible to say for sure whether he had deserved such a reputation. There were two sides to the McClellan story, neither of which could be disproved. He was conceited and Messianic, considered himself the chosen of God to be the savior of his country, (in letters to his wife he marveled at this role), let slip continual disturbing references in public to "his" army, and made his general distaste for the civilian management of the war clear. He snubbed Lincoln, and in a particularly vexed moment in the summer of 1862 wrote a letter to the President laying out the proper political objectives of the war — no confiscation of property, no territorial organization of conquered States, and no forcible abolition of slavery. The gesture was more Napoleonic than a good many democrats desired; there was, after all, one Napoleon then on the throne of France who had upset a republican government. In the field, McClellan was a slow mover, and in all his campaigns never seemed to capture a major objective or to bag an enemy army.

On the other hand, he never really had a free rein from the beginning. An article of the Radical faith was that the regular army was shot through with political sin, pro-Southern and proslavery at heart. McClellan was the personification of the regular officer. As a war hero, he was a convenient focus around which the opposition could rally, a thought which was in itself fearful to contemplate for the superorthodox Republicans. Beginning in 1861, he was attacked by a potent segment of officialdom, including Congressional leaders, Republican governors, and cabinet members. The Secretary of War, by 1862, was joining in the pursuit and he had the power to make his opinions carry weight. McClellan's command was progressively whittled down, until one point in August of 1862 when, although still technically a commanding general, he had nothing but his personal bodyguard directly assigned to him. His excellent paper plans were changed by having troop dispositions, subordinate commands and routes of attack juggled at the last minute in Washington. He hammered the army into a first-rate fighting force, but he never enjoyed the unrestricted use of it.

Whatever all this might add up to, for James Gordon Bennett there was no doubt of "Little Mac's" greatness.

McClellan's conservatism on the war program jibed perfectly with the editor's sneering contempt for the engineers of the Radical program, the "cranks" and "abolitionists" whom he had loudly detested for two decades. There was something more, perhaps. Bennett was, in his curious bourgeois fashion, a romantic, and McClellan, standing strong, dynamic and alone above the pack, was as romantic a hero as the Scots journalist himself. In him there seemed to be a genius for military management equal to Bennett's own genius for public enlightenment. Bennett felt a sympathetic thrumming of mighty minds when he considered McClellan, and from the beginning he and his reporters let it be known that McClellan's little finger was thicker than the loins of all other captains put together.[13]

Just how publicity-wise "Little Mac" himself was is hard to say. According to the highly suspect testimony of Ives, however, he was spectacularly aware of the stuff of which greatness was made in 1862. Ives wrote a letter to the *Herald's* owner on January 15, 1862, which began by claiming that Stanton, of all people, had arranged an interview with the general for him. The Pennsylvania lawyer at the time had not yet received his appointment to the war office but was expecting it daily, and he told the New York reporter that when it materialized he would "show that he was no middle measures man, but should throw

[13] McClellan himself is best revealed in the collection of letters entitled *McClellan's Own Story* (W. C. Prince, ed., New York, 1887); for other bird's eye views, see T. Harry Williams, *Lincoln and the Radicals* (Madison, 1941), pp. 77-196; Burton J. Hendrick, *Lincoln's War Cabinet* (Boston, 1946), pp. 265-321.

overboard the rest of the press and cling to the Herald alone."

McClellan, Ives continued, had immediately taken him to his bosom, told him that on the previous day he had refused to reveal his future plans to a meeting of the cabinet, but hastened to add that he would now tell all to the *Herald's* representative. As Ives's sycophantic pen flew over the sheets, apparently, his enthusiasm mounted, and the letter took on more and more of an overexcited flavor:

> After informing me that Mr. Hudson's name was a household word with some of his nearest friends . . . he surprised me by establishing a claim of my own upon his confidence . . . and added: — but I particularly wish to charge you with a message to Mr. Bennett: — "Mr. Bennett has stood by me in the hour of the bitterest anxiety of my whole life. . . . He has done so disinterestedly, nobly, and with the whole force of his paper. He and he alone, has upheld me, cheered me and encouraged me, when every other newspaper heaped upon me calumny and abuse, at the very time that I was saving them from the horrors of an invasion. . . . I shall *never, never, never* forget his kindness, and I want him to know that I cherish him in my heart, and that I shall strive with all the energy my Maker has given me to prove, as I have no doubt I shall, that his confidence has not been misplaced." He then rather apologized for saying that it was his duty to require a solemn pledge from me not only that what he was about to tell me should be revealed to no living being, excepting yourself and Mr. Hudson, *exclusive of every one else;* but also that we would not even let the fact of the possession of such knowledge be known.

Ives then added a long list of supposedly pending movements, and followed his advantage up the next day with the story that McClellan had invited him in to have a private look at the latest letters of Generals Halleck and Buell. Some ten days later he had still more to say; this time, the general had confided that the army would advance into Virginia in the first days of March, come what might. At this point it occurred to him, evidently, that information which could be disclosed to no one was of dubious value to a newspaper, so an arrangement for a tip-off was made. Just before the moment to begin the advance, McClellan's aide-de-camp would telegraph to Bennett the two words "Come on," which would be the signal to start the presses rolling. Until then, the *Herald* could help to throw dust in the eyes of the enemy by printing false leads, hinting heartily meanwhile that they were straight from inside sources.

Bennett and managing editor Hudson, reading these letters, may have begun to worry about what damage Ives, on the loose in the capital, could do to the paper. On the 28th of January, S. P. Hanscom, quite possibly acting for Hudson, went to the War Department and declared that Ives had only a "local employ" with the *Herald* in New York, was in Washington on private business, and was not officially entitled to any handouts. This precaution did not quiet Ives, who, upon finding it out the next day, wrote petulantly to the home office claiming that Hanscom had undertaken the errand on his own initiative out of pure jealousy. He had the word of Chevalier Wykoff and of Mr. Shaw, another of Bennett's Washington reporters, to prove it. He did not expect any damage, thinking that his hold on McClellan was "sure," but he wanted to come back to New York to straighten the record. On the 8th of February he was out of his uncharitable mood, however, and wrote hastily to explain that he now had made certain of the co-operation of the Navy Department and the Treasury, and was off to the War Department that afternoon to make fresh arrangements. It was on that day that he was arrested.

Ives was decidedly unbalanced, but even if there were the merest kernel of truth in his story, then McClellan had discovered a dazzling new concept of military-journalistic rapport. The *New York Tribune*, as a matter of fact, may have believed that there was something in it, for a story was run in its columns which said that Ives had entertained the general's staff at breakfast at Willard's Hotel just before his arrest. The *Tribune*, however, was poisonously anti-McClellan, and the *New York Times* promptly announced that its esteemed contemporary was lying.[14]

Still, McClellan was able to be kind to *Herald* men whose word was less suspect on grounds of flightiness than that of Ives. The general's chief of staff, Randolph B. Marcy, had written occasionally for the lively New York journal while on the brief expedition of part of the regular

[14] *New York Times*, quoted in *Cincinnati Commercial*, February 13, 1862; Ives's letters to Bennett are in a folder of Bennett Papers in the Library of Congress, dated January 15, 16, 27, and February 8, 1862. Excerpts were reprinted under the title "Federal Generals and a Good Press," *American Historical Review*, XXXIX (1933-1934), 280-289.

army to Utah, in 1858, and had known Frederic Hudson for some time. Friendship had its advantages, and the Washington bureau chief was once able to write Bennett: "I presume you have heard from Wilson, who was smuggled into the Army of the Potomac by General Marcy," at a time when McClellan's assistant adjutant general was banning other correspondents from camp in "the best interests of the service." When the army finally gave up the Peninsula operations and embarked for its base near the mouth of the Potomac, W. H. Stiner, a kind of field superintendent of *Herald* interests in the campaign, rode in the ship carrying McClellan and the staff "by the kindness of General R. B. Marcy." [15]

McClellan, as he appeared in the columns filed by *Herald* men covering operations, was almost legendary. In October of 1861, a Maryland correspondent told the world that at the battle of Ball's Bluff a hesitant regiment was exhorted by an officer: "Forward, my brave men, forward, for McClellan and our country," a cry which seemed to "electrify the whole brigade," for it thereupon "advanced with the determination to conquer or die." The next spring a correspondent in Cairo met a close friend of General Halleck, who explained to him that even the victories in the West — the capture of Forts Henry and Donelson and the cleaning up of Missouri — were part of a master

[15] Jesse A. Gove, *The Utah Expedition* (Concord, New Hampshire, 1928), p. 182; Frederic Hudson Diary (in possession of Mrs. Wesley P. Wilmot), January 9, 1855; Bennett Papers, Whitely to Bennett, July 29, 1862; George B. McClellan Papers, Library of Congress, 2nd Series, Seth Williams to John C. Jacobs and John Whittemore, July (N.D.) 1862; Bennett Papers, Stiner to Bennett, August 23, 1862.

plan laid down by McClellan. The Army of the Potomac was to pin down Confederate strength in Virginia while the entire Western theater was overrun in the healthful spring weather, and in the autumn the decisive attack on the Confederate capital would be launched. This information, according to the reporter, would be of special interest to the Radicals who were howling for an immediate advance on Richmond, and cursing McClellan for his refusal to "sacrifice the chivalry of the nation upon the altar of their negro mania." [16]

The campaign of 1862 in the Peninsula was McClellan's most ambitious effort — a win-the-war offensive, to which the reporters came like locusts. At Michie's plantation, near the Chickahominy, there were no fewer than twelve representatives of five papers sitting down to the hospitable table of the Virginia owner during one period. They included Henry J. Raymond, owner of the *Times*, and George Alfred Townsend, Bennett's exuberant twenty-one-year-old correspondent, who wrote poetry in the albums of the Misses Michie, in quiet moments. Townsend and other writers of the *Herald* had nothing but praise for the management of the operation. "The officers . . . from the highest to the lowest, love and respect him," ran one dispatch about McClellan, and another indignantly reproached those of little faith who were expecting results prematurely. If the public really grasped the situation, it would place implicit confidence in "Little Mac" and bid him "an encouraging Godspeed." A descrip-

[16] *New York Herald*, October 28, 1861, February 25, 1862.

tion of the general's appearance during a May skirmish struck the heroic note:

> There was a large welcome in every heart for that stout little figure and blue soldier's overcoat . . . He came, and listened, and spoke — that was all — and the mass of blind, purposeless movement unravelled itself and there was a plan and a battle.[17]

At the end of June, in the murderous week of fighting known as the Seven Days' Battles, the Confederates upset McClellan's plans and crowded him into a first-rate exhibition of defensive skill. They got around his right flank and unhinged it completely. McClellan thereupon moved the entire army southward, fighting all the way, to a new base on the James, where the navy could cover his left wing. He claimed that he had intended this approach from the start, but that on orders from Washington he had chosen the northerly route along the York and Chickahominy rivers, so that he might keep one hand outstretched to contact another force working down from Washington. The army was safe, but it had suffered fifteen thousand casualties (in addition to those already laid low by swamp fevers), much of its equipment, and any prospects of an early victory. The young commander was keenly aware that the campaign was not taking a precisely Bonapartean turn. He sent a scalding telegram to the Secretary of War, claiming that the government had done its best to

[17]George Alfred Townsend, *Campaigns of a Non-Combatant* (New York, 1866), 138-143; *New York Herald*, April 15, 30, May 10, 1862.

sacrifice the troops, and then insisted loudly that he was now in a better position than ever: give him reinforcements, and Richmond would be bagged. McClellan's newspaper supporters were also obliged to make it clear that the change of base had not been a retreat, a task which was difficult in a day that had not yet seen the invention of the term "retrograde disengagement." Still, they worked at it. A correspondent claimed from the Peninsula itself that the evacuation had been part of a predetermined plan, and another in the safer location of Fortress Monroe, at the mouth of the James, explained that "the young chieftain" had "out generalled the rebels two to one" in escaping destruction. From the new base came the report of a *Herald* observer containing a smoldering attack on the government:

> Not a breath of complaint escapes officers or men of General McClellan, but the curses loud and deep . . . against the real authors of this withdrawal . . . are ominous. . . . How long will this bloody mockery last, when men are bidden to make their graves and lie in them by the unprincipled and incarnate abolitionists, who by some means appear to have obtained control of army movements . . . [and] unconcernedly allowed this time to pass by without reinforcing our army here, virtually consenting, not to say conniving at McClellan's defeat.

Backed up by the Fortress Monroe man's report of "bitter feeling against Mr. Stanton in the army," this made it clear to discriminating readers that the politicians of Washington had attempted to undo the brilliant field commander, who had thwarted them by his great side-stepping maneuver.[18]

It was worth noting, however, that Bennett's readers on the Fourth of July had five full pages of closely printed details of the fighting, by the courtesy of Townsend, whose odyssey from the battle highlighted the adventurous side of journalism in the sixties. Townsend had caught a fever shortly before the main fighting began and spent several days in delirium at Michie's. During the retreat he picked his way in the wake of the army, cataloguing one horror after another in the choked and stinking hospitals, and nearly starving among the sweltering, cursing confusion of the movement. His baggage was left at Michie's, whose frame house, lawn and oak grove were turned into a pawed-over shambles when the withdrawing troops camped there. At the James he got a ride on a transport whose stairways, gangways, saloons, cabins and holds were crammed with glassy-eyed stretcher cases. At Fortress Monroe, still hollow-eyed and weak with fever, he transferred to a Baltimore-bound steamer; at Baltimore, clutching a bundle of notes, he was driven wildly through the streets to connect with a Philadelphia train. During the four hours it took to reach the station at Broad Street he scribbled copy, paused only to rush across town to catch a ferry to Camden, where he boarded a New York-bound steamer. He wrote uninterruptedly in the captain's cabin until the ship docked, leaped into a cab that took him to the *Herald's* office, continued writing far into the night and finally

[18] *New York Herald,* July 2, 7, 1862.

dropped from exhaustion.[19] That kind of news-gathering had more to do with Bennett's success than any of his opinions on the greatness of soldiers or the meanness of politicians.

Within a few weeks, however, it almost appeared as if McClellan's gallery would have the last word. The army was brought back to Washington, and its units fed into new commands, leaving McClellan finally with nothing at his disposal but an escort. In the last week of August, however, the second battle of Bull Run was fought. It was, to use the euphemism of the day, a "disaster to Federal arms." The army back-pedaled northward; for the second time in fourteen months there was serious doubt that Washington could be held — even McClellan was at one point writing to his wife that he would try to slip into town and have her silver shipped off — and in the first days of September the President, Stanton and Halleck restored the army to its old master and waited prayerfully. At that point, on September 11, the *Herald* made its most unrestrained suggestion, namely, that McClellan should become a kind of American Cromwell. He should "insist upon the modification and reconstruction of the Cabinet, in order to have it purged of the radical taint." He could "demand indemnity for the past and security for the future," since "the game" was now in his hands and he was "master of the situation." This excited appeal to shoot the bottom out of the Constitution was quite possibly inspired by the terrors of Bennett's Washington agent, Whitely.

[19] Townsend, *Campaigns of a Non-Combatant*, pp. 152-216.

Perhaps overstimulated by a week spent in daily anticipation of awakening to find Confederate cavalrymen trotting down Pennsylvania Avenue, Whitely had written to Bennett on the 9th:

> I sent you a dispatch last night in regard to abolition movements. These are much canvassed here. They mean revolution, anarchy and secession. These men are mad. They openly threaten to depose the President if it can be accomplished. The gait they are going will go near to drive the army and the people to anticipate the abolition programme by declaring McClellan military dictator. The idea is becoming familiar to people here.[20]

In the face of Whitely's loss of journalistic detachment, the editor in New York might easily have concluded that McClellan should take matters into his own hands. The notion must have seemed even more appealing to Bennett later in the month, when Lincoln issued the Emancipation Proclamation, and Whitely wrote agitatedly that the air was "thick with revolution." But McClellan was no Cromwell after all. He had his hands full with the army. After beating the Confederates at Antietam on the 17th of September, he had promptly settled down into camp and an angry correspondence with the War Department, in which he responded to appeals to pursue Lee southward at once by irritably pointing out that his veteran outfits, riddled with shortages in personnel and equipment after six months of steady fighting, were in no shape to move anywhere without refitting.

[20] Bennett Papers, Whitely to Bennett, September 9, 1862.

Seven weeks of this finally decided Lincoln that the risks of removing McClellan were no worse than those of leaving him where he was. On November 7th, his command was taken from him. A *Herald* reporter contributed a last flick of the polishing rag to the McClellan legend. For over a year, the passionate attachment of the army to its leader had been good for a paragraph on a slow morning. Now the principals were being wrenched apart, and the correspondent made the most of it in his account. Headquarters, on the morning of the general's departure, wore a dismal and deserted look. Morose staff officers gathered with McClellan for a last glass of wine. As he paraded his horse between ranks drawn up for final review, "tears were shed in profusion," men broke ranks to touch his horse, and others ran after him, some weeping aloud and crying "Fetch him back, Fetch him back!" Combat-wise infantrymen supposedly behaved towards the two-star general like supporting members of a melodrama's cast.[21]

McClellan retired to await, in sullen dignity, the Democratic nomination for 1864. The *Herald* would editorially take him up again, but the field correspondents were shut out. Other commanders who failed with the Army of the Potomac were sent to lesser commands to salvage what they could of their reputations, or at worst to the West to try their mettle against the Sioux. Stanton was taking no chances on McClellan. The young Napoleon's last orders in Virginia assigned him to Trenton, New Jersey,

[21] *New York Herald*, November 12, 1862; Bennett Papers, Whitely to Bennett, September 24, 1862.

where even the *Herald* and its staff could not very well make his name immortal.

The reign of McClellan in the news columns showed how indispensable the co-operation of reporters was becoming to the well-dressed public lion. Elsewhere, *Herald* scribes polished up their public relations techniques, sometimes working for political reasons, sometimes merely with an eye to an obviously useful contact. There was, for example, the case of General Don Carlos Buell, whose Latin-sounding name gave an entirely illusory promise of fire and dash. As a conservative and as McClellan's picked candidate for command of the armies in the West, Buell was set adrift in the political typhoon belt whether he wished it or not.

A cold man personally, Buell was inflexibly discourteous to reporters; one might as well have looked for roses in December as favors at his headquarters, according to a Cincinnati correspondent. Henry Villard, campaigning with him, thought that he was as hostile as Sherman but not so redeemingly human. For all that, Buell had an excellent press in the *Herald*, due mainly to the efforts of William F. G. Shanks, who corresponded for Bennett and held a passkey to the camps in his extra capacity as aide to a division commander, General L. H. Rousseau.

Shanks knew his way in the newspaper profession well; he was, as a matter of fact, a future editor of *Harper's Weekly*, the *New York Times*, and the *New York Tribune*. Buell was the great arbiter of who did and who did not stay with the army. Buell was a general whose political (or nonpolitical) bent stirred the rare kindly feelings of Shanks's editor, Bennett. As a Kentuckian, too, Shanks was likely to find something attractive in the commander's refusal to lend a hand to the "abolition programme." With all this taken into consideration, nobody should have been surprised at the kindness with which Buell was presented in *Herald* correspondence from August to November of 1862. His critics were damned as "croakers," and he was given "all credit for . . . achievements in the West," where things had patently gone better for the Union than in Virginia. Buell, said the *Herald's* letters from Alabama, Tennessee and Kentucky, was not receiving his due honors because of the hostility of a powerful clique of Republicans and his own refusal "to make the Negro question superior to the question of the Union." (Buell did not permit fugitive slaves to remain in his camps, a practical kind of emancipation allowed by some commanders.) Like McClellan, he was accused of conducting warfare at an almost languorous pace, but from Louisville in October the *Herald* reporter wrote that when pressed Buell could "*make as rapid strides as any commander.*" In fact, Buell was as much of a misunderstood genius as McClellan himself, but one day the country would "rise up in the majesty of its sustained honor . . . and call these two men blessed." While these stories were appearing, reporters for an arch-Republican paper such as the *New York Tribune*, supposedly covering the same campaigns with the same disinterested yen for truth, were writing that Buell's career was "inglorious" and "disastrous," that he was regarded with "disgust and contempt" by knowing observers, and that he had been "playing false to the Government" by "strange management." [22] A newspaper reader's view of the war depended on the politics of his paper.

That was even more noticeable in the case of John C. Frémont, the Union commander in Missouri in 1861. Frémont took over his duties in August with loud announcements that he was about to pacify the entire Western theater. Energetically he began to recruit troops and order supplies — without waiting, in some cases, for the rheumatic process of official authorization from the War Department. The *Herald* was impressed profoundly with an officer who bustled and proclaimed his way through red tape, and editorially Frémont was declared "just the man" for the touchy job of taming Missouri with the proper spirit and zest. The paper's St. Louis correspondence, most probably coming from Thomas W. Knox, promoted the colorful general's cause; he was "busy night and day pushing forward matters for a vigorous campaign," and getting set to deal "aggressive blows at the enemy" — information especially gratifying to a Northern public with no major engagement to look back on but Bull Run.

Early in September, however, Frémont took matters more firmly in hand by declaring martial law in his department, announcing that all persons taken in arms

[22] Williams, *Lincoln and the Radicals*, pp. 192-194; *Cincinnati Commercial*, May 16, 1862; Henry Villard, *Memoirs* (New York, 1904), I, 213; *New York Herald*, August 24, September 6, October 3, 4, 10, 12, 20, 1862; *New York Tribune*, October 8, 25, November 12, 1862.

against the government would be shot, and ordering the confiscation of all property of known rebels — slaves included. This was abolition by military directive, and sent shudders through conservative circles. To Lincoln, still trying to preserve the tenuous loyalties of the border States, the proclamation was politically tainted and inconceivably risky, and he revoked the edict almost immediately. The *Herald*, meanwhile, at first startled into approving the straight-from-the-shoulder style of the proclamation, reversed its field and was presently declaring that Frémont's career "both martial and political" had "proved very unfortunate." Within a week of the appearance of that opinion, a letter from a Cairo correspondent was printed. According to the writer, feeling in the West towards the commander had "vastly changed." There was good reason, too. Frémont, the master strategist, had left Cairo without an adequate garrison, tempting bait for Confederate raiders. Frémont, the hustling dynamo who got things *done*, had been gulled by contractors; a large stock of European arms which he had ordered proved to be defective. When Bennett was reproached by the *New York Tribune* for his mid-air somersault, he snapped back that he was no party organ-grinder, whose tunes were dictated by authority. It was apparently not altogether certain that his reporters could make the same boast. A New York reader who approved of the proclamation, however, had only to do a little shopping among the city's papers. In the *Tribune* he would find another set of "facts" which satisfied; Greeley had correspondents who recorded "overwhelming" public support for Frémont in the face of "relentless and vindictive personal attacks." [23] There seemed to be no end of correspondents, in fact, who furnished brands of information pleasing to almost any taste.

Other military nabobs drew mixed notices from *Herald* men, and in many cases at least a suspicion of political color could be sustained. Generally good treatment was given to General Nathaniel P. Banks, an amateur warrior who had served a turn as governor of Massachusetts. In 1864 he told a New Orleans correspondent of Bennett that he was grateful to the paper for having been his "fast friend." Although a Republican, Banks was no friend of the Radicals, since he had refused to reconstruct Louisiana according to their vigorous notions during his period in command there. In the Army of the Potomac, changes in leadership were commented on unrestrainedly by *Herald* men. In the midsummer of 1862, field operations in Virginia were given over to General John Pope. One of the more painful highlights of his tenure was the raid on his headquarters by Jeb Stuart which resulted in the capture of many of his personal possessions and official papers. A *Herald* man's yeasty account of how Stuart's men had dressed a fugitive Negro in Pope's best uniform and ridden him on a mule through Warrenton did little to furnish a tonic to Pope's reputation. As it happened, Pope was highly esteemed by the Radicals, who blamed his failures on lack of co-operation from subordinate commanders loyal

[23] *New York Herald*, August 10, 23, September 2, 21, 25, October 4, 8, 10, 1861; *New York Tribune*, September 20, October 5, 1861.

to McClellan, whose place he had in effect taken. General Burnside, who had the army in the winter of 1862-1863, was described by a *Herald* man as an "earnest, laboring, zealous patriot." He was, at that time, a first-name companion of McClellan and had handled the question of escaped slaves in a carefully conservative manner while commanding an expedition in tidewater North Carolina. General George Meade, who took over the Army of the Potomac at Gettysburg, was politically neutral; the *Herald* had kind words for him, and when, in 1864, Grant was placed above him in over-all command of operations, correspondent F. G. Chapman was careful to point out that the soldiers' contentment with Grant did not imply any unhappiness with Meade.[24]

So much might be coincidence, but an occasional correspondent candidly admitted that political factors weighted his estimate of a soldier. A Kentucky-based *Herald* agent wrote, in 1862, that General Quincy A. Gillmore, an army regular, was a fine top-level officer — among other things, because he frankly cared "nothing one way or another about the nigger" and kept escaped slaves out of his positions. On the other hand there was the case of General David P. Hunter, heading a department which embraced the occupied islands off the South Carolina coast. In September of 1862 Hunter, like Frémont, issued a proclamation freeing the slaves in his zone, and, as with

[24] Williams, *Lincoln and the Radicals*, pp. 274-277; Bennett Papers, William Young to Bennett, May 20, 1864; Thomas Knox to Hudson, June 28, 1862; *New York Herald*, August 29, 1862; November 14, 1862; W. C. Prime, ed., *McClellan's Own Story*, p. 245; *New York Herald*, March 21, 1864.

Frémont, it was promptly canceled by Lincoln. The *Herald* man on the scene, unencumbered by any notion that his job called for nonpartisanship, wrote that the government had been "losing money" on Hunter since he came into the department. "We must get along without our radical generals," moralized the newspaperman.[25]

The *Herald*, however — or at least the more knowing of its agents — was never the paper to let political animosities seal it off from a news source. Besides, individual reporters occasionally developed attachments for certain officers who, whatever their views on questions of state, knew when a hard-working chronicler of the war could use a pass, a dinner, or a nip of old Monongahela rye. Sometimes this engendered confusing situations.

In the spring of 1864, plans were made to have a Union army move up the James River to complete the stranglehold which would be put on Richmond; it was to be under the wing of General Benjamin F. Butler. Butler was the *ne plus ultra* of Radical generals; he had originated the idea of rounding up escaped slaves for use by the army as labor battalions; he had been in charge of occupied Louisiana for a time and made it howl; he had a tongue that dripped acid on adversaries of any kind. He was clearly unfit for top commands, but was too well dug into his position in the party to be dislodged before the election. Rarely did the *Herald* have so good a target.

Yet W. H. Stiner, one of Bennett's veteran army reporters, wrote to New York in April and reminded Hud-

[25] *New York Herald*, September 10, November 14, 1862.

son that talkative army chiefs were worth cultivating. "As General Butler takes *chief command* of the operations in this Department," he noted prudently, "it might be better not to offend him. In fact your promise and that of Mr. Bennett to me, was to the effect that nothing should be said against him." Stiner did not always get full payment on that promise; in May, for example, a long editorial said that Grant had been forbidden to fire generals like Butler, "unfit for their positions," because any such move would be "a cut at Mr. Lincoln's Presidential arrangements." But Butler was not sensitive by nature, and Stiner was not sent off into exile. In fact, he was contentedly reporting a three-hour chat in the general's tent, brimful of news, almost at the very time the Grant story appeared.[26] There was evidently an understanding between realists. To Stiner, a source was a source; to the sardonic politician, publicity was publicity.

Stiner had more to worry about, however, than sabotage of his diplomatic relations with Butler by a nettled editorial writer at a desk in New York. The army's commander had subordinate officers leading corps, and they had reporters at *their* headquarters who looked to them for favors received. Oscar G. Sawyer, for example, was the *Herald's* man at the command post of the 10th Corps, led by Quincy A. Gillmore, whose vinegary relationship with Butler was common knowledge. Sawyer wrote a number of letters for publication gilding the accomplishments

[26] Bennett Papers, Stiner to Hudson, April 21, May 22, 1864; *New York Herald,* May 28, 1864.

of the corps and pointedly omitting any credit lines for Butler. Evidently Stiner took him to task and pointed out that this was not the way for a *Herald* man to win his letter in Butler's army, for Sawyer lodged a loud complaint with Hudson that Stiner was tied to a "lick-spittle style." Stiner, for his part, swore that Sawyer had been "very indiscreet," going about and talking of the "blunders of General Butler" and inflating Gillmore. Sawyer italicized his own distaste for the situation by refusing to send his dispatches any longer through Stiner, the chief agent in the area. Overflowing with the justice of his cause, Stiner wrote to New York and advised Hudson not to blame *him* if news came late from 10th Corps. In all, not a word was said about politics. It was evident that editorial consistency was not going to deny a clear track to any *Herald* correspondent moving in on a firsthand story.[27]

Bennett's men were not reluctant to undertake the education of public opinion on other topics either. There was the matter of fugitive slaves. The war was not more than a few months old when it became evident that the military government of occupied Southern territory would carry with it a number of problems inescapably political. When the Union army's lines began to move over seceded farmlands, hundreds and soon thousands of plantation Negroes walked easily out of the slave quarters, no longer guarded by the absent white men of the region, and into

[27] Bennett Papers, Stiner to Hudson, April 21, May 28, 30, 1864; Sawyer to Hudson, May 26, 1864; *New York Herald*, July 22, 23, 1864.

the camps which had sprouted around them. They were curious, unsure of what to expect, cheerfully dependent, and hungry. What to do with them was a slippery question. There was a military argument for organizing them into work gangs, for use in the endless loading, hauling, road building, canal digging, and clearing that warfare in rugged terrain required; some military men said that, however many extra rations they ate, they were useful contraband of war, as valuable as captured gun caissons or barrels of powder.

The Radicals were in emphatic agreement. They were, in fact, in no mood to have the slaves restored to their own farms, a practice which would amount to using the United States army as an enforcement agency for slavery. The most bellicose, in fact, had even more spectacular ideas, and wanted to uniform the fugitives and use them as a kind of native auxiliary corps. A few of them dusted off their French, looked at North Africa, and murmured about a *Corps d'Afrique*, seeing Spahis and Senegalese rising from the cottonfields. In time, Negro troops would, in fact, perform excellently, but the motives of their Republican promoters were clearly political as well as martial.

For the Democrats, however, matters were more complicated. There was no hope of a compromise peace with the South if the issue of the war changed from one of allegiance to the Constitution pure and simple to one of emancipation. The Confederacy would hold out to the last bullet against that; and until the Southern States returned to the Union with full voting rights and their normal, satisfying Democratic majorities, the Republicans would remain in the pilot's cabin. For all the scattered opponents of the Republican program a "contraband" policy which unlocked the door to abolition by chipping at the legal foundation of slavery (already weakened by the collapse of local governments in the fighting zones) was a nightmare. Even a few conservatively minded Republicans squirmed when they thought of the implications of a free-handed wiping out of property rights, and in the eighteen-sixties war was still conducted with a certain gingerly care for private possessions. Antiadministration orators had to fight off a tide of sentiment in favor of using escaped Negroes by arguing that they were not really valuable at all, unable to make up for the extra logistical load which they threw on the shoulders of the Union supply and transportation system.[28]

They got considerable help from the correspondents of the *Herald*. Early in 1861, stories from Fortress Monroe appeared which said that the slaves were coming into the lines looking for "the blessed land of Canaan" in the shape of "little work, [and] plenty of hog and hominy." Union officers disappointed these alleged hopes in setting them to work in the warehouses and on the docks of the base; rations and quarters were furnished for these new hands, and the *Herald's* correspondents took the opportunity to grumble that the accommodations were better than those provided for the troops themselves. In order to ease shortages of fresh

[28] A thoroughgoing discussion of the whole question is available in Bell I. Wiley, *Southern Negroes, 1861-1865* (New Haven, 1938), especially pp. 175-344.

food, the Negroes were allowed to put in time cultivating the gardens of abandoned "rebel" homes. To one of Bennett's Virginia reporters this was coddling an "unbridled and ignorant class." It would be necessary presently to detach a brigade to "hunt them like hares" in order to clamp down on their "atrocities" — a staple of proslavery argument being that the Negroes, left to themselves, would run wild among the unprotected homesteads behind the lines. At Norfolk, according to another *Herald* man, idle house servants were roaming the streets in gangs; those employed by the army rarely showed up at work and rarely missed meals.[29]

On the sandy islands off the South Carolina coast, where regiments from New England and the Atlantic States braved sand flies, fleas, and diarrhea to guard against blockade runners, a social experiment was tried in 1862. Advance patrols of missionaries and schoolteachers, sent out by antislavery societies of Boston, New York and Philadelphia, took over abandoned cotton plantations and attempted to work them with paid Negro hands, backed by the reluctant approval of the government, which wanted the cotton to be grown. Along with their first taste of wage labor, the ex-slaves were patiently led through spelling books and arithmetics by their conscientious though inexperienced new employers. This brought no sympathy from the *Herald* correspondent at Port Royal, South Carolina, who dangled a favorite Southern scarecrow; such interference by

[29] *New York Herald*, August 9, 26, 1861, January 19, April 23, May 16, 1862.

"mischievous, pestilent missionaries" would "create negro insurrection, and result in the indiscriminate slaughter of the white race, of every age and sex, in every section of the South." Another slightly more charitable reporter advised subscribers, with a figurative wink, that of course the Negroes were incapable of learning anything, but they would afford the missionaries "a good deal of fun." Bennett liked to boast of his paper as an instrument in the education of the workingman, but black laborers were not included in his proposed student body.[30]

On the Peninsula, the army was racked with swamp fever. Republicans, always ready with a topical argument, protested that the men were easier victims of it because they were exhausted by the hard labor of digging the entrenchments and leveling the camp sites demanded by McClellan's elaborately slow advance. If the road to Richmond had to be laid foot by foot through bog and fen, they said, the job should be done by escaped Negroes who were accustomed to the climate. For the faithful believers in the *Herald's* political gospel, there was a counter-argument in the "facts" furnished by the correspondents of their favorite daily. Negroes ordered to work at Newport News (said a story filed there) grumbled loud and long; they had enjoyed an easy living running errands and snaring shellfish to sell to the perennially hungry soldiers. Ex-slaves at the larger bases worked long enough to accumulate a dollar or so, and then fled to enjoy their fortunes

[30] Wiley, *Southern Negroes*, pp. 177-181; Williams, *Lincoln and the Radicals*, pp. 137-139; *New York Herald*, May 20, 25, April 4, June 17, 1862.

at leisure; the "everlasting cant about making negroes dig trenches," according to one account, was out of plumb with the facts. (Frederic Hudson was guilty of a slippery memory when he ordered this set in type. A year earlier he had noted approvingly in his diary the idea of a visitor that it was "the mission of the negro to clear away the miasmatic country around the Gulf for white men.") [31]

The earnest American Victorians of 1862 did not admit that respectable white men occasionally found exertion distasteful; when a *Herald* man on the Peninsula revealed that the "happy, careless, good-for-nothing" fugitives enjoyed Sunday because they were "not obliged to work," it was, therefore, presumable proof of their racial inferiority. Nobody could seriously expect to emancipate a people with a "chronic antipathy to labor." The maxim of those who opposed the efforts to convert the ex-slaves into wage earners was delivered by a *Herald* correspondent with General Pope's forces in northern Virginia: "A nigger's liberty is laziness, and unless he be smart, freeing him is doing him a great injury." Out West, a reporter in Nashville warned darkly that freed Negroes were drifting into Illinois, Indiana and Ohio in "sufficient numbers to alarm the working people and the taxpayers." [32]

How much of this was believed by the reporters themselves was not certain. Undoubtedly, a certain hospitality to the editor's viewpoint kept them working for the paper. The war was changing their status, but as yet they were

[31] *New York Herald*, July 30, July 17, August 2, 1862; Hudson Diary, January 22, 1861.

[32] *New York Herald*, August 6, 14, October 27, November 8, 1862.

not a completely professional corps, selling their services impartially to the high bidder. They rather looked on themselves as a volunteer company of gentlemen adventurers. Townsend, for one, seemed to speak his own mind. In 1866 he hustled his war memoirs into print, in a period when extolling the freedmen was certain to be helpful to sales. Yet his whole book abandoned the overwrought sentimentality of then popular works and spoke his mind with crisp realism. When he came to write of Negroes on the Peninsula, he clearly showed a racist bias, noting that they "slept and danced and grinned" in approved "coon joke" fashion, and that "their Elysium had come; there was no more work." When the Emancipation Proclamation was announced, the nervous Whitely, in Washington, was convinced that the abolition cabal meant "revolution, anarchy and secession." [33]

It was a pity, for the correspondents were missing a chance to pin on their new profession the blue ribbon of a necessary job well done. There was the story of a century in the freedman and his bewildering position. He was pushed into a glare of publicity and overwhelmed with contradictory instructions, trying to weigh freedom, wages, education and uniforms against cuffs, segregated camps, political hornswoggling and menial jobs. The slave was kicked, in one tremendous kick, from the age of Cain and Noah into a modern society too complicated for its most learned members to understand. The reporters who watched

[33] Townsend, *Campaigns of a Non-Combatant*, p. 146; Bennett Papers, Whitely to Bennett, September 9, 24, 1862.

his fumbling actions in the first months of liberation could have told a story that would later untangle a good many prejudices and erase a variety of stereotypes. But the caustic correspondents of the Democratic press had no interest in a careful portrait, and neither had those of the arch-Republican papers, who only swore out loud that every escaped Negro was as noble as Uncle Tom or as clever as Toussaint l'Ouverture. For all its lofty pretensions, journalism was not yet adult enough to make a responsible presentation of the problem. Possibly it was as well, for it was not certain that the audience was sufficiently mature to listen.

Herald men occasionally did some straight-out politicking. When the Democrats carried the New York State elections in the autumn of 1862, a dispatch from Virginia spoke of "joyful visages" among the troops, assured at last that "friends . . . of the Union" were "in preponderance." In Nashville, the same news moved one correspondent to say that everyone was pleased with the development save those who had been "gorging themselves to the chin with the fat pap Uncle Sam [had] to give." Finley Anderson, who could speak with a certain authoritativeness on the Southern scene after his year in a Confederate prison, said that he had received assurances that if Lincoln were replaced by "a fair, conservative President" peace talks might ensue. There was not a chance of them so long as he occupied the White House.[34]

When Bennett tried to inject life into a Grant-for-

[34] *New York Herald,* November 8, 12, 1862; March 24, 1864.

President boom in 1864, he had some help from his reporters afield. William Young, reporting from Army of the Potomac headquarters in February of 1864, warned professional managers of the "affection of the soldiers everywhere for General Grant" and their "determination that the next President be a military man." Grant's arrival to take command was, according to *Herald* accounts, met with "such an outburst of enthusiasm as no other general (except, of course, McClellan) could inspire." But McClellan was being prepared for a push over the side. While a reporter at the headquarters of the 5th Corps found the news of his nomination by the Democrats bringing "general satisfaction," Anderson, with another corps, spoke of the sorrow that the ousted general's failure sufficiently to damn the peace faction in the party had brought. People would be compelled "out of two evils to choose the less." It was Bennett's attitude precisely, once Grant was clearly out of the race for the nominations.[35]

After 1863, for the most part, however, the chances for political sermons by correspondents were dwindling. One by one, time settled the political issues of the war. The Negro got freedom and guns; the fighting went on until the exhaustion of the South; Lincoln kept his hold on the reins for all the rearing and bucking of the yoked Radical politicians; combat weeded out winning commanders from political officers.

The *Herald's* main business was news, after all. Town-

[35] *New York Herald*, February 1, March 23, September 3, November 11, 1864; Bennett Papers, Anderson to Bennett, September 10, 1864.

send had been impressed, while following McClellan in 1862, with the single-mindedness of the paper's superintendent of news services on the Peninsula. He wrote:

> Such a thorough individual abnegation I never knew. He was a part of the establishment, body and soul. He agreed with its politics, adhered to all its policies, defended it, upheld it, revered it. The Federal Government was, to his eye, merely an adjunct of the paper. Battles and sieges were simply occurrences for its columns. Good men, brave men, bad men, died to give it obituaries. The whole world was to him a Reporter's district, and all human mutations plain matters of news. I hardly think that any city, other than New York, contains such characters. The journals there are full of fever, and the profession of journalism is a disease.[36]

Townsend himself had the disease. He had nearly died of the fever following McClellan, and three months later had undauntedly bought a folding camp bed and a horse, using a hundred and fifty dollars of the *Herald's* money, and gone out to follow Pope. He tried Europe for a year, but was back in the field in 1864, crunching his hardtack, rubbing saddle blisters and penciling copy by firelight in the Shenandoah Valley. After the war — years after — he built his home on South Mountain battlefield, and led in the campaign for money to erect the freakish monument in stone to his collaborators in journalism.

With such men working at the profession, it was no mystery that the *Herald* should emerge from the war bigger

[36] Townsend, *Campaigns of a Non-Combatant*, pp. 90-91.

and brassier than ever. The reporter, too, grew with it; he became an intimate, adviser, teacher and oracle to millions. Bennett's paper was a leader in creating a new American personage.

CHAPTER VI

Mr. Greeley's War

IN the summer of 1861 the Washington correspondence of the *New York Tribune* was supervised, and in part written, in an office on 14th Street near Pennsylvania Avenue by Samuel Wilkeson, a man well seasoned in the high-level intricacies of journalism and politics and a onetime star witness on censorship during the Hickman investigation. He had worked at one time with Thurlow Weed, New York's cagey Republican boss, who ran an Albany newspaper. Horace Greeley, his present employer, had formerly been teamed with Weed in managing the public relations of William H. Seward, now Secretary of State, when he was governor of New York. Wilkeson's capital connections were plentiful and weighty, which was fortunate, since his job called for a veteran's skill. A typical morning's letter from Greeley presented unique problems:

> I am amazed at your simplicity in asking me to go away at this time. Why don't you go to one of McClellan's sentinels over the river and tell him he will catch his death by cold if he don't quit his post and go into his tent? You know well that no one can manage a newspaper for another in such a crisis as this . . . I must stay about the Tribune now or let everything go to destruction.

. . . .

> You see that the Northern Democracy have conspired to force us to a shameful peace; but you do not know that the Catholic hierarchy are in the same boat. . . . I guess there was nobody really in earnest in opposing the Jeff. Davis rebellion but the Tribune. And the C.S.A., backed by the Northern Democracy and the Catholic priesthood make a pretty strong antagonist for one newspaper.[1]

Wilkeson knew by experience the trials of managing any newspaper office, but he must occasionally have felt that he was undergoing special testing by Providence, which had set over him a chief who was convinced that the Civil War was his personal battle.

Greeley was not fundamentally upset to find that his newspaper was alone "in earnest" in pushing on the war; it had long been his conviction that the *Tribune* was fighting against the demon rum, the Slave Power, free trade and other heresies virtually singlehanded. Commuting daily to a downtown Manhattan office from his farm in Chappaqua, New York, the myopic editor with the round face and neck whiskers conceived innumerable schemes for simultaneously ending the Confederacy and re-energizing democracy; he would rush them into print, wait tensely for the reaction, shriek that his critics were sneaks, traitors and bullies, and then be lifted on the surge of a new idea. He alternated strident demands for a vigorous war with clumsy personal attempts to end the fighting by negotiation; in 1864 he went so far as to travel to Niagara Falls in order to meet briefly and fruitlessly with Confederate

[1] Horace Greeley Papers, New York Public Library, Greeley to Wilkeson, August 27, 1861.

peace emissaries. Lincoln supposedly once asked Homer Byington, another *Tribune* Washington correspondent, "What in the world is the matter with Uncle Horace? Why can't he restrain himself and wait a little?" — a question entirely beyond the capacity of Byington or anyone else to answer.[2]

Greeley's erratic enthusiasms were a matter of concern to the President, for the *Tribune* stood high in favor among the Republican elect, and its popular circulation was impressive. Although the editorial staff was well sprinkled with pundits, the daily issues contained enough financial, theatrical, sporting and police news to magnetize a grosser audience, and in the rural world its readership was plentiful, since Greeley, himself a farmer, saw to it that there were frequent helpful articles on gauging markets, guessing planting times, building hencoops and gentling new horses. Good relations with the *Tribune* were worth the efforts of administration officials, always anxious for popular support for the war and apt to brood on future political possibilities even in its tighter moments.

A good place to begin the cultivation of *Tribune* friendship was in the office of its Washington correspondents. The top capital reporter of a newspaper was able to play the part of contact man easily; he was mobile, presumably trained to be discreet, and able to widen his acquaintances without embarrassing questions. If his paper happily belonged to the incumbent party, his work load was increased along with his satisfactions. The channels were not espe-

[2] William A. Croffut, *An American Procession* (Boston, 1931), p. 123.

cially winding, either. Friends and claimants of the editor would make their special requirements known to him; a letter would go to the chief Washington agent, who dutifully sallied out to conduct "interviews" with the proper parties. Presently he would return to file a private report with his managing editor, indicating what officials were entitled to a beneficial paragraph or two in a column likely to attract notice. Publicity was always negotiable currency in Washington.

Wilkeson chose as his chief protector not Seward, with whom Greeley had long since quarreled, but the Secretary of War, Simon Cameron. White-haired and long-faced, Cameron was turning army procurement into a fish fry for manufacturers of his native Pennsylvania. Not a word of criticism, however, came from the *Tribune*, normally freighted to the water's edge with brickbats for public officials suspected of mischief; in fact, the Secretary's report of his first nine months in office, submitted in December (and given to the *Tribune* before its official release), was hailed as "simple, lucid . . . beyond the need of apology or vindication." Part of this enthusiasm was due to the fact that Cameron, in an early draft, proposed a favorite Greeley scheme of arming escaped slaves. Part of it, however, mirrored the touching understanding between the war minister and his favorite news-gatherer. Wilkeson would send to Cameron a clipping of one of his more flattering articles on the existing management of the war, and Cameron would respond in a way that counted, by dropping a note to the telegraph censor and requesting that

Wilkeson's dispatches be sent through untouched. When Cameron traveled to Missouri in October to observe a part of the war for himself, Wilkeson made part of the official retinue. Undoubtedly Wilkeson's staff of Washington reporters were able to capitalize on this friendship in lower echelons of the War Department. For the bureau superintendent, however, it meant the undertaking of considerable work which would never, in later years, be part of the curriculum of a school of journalism. Just before leaving for a stretch of front-line correspondence with McClellan's army in April, 1862, Wilkeson admitted his gratitude at being relieved of

> the business of general agent in the city of Washington for all people who happen to take the New York Tribune or who know me in person or by name. . . . For nine months I have borne its burdens, being afflicted during that long time with applications for about everything that the heart of man can desire out of a national capital in a time of peace or a time of war. I was bored only with reading the letters of the man who wanted the Peruvian mission. He never got me to draw on my boots on his behalf. But, from this person's misdirected ambition, down to the prayer of a ragged lad who begged me to place him as an ostler in a government stable — from requests for authority to raise brigades down to the procurement of discharges from the ranks of boys, runaways from their mothers' homes — from entreaties to assist in the manufacture of brigadier generals, inspector generals, colonels, majors, captains, lieutenants and department clerks, way down to orders for garden seeds from the Patent Office, and memorial bowie knives from . . . Bull

> Run — from requests to forward countless bushels of Congressional documents, up to entreaties to get from the War Department consent that Indians and negroes should be mustered into the service — from the torment of . . . the warrior with the impregnable military vest, down to the versatile bore who would have me assist him in running down the government with a choice between his unequalled breech-loading carbine . . . and his cannon that would keep firing just as long as any one would turn the crank — through services in getting back pay, in hurrying requisitions through the Treasury for needy creditors of the government, and in presenting the interests of manufacturers to members of committees charged with framing tax and tariff bills — in and through all this inevitable Washington work I have labored gratuitously for three quarters of a year.
>
> . . . .
>
> I give notice that the business of general charitable agent in the Tribune bureau at Washington is at an end. The sign is taken down, and another slave is emancipated in the District of Columbia.[3]

Though there was no suggestion throughout this manifesto of anything in the business of expediter for Wilkeson, the *New York Herald* ferreted out of an investigation of Cameron's contracts a story which charged that the Washington correspondent and two of the *Tribune's* commercial and financial writers had secured the charter of a Connecticut gun manufacturer and submitted a bid to supply the government with 25,000 muskets at twenty dollars apiece. Wilkeson (whose name was twisted by the *Herald*

[3] *New York Herald,* May 1, 1862.

to Wilkinson) had supposedly used his influence to have the Ordnance Department hurry matters along. The *Tribune* denied that any of its men had owned any part of the contract in question; Wilkeson admitted to an act of "disinterested kindness" and nothing more, but soon thereafter left Washington for the army. In any case, Secretary Cameron had been relieved of his cabinet post in January of 1862, and the practical value of his friendship had dropped to nothing.[4]

The change in the war ministry, however, did not close the door of the *Tribune*. Stanton, almost as soon as he was installed at his desk, wrote to Charles A. Dana, the managing editor, confiding that his mission tended toward the same end as that of the paper. In an early entanglement over a censored dispatch Stanton admitted that he and Dana were of "one heart and mind" in the cause of victory. He meant it, apparently, for Dana subsequently left Greeley's pay roll and, under the title of Assistant Secretary of War, ventured afield to keep an eye on various headquarters for Stanton.[5]

The *Tribune*, in fact, sometimes seemed to be regarded as an official gazette of the Radicals, despite the fact that it rarely stood still long enough to be identified with any particular cluster of ideas. If this was an advantage at cer-

[4] See also, in the Simon Cameron Papers, Library of Congress, a letter from Wilkeson to Cameron, August 25, 1861; Burton J. Hendrick, *Lincoln's War Cabinet* (Boston, 1946), pp. 219-223; Ralph R. Fahrney, *Horace Greeley and the Tribune in the Civil War* (Cedar Rapids, 1936), p. 163; *New York Tribune,* December, 4, 1861.

[5] Miscellaneous Papers of Charles A. Dana, Library of Congress, Stanton to Dana, January 24, February 19, 1862.

tain times, it was occasionally an embarrassment. When mobs of antidraft rioters howled through lower New York in July, 1863, the *Tribune* building, clearly a symbol of abolition war, narrowly escaped being burned down, and, according to some rival editors, Greeley himself had to take cover in the back room of a downtown restaurant in order to avoid the leading role in a lynching. (Despite the obvious prudence of such a defense, Greeley, in a nettled editorial, denied that he had done any such thing.) The editor was luckier than two of his prize correspondents, however, Albert D. Richardson and Junius Browne, who were captured near Vicksburg in 1863. Ordinarily the ground rules of the fighting allowed the quick release of seized newspapermen, who were not deemed especially useful to the enemy war effort. Months went by, however, without the return of the men, even though a list of notables which read like a blue book of the Northern high command was prevailed on to make contact with the Union exchange agent at Fortress Monoe and ask for speedy action — Lincoln, Stanton, Generals Ethan Allen Hitchcock (a top-rated War Department adviser), Grant and Butler, and the governor of Ohio, where both correspondents had lived for a time. All these efforts failed to impress the Confederate commissioner of exchange, who explained clearly enough why he was holding on to Browne and Richardson. "Such men as the Tribune correspondents," he wrote, "have had more share even than your soldiery in bringing rapine, pillage and desolation to our homes. . . . They are the worst and most obnoxious of all non-combatants." Stuck with Greeley's reputation, the two reporters remained in captivity, growing progressively more desperate and undernourished, until December of 1864, when they broke out of a North Carolina prison camp and crossed the Blue Ridge mountains afoot in the dead of winter to rejoin the Union lines.[6]

Still, it was helpful to wear the *Tribune's* livery in the field. The paper's men were often able to hold down important attaché assignments thanks to a judicious appreciation by sensitive commanders of the fact that the pen could, at times, really *be* mightier than the sword. When Wilkeson left Washington in the spring of 1862, he went to the Peninsula as "volunteer aide" to a corps commander, Samuel P. Heintzelman. Benjamin Butler kept the *Tribune's* W. H. Kent among his stable of reporters. "Fighting Joe" Hooker, leading a corps at Antietam, made use of still another *Tribune* man, George W. Smalley, to carry messages down to division commanders, a job which had the advantage of considerably widening the reporter's view of the battle. There were others, too, who managed to play a triple role. They gathered news to feed to the faithful each morning, they informally managed the public relations of their benefactors, and, in so doing, they filled the important political assignment of building up, in the public eye, a corps of generals avowedly loyal to the principles of Republicanism. For Greeley and the Radicals that was what counted. A general should make it clear

[6] *New York Tribune*, July 16, 1863; *Official Records*, Ser. 2, V, 723, 746-747, VI, 59, 183-184, VII, 3, 10, VIII, 810, Ser. 1, XLII, Pt. 3, 782.

whether or not he stood "square on the line of 54-50" or was "squinting toward 36-30," the Missouri Compromise line dividing free from slave territory, which certain moderates in 1861 thought of running westward to the California border as a bloodless solution to the war's main issue. If a commander was guilty of squinting, he was unfit to command Union forces, and none of "the gas about . . . military knowledge" was relevant. The *Tribune's* editor thought so little of professional military training, in fact, that one of his win-the-war suggestions, in 1863, was to close West Point and pack off its personnel into active service. Presumably a soldier's education could be acquired from *Hardee's Tactics With Johnson's Manual of Arms and a Chapter on "How to Preserve the Health of Soldiers,"* advertised for twenty-five cents in the *Cincinnati Commercial.*[7]

Ready-made for a Radical counterpart to the dashing McClellan was General John C. Frémont, whose first wartime assignment was to hold for the Union the doubtful State of Missouri, ready to fall to whatever side most quickly organized a force impressive enough to control it. Frémont could hardly have been a better Republican; he was the party's first Presidential candidate in 1856, and had been baptized in California politics from the time he had assisted in snatching the territory from the Mexicans. Moreover, he matched McClellan's appeal to the sense of

[7] *New York Tribune,* July 1, 1861, January 22, 1863; *Cincinnati Commercial,* August 18, 1862.

the romantic. He had helped explore the Far West with Kit Carson and other mountain men, and his public nickname of "The Pathfinder" rang even more bell-like tones than "The Young Napoleon."

Frémont set out to rescue Missouri with abundant sound and fury. Within a short while, thousands of newly recruited soldiers were making dirt fly as they worked on fortifications around St. Louis, and contracts for shoes, powder, blankets, mules, wagons and tents were fluttering in a paper blizzard from headquarters. Frémont had a lively sense of what was due to him as a commander, and he surrounded himself with a special bodyguard and traveled through the streets in an ornate equipage. Sentries with drawn sabers guarded his offices, in whose anterooms crowds of citizens cooled their heels waiting for business and official interviews. All of this looked suspicious to some Westerners, accustomed to militia generals who stuffed their pants into their boots and spat in public. The Pathfinder, unperturbed, continued with his individual prescriptions for winning the war in the West, suppressing a St. Louis newspaper for criticizing him with excessive vigor, and issuing his September proclamation on slave confiscation and firing squads for rebels. Lincoln had promptly revoked the order, but to the Radicals, immediate emancipation by the army represented the very way to get on with the war without any nonsense; better the immediate secession of the doubtful States and the loss of new battles and more lives than any infamous temporary compromise with the devil. For Republican extremists, Frémont was trumpeter of a reveille that could not be ignored for long.[8]

Editorially, of course, the *Tribune* placed itself squarely behind the general. Readers could naturally expect then that its correspondents would do the same, and in fact they lined up briskly on the mark. From St. Louis came a news report that all Union men endorsed the proclamation, which had caused a "great sensation." From Chicago a letter said that it was greeted with cheers by "all loyal men." From Cairo, word of "entire satisfaction" at the order. When countermanding orders came from Washington, the *Tribune* man at Frémont's headquarters foamed.

> Mr. Lincoln and his advisers may not yet be aware of the fact; but there is war in Missouri. A desperate, unscrupulous, bloodthirsty foe is over-running the State. . . . In such a condition of affairs, Gen. Fremont's policy was *simply a military necessity*. . . .
>
> But even rebellion, it seems, cannot destroy the sacredness of Slavery.

In Washington, a *Tribune* correspondent who could keep his ear to the ground for distant rumbles from the Mississippi valley said that Frémont stood so high in the West's confidence that his removal would stop enlistments.[9]

Talk of Frémont's relief continued to grow when the

[8] Lucy L. Tasher, "The *Missouri Democrat* and the Civil War" (unpublished Ph.D. dissertation, Department of History, University of Chicago, 1934), pp. 84-103.
[9] *New York Tribune,* September 6, 11, 16, 19, 20, 25, 1861; Fahrney, *Greeley and the Tribune in the Civil War,* pp. 115-117, 187-188.

army finally moved out into southwestern Missouri ready for action. About twenty correspondents had been waiting for this event, crowded into half a dozen rooms in the principal hotel of Jefferson City — a carelessly put together house, where a piano stood in the ladies' parlor and Negro children parked behind guests at the dining room tables and waved flies away from the fried ham and corn bread. The newspapermen enjoyed the absence of Eastern society's restraints. Romantically naming themselves "the Bohemian brigade," in self-conscious advertisement of their gay character, they played poker, smoked, borrowed each other's clothing, and engaged in roughhouses with their baggage and bedding.[10] When the wagons began to roll, they settled down to the business of reporting the campaign.

Since major battles were slow in developing, the correspondents for certain papers, the *Tribune* in particular, were able to put in some time in counteracting the growing outcries against Frémont. Stories filed back in St. Louis said that the major-general was losing money in the country's service, since he was paying an agent no less than $24,000 a year to look after his business affairs, while drawing only $6000 in salary, and that he was continuing this sacrifice despite "relentless and vindictive personal attacks." He had been cramped by the niggardliness of Washington in his efforts to hold Missouri, while a mammoth army sat idly in front of the capital absorbing men

[10] Albert D. Richardson, *The Secret Service, The Field, The Dungeon and The Escape* (Hartford, 1866), pp. 189-193.

and money. Since criticisms of his "extravagance" had come only *after* the proclamation, it was plain that proslavery skulduggery was at work. At Jefferson City a *Tribune* reporter bid for sympathy with a human-interest story on the general's wife, Jessie Frémont, the handsome daughter of Missouri's onetime distinguished Senator Thomas Hart Benton. Jessie had "peculiar grace of movement," a rich, musical voice, a comprehensive intellect and feminine intuition, qualities which might increase the warmth of sentimental readers' wishes for her husband's success. Out in the field at St. Joseph, another *Tribune* account pictured the Pathfinder as "the object of political jealousy and persecution." [11]

When the expected ouster finally came through, an unsigned *Tribune* story from headquarters foreshadowed the "all-is-lost" prose which was to flow from pro-McClellan journals when that ill-starred officer bit the dust. According to Greeley's witness, impromptu indignation meetings were held throughout the camps, officers publicly blustered about resigning, and, in a curiously touching gesture, regimental bands marched out to serenade Frémont and cheer him whenever he showed himself. "Universal gloom prevails throughout the camps," the jeremiad concluded, and the troops, though they would stand firm, were reportedly disheartened and unenthusiastic.[12]

Frémont was perfectly aware that he showed up as handsomely in certain papers as he did in his barouche,

[11] *New York Tribune,* October 3, 11, 22, November 6, 1861.
[12] *New York Tribune,* November 7, 1861.

rolling behind a liveried driver through the bustling streets of St. Louis. His relations with various correspondents were, according to some charges, almost textbook maneuvers in the procurement and co-ordination of journalistic supporting fire. Most striking of all was a possible link to the *Tribune's* leading Western correspondent, Albert Deane Richardson, through the opportune channel of army contracting.

Richardson was a prim, thirty-five-year-old Yankee, gone West to newspaper work in Cincinnati after a spell of schoolteaching. He had carried the banner for the Free State side in Kansas, and been a companion to Greeley in 1859 when the editor jounced his way out to Pike's Peak for his personal sniff at the West. In the fall of 1861 he was Greeley's chief agent in St. Louis, and hence was encountered by Samuel Wilkeson when the *Tribune's* Washington scribe was visiting Missouri as part of the entourage of Secretary Cameron. Wilkeson later wrote to Greeley that the train to headquarters had been "stuffed" with contract hunters, eager to keep Frémont in command if only because he seemed to them a blue-uniformed Santa Claus. Among others, said Wilkeson, "Richardson your special St. Louis correspondent was along — interested in Wheeler's contract for 2000 mules." [13] The letter went on to spell out Frémont's complete incompetence in command. None of it ever saw print, nor did the *Tribune's* attitude change, for Greeley believed that it was the function of journalism to lead and uplift, and there could ob-

[13] Greeley Papers, Wilkeson to Greeley, October 15, 1861.

viously be nothing uplifting about contributing to the removal of a "loyal" officer. Richardson continued to uphold the reputation of Frémont, who, whatever his limitations, had style. Any general might appoint a reporter as an aide-de-camp or pass on to him the first copy of an official report. It was Frémont's peculiar excellence to say it with a contract.

Richardson, however, was not exclusively lucky. Rumors that several correspondents were involved in "iniquitous 'deals'" became thick enough for one of the general's backers, the St. Louis *Missouri Republican*, to spend editorial space on denying them. One of the reporters allegedly involved was the *Republican's* own man, Junius H. Browne, a bald, frail-looking bachelor, who also wrote for the *New York Tribune*. Browne, gifted with a tiger's heart wrapped in an essayist's hide, sent in a bristly note from the field saying that he was clean-handed and ready to face any court of inquiry. No one took him up.

At a later stage in the war, the correspondents' special freedom of movement and association gave some of them tempting opportunities to enlarge their prospects. As the armies moved deeper into the cotton belt, bales of the harvested crop were left abandoned by the thousands in storehouses and on levees. Prices were at gold rush levels, and a scramble quickly got under way among private buyers to collect the cotton and ship it northward. The government tried to monitor the traffic by establishing a system of permits without which the bales could not be moved. These permits came, in some cases, from the generals commanding occupation zones. Correspondents who were on supper-table terms with certain of these officers held a strategic position, which many were ready to recognize. The *New York Times's* Franc Wilkie, with the candor of an adopted Westerner, claimed in his pointed memoir of the war that he had once gotten for an acquaintance a permit from Grant allowing the transport of fifty bales. It took him a matter of minutes and netted a hundred-dollar bill. Other newspapermen were more expansive in their operations. Albert H. Bodman, who covered the Mississippi theater of war for the *Chicago Tribune* at sixteen dollars a week, was rumored to have bought a house in the city for $22,000 in cash after a few months of arduous field service. William Webb, a St. Louis journalist, while recuperating at home from a campaign, blossomed forth temporarily with a Negro valet and the white gloves and vest of a Civil War dude. One of the artists for *Frank Leslie's Illustrated Weekly*, Henri Lovie, reportedly invested in real estate the profits of a flyer in cotton. The profession of reporter offered a number of interesting byways into politics and finance.[14]

At any rate, whether politics or business won Richardson to the Frémont side, he fulfilled Thaddeus Stevens's definition of an honest man: once bought, he stayed bought. In the spring and early summer of 1862, a generally cheerless season for the Union in Virginia, the Pathfinder was given a command in the Shenandoah val-

[14] *Missouri Republican*, November 10, 16, 1861; Franc B. Wilkie, *Pen and Powder* (Boston, 1888), pp. 51-52, 75, 225-229.

ley and within a short time was thoroughly beaten by Stonewall Jackson, a general whose attention was less distracted by civic ambitions. Once again, Frémont was superseded in command. A letter over Richardson's initials appeared in the *Tribune*, keening over the discrimination against an officer who had served "untiringly, devotedly and efficiently" and with "self-denying fidelity." Richardson had technically wandered off his beat to answer the alarm, as he was then in Memphis. The *Tribune* correspondent at Frémont's headquarters did his share for fearless and impartial reporting by describing the relief as a "causeless" and "utterly inexcusable" stroke. The general warmly shared these opinions, and resigned in protest. A year later, one *Tribune* correspondent with the Army of the Potomac cautiously hinted that the very man to lead the troops to victory over Lee was John C. Frémont. There was no follow-up, however. Other things were in prospect for Frémont, who emerged in the spring of 1864 as the Presidential candidate of a hyperactive Republican faction which saw in him the zest for the Radical faith lacking in Lincoln. In campaigns of this kind, the support of reporters was possibly a more usable advantage. One did not have to face Confederates who had not read the press notices.[15]

Tribune correspondents were active in the journalistic campaigns fought over McClellan. In the honeymoon tenderness of the first days of his command, the paper led

[15] *New York Tribune*, July 2, 23, 1862; May 23, 1863.

with its ace in his support. During September, 1861, Greeley sent Bayard Taylor to Washington to do a few columns on the young Napoleon. Taylor, at thirty-six, knew his way around Russia, Japan, central Africa, the *Tribune* editorial rooms on Nassau Street in Manhattan, and the inside of a Goethean stanza. (He was to be the author of a widely used translation of *Faust.*) He pushed intrepidly through the traffic and hotel barrooms of Washington and arrived on the farther side of the Potomac to watch McClellan conduct a review, surrounded by such choice imported members of his staff as Colonel de Trobriand, the Duc de Chartres and the Prince de Joinville. Taylor scanned "his figure, his attitude, and the square, tenacious set of his jaws," and saw nothing that was not "cool, firm, prompt, determined and self-reliant." The more cosmopolitan part of the *Tribune's* audience, at least, was reassured that all was well.[16]

As the rest of 1861 disappeared without the immediate capture of Richmond, however, a querulous note slipped into the *Tribune's* editorial treatment of McClellan. Early in 1862, Greeley wrote to a Congressional friend to find what the "House members of the War Investigating Committee" thought of the general's management. It was not a particularly reliable source. The Joint Congressional Committee on the Conduct of the War had been set up and was dominated by the Radicals, ostensibly to provide a legislative check on the employment of the national

[16] *New York Tribune,* September 10, 1861.

strength in the fighting, and actually to make sure that the war was conducted on approved Republican principles. The committee had a rich store of the peculiar military intuition of legislators, an occupational thirst for publicity, and it knew to a T how to choose a witness and then pilot him through a set of loaded questions into the safe harbor of a predetermined conclusion — almost invariably a documented tale of Democratic, or at least conservative, villainy at work undermining the war effort. No doubt the report made to Greeley did nothing helpful for McClellan's standing, and by mid-March an editorial article was complaining of "delays and procrastinations" and wondering solicitously if the general might not be surrounded by politicians "more anxious for the preservation of Slavery than for the exemplary crushing out of the rebellion." [17]

An echo almost immediately bounced back, first from a Washington reporter who clucked over the "crowd of sycophants" surrounding McClellan, and then from an army correspondent who was moving out with the lead elements of a force sent by the general to occupy positions just outside Washington abandoned by Confederates at the beginning of March. The Army of the Potomac, then in the process of organizing for the trip to the Peninsula, discovered that the supposedly formidable defenses barring the road to Richmond all winter past had been manned by numerically inferior forces and equipped in

[17] Greeley Papers, Greeley to S. Colfax, January 24, 1862; *New York Tribune,* March 12, 1862.

part with dummy guns of wood. Greeley's reporter filed a crackling dispatch on the wait-and-see strategy which McClellan had followed for months. It was fitting, he said, that the people who had footed the bills for the "expensive entertainments . . . furnished to sightseers for the last seven months" should know what supposed obstacles had kept the army parading in Washington when it might have been battling towards the enemy capital. When the first regiments arrived in the empty fortifications, the account went on, they "burst out into tears and imprecations upon the mismanagement" which had made them "a laughing-stock to the whole civilized world." Being unblooded volunteers mostly in their teens, a few green troops may have shed an unlikely tear at missing a battle, but the important thing was that the restless reading public at home undoubtedly added a few imprecations of its own, carefully directed by the story at McClellan.[18]

To add an extra barbed touch, the Committee on the Conduct of the War called in Bayard Taylor for questioning. The *Tribune* correspondent had evidently failed to find the generalship in McClellan which his first look had led him to expect. He tapped his professional erudition for a few welcome judgments. Probably no heavy guns had *ever* been emplaced in the works, he thought, and no more than 75,000 men had held them. "Could you see any reason," the committee asked, "why one hundred thousand men should not have captured the whole force there months ago?" "Not the slightest," retorted Taylor

[18] *New York Tribune*, March 13, 14, 1862.

imperturbably, leaving it clear, apparently to general satisfaction, that McClellan was the goat of the episode.[19]

Once on the Peninsula, the commander's treatment by the *Tribune* was not entirely destructive. There was a story to the effect that McClellan, a touchy man about the disciplines of war, had placed guards over "rebel" barns while his own men were on short rations. A Congressman into whose hands this fell was instantly spurred to demand an investigation, the unfailing sequel to a case of Congressional indignation. Another *Tribune* report carried the announcement that a surgeon had been unable, because of McClellan's orders, to requisition a private home for use as a hospital. But to offset this, when McClellan was driven to change his base during the Seven Days' Battles, one *Tribune* reporter described it as a "masterly movement" — a descriptive phrase virtually copyrighted by the pro-McClellan press — and another compared the general to a chess player sacrificing a pawn or two in order to drive on to a checkmate. More impressive than either of these, however, was a battlefield report from Samuel Wilkeson. Wilkeson was technically serving as a special aide to General Samuel P. Heintzelman, a gray-haired corps commander who, like other older officers, was a shade regretful at serving under a thirty-six-year-old-military *Wunderkind*. Moreover, Wilkeson knew perfectly well what Greeley thought of McClellan by that time. But he had no urge towards a subtlety that would conciliate either his military

[19] "Report of the Joint Committee on the Conduct of the War," *Senate Reports*, 37th Congress, 3rd Session, No. 108 (Washington, 1863), I, 246-250.

patron or his employer after he went through the retreat itself, a week made nightmarish by fatigue, combat, continual fear of becoming lost, and rumors of impending capture. Wilkeson wrote a story for the *Tribune* describing the entire episode, and then turned on the critics:

> The army . . . will feel for its commander, the admiration and gratitude that saviors of men ever enkindled in loyal hearts. But the brilliancy of this movement will not . . . dazzle the sight of the angry people so as for a moment to obscure their perception of the *crime against the nation. . . . The politicians . . . who left us here to be outnumbered and cut off from our supplies . . . are doomed men.*[20]

Wilkeson was able to set a pattern of sturdy and independent reporting. It was the second time in nine months that he had told Greeley unpleasant facts about the *Tribune's* political collaborators, the first occasion having been in the previous October when he privately exposed the contracting sleight of hand in Frémont's headquarters. But his defense of the Peninsula evacuation was McClellan's last visible kindly notice from a *Tribune* correspondent. When the army came back to the Potomac it arrived just in time to be fed into the campaign which ended disastrously in defeat at the second battle of Manasses. A cry went up from the panicky Radicals that McClellan, in effect sulking in his tent, had been deliberately slow in sending off his units to join Pope's hard-pressed

[20] War Conduct Committee Report, I, 98; *New York Tribune*, July 1, 2, 3, 4, 7, 1862.

northern Virginia command. One *Tribune* reporter in Washington, which was once more practically front-line territory, repeated the charge. He said that if McClellan's troops "had been sent forward when they were ordered" a different story might have resulted. Another letter datelined Washington stated as a fact that an entire corps had been kept in camp three days after it was ready to march, with McClellan countermanding movement orders as fast as they were taken off the telegraph line from Washington.[21]

McClellan got another chance, nevertheless, and for a moment seemed to have gotten the upper hand of his enemies by his victory at Antietam. The battle was covered by four *Tribune* men with considerable enterprise. They met in the evening to co-ordinate their accounts, and then George W. Smalley, who had been twice grazed by bullets during the day, headed northward with the news. He rode thirty miles on horseback, flung a short bulletin into the telegraph system, caught one train, barely made connections with another, and finished a five-column story crouching in a coach under a swaying oil lamp. At seven A.M. the morning after the battle he staggered into the *Tribune* press room with his copy.[22] The paper expected the same high standards of energy to be met by the general, for while McClellan remained in Maryland for weeks

[21] *New York Tribune*, September 2, 1862.
[22] F. Lauriston Bullard, *Famous War Correspondents* (Boston, 1914), pp. 400-401; Richardson, *Secret Service, Field, Dungeon and Escape*, p. 286; George W. Smalley, *Anglo-American Memories* (New York, 1911), pp. 154-158.

following the engagement, insisting on the army's need for a refit, *Tribune* reporters hinted broadly that nothing kept him waiting except his chronic timidity.

One reporter, Nathaniel Paige, said that when news reached the camps of the southward withdrawal of Lee, "disappointment and chagrin" were rife, and that soldiers expressed their feelings in a "whole vocabulary of oaths." (According to journalistic accounts, Civil War fighting men had the temperamental instability of operatic leads. They burst into either tears or "oaths" at any unusual development in the news.) Paige railed that every "sensible" officer expressed readiness to fight at once, and insisted that the army needed nothing more for its efficiency. One of the Washington correspondents backed him up with an article asserting that the supply departments had promptly filled every requisition made for the encamped regiments, so that there was no foundation to the complaints of logistical deficiencies. Another army reporter, signing himself "J.R.S.," asked his readers to speculate with him on why the Confederates, barefoot and coatless, were able to move freely in Virginia while the Union army went through a lengthy build-up in fixed positions. Richardson, borrowed from the Western theater to cover Antietam, even suggested that the much-publicized enthusiasm of the troops for McClellan was dwindling. He had watched two corps parade past the general in review, with only "faint cheers" being sounded. Richardson was not apt to be carried away by demonstrations for McClellan. Whereas Bayard Taylor, on his first view of the young Napoleon, had found promptness, coolness, iron determination and other fourteen-carat virtues in his features, Richardson, less susceptible, had been struck only by a "mild, moony face, with one cheek distended by tobacco." [23]

The more devoted members of the general's staff had good reason to detest *Tribune* reporters, and at a review at Warrenton, Virginia, several of them surrounded one of the paper's men, rode him off to one side, and "forced him to dismount, somewhat bruised." This was after McClellan had finally begun to move southward. He did not proceed very far before orders for his relief caught him. The journals which had supported him pictured general moroseness throughout the army, but if the troops were stricken by his removal it was not so that the *Tribune's* witnesses could notice it. "J.R.S." saw "no perceptible effect" resulting in morale, and Nathaniel Paige cited conveniently anonymous corps commanders who admitted, now that they were no longer bound by formal loyalties, that they placed McClellan "below his most incompetent Brigadier-Generals." (Every army, during the early part of the war, was well supplied with corps commanders who knew how to manage the campaign better, as they could demonstrate to reporters at the drop of an epaulet. Corps headquarters were happy hunting grounds for a sharp-eyed newsman at any time, but particularly so after a battle or a shake-up in command.) Another writer in Greeley's

[23] *New York Tribune,* September 23, October 20, 27, 30, November 5, 1862; Richardson, *Secret Service, Field, Dungeon and Escape,* p. 143.

pay was at a way station when the train carrying McClellan passed through, to the tune of "a few faint cheers, anything but hearty"; Richardson listed reports of disaffection in the ranks as "sensational falsehoods."

Four months later, a *Tribune* correspondent at Army of the Potomac headquarters scoffed at the idea that the troops were pining for Little Mac. "The soldiers don't care half so much who is over them as certain persons would make us believe," he wrote. It would have been interesting to the authors of the copy concerning Frémont's dismissal to learn that. The army's devotion to a commander burned more brightly in the unfettered prose of the correspondents than anywhere else, and its intensity there was usually determined by whether he voted the paper's ticket.[24]

Tribune reporters showed no mercy to General Buell during his command in the West. Junius Browne devoted columns to Buell's "inglorious, disastrous career," his "waning reputation," the "lamentable failure" of his plans and the "disgust and contempt" which he supposedly aroused among the knowledgeable civilians of the Ohio valley States.[25] Browne's pugnacity increased with every month of fighting. Normally a suave and inoffensive man of noticeable delicacy, which suited his small stature, he had amused his colleague Wilkie of the *New York Times* while waiting for Frémont to move in St. Louis by filling himself

[24] *New York Tribune,* November 10, 12, 13, 14, 1862, March 3, April 7, 1863.
[25] *New York Tribune,* October 1, 4, 8, 25, November 12, 1862.

with liquor and threatening, *mezzo forte,* to lick any secessionist in town. At the battle of Fort Donelson, in February, 1862, he came upon a trio of snipers trying to neutralize a battery bearing on Union positions. Unhampered by any red tape concerning the activities of noncombatants, Browne borrowed a rifle, squeezed off a shot which silenced the Confederate gun temporarily, and decamped before his luck could be explored any further. By the second autumn of the war, he was fully ready to take on a major-general, especially when the general was a regular, a friend of McClellan, and a proven skeptic concerning the Republican program. *Tribune* correspondents were always showing unwittingly by their writing that one of the ancestors of the reporter was the pamphleteer. Together with Greeley, they seemed to entertain a high respect for that tradition. In contrast to the treatment of Buell in the *Tribune,* was a glowing report from Richardson, in September of 1862, on the excellences of General Lew Wallace, who was then responsible for guarding Cincinnati against a possible sneak attack by Confederate cavalry operating in Kentucky. Wallace was, unlike the professionally schooled Buell, a lawyer and a novelist. His legacy to the republic, in fact, was not to be the salvation of Cincinnati, but *Ben Hur.* When examined by the Committee on the Conduct of the War shortly before taking his Cincinnati command, he had come out squarely for unrestrained confiscation of "rebel property" and the arming of escaped Negroes. In the *Tribune's* editorial judgment, *there* was a general! It was not often that the paper's opinions were contradicted by the "facts" which its reporters gathered.[26]

On rare occasions, apparently, a correspondent was in fact sent to gather information for limited consumption only. In May of 1863, Sidney H. Gay, then Greeley's first assistant, ordered George W. Smalley southward from New York to Army of the Potomac headquarters. The *Tribune* was especially discontented with the command situation there. Six months had elapsed since McClellan's removal, and the situation was unchanged except for new defeats. Moreover, McClellan's successor, General Ambrose E. Burnside, had been more or less "converted" to abolitionism in January, 1863, and *his* successor, "Fighting Joe" Hooker, had endeared himself to the Radicals by explaining to the Committee on the Conduct of the War that McClellan's incompetence alone had kept him from taking Richmond during the Peninsula campaign. It was therefore inconvenient to blame the situation on the sagging moral fiber of proslavery commanders, normally a popular device in Radical circles, though there was some murmuring about disloyal subordinates. Smalley's mission was to find out as diplomatically as possible what the officers directly under Hooker actually thought of him, and what successor, if any, they would prefer.

The *Tribune's* name was impressive enough to Hooker for him to offer its emissary accommodations even after the correspondent had candidly explained his mission.

[26] Wilkie, *Pen and Powder*, pp. 75, 107; *New York Tribune*, September 12, 1862; War Conduct Committee Report, III, 347-353.

Perhaps "Fighting Joe" felt that dismissing Smalley would lose him the *Tribune's* useful favor in any case, whereas he might have some chance in a popularity poll among division and corps commanders. Smalley spent several days in his interviewing; most of the generals were willing to talk to a newspaperman, and in fact began tugging their coats straight and smoothing their mustaches for a public portrait the moment a correspondent appeared in camp. The general opinion was that George G. Meade would be the best candidate, though Meade himself impatiently disclaimed any interest in the survey or its result. With the information in his pocket, Smalley headed for New York and reported to Gay. The managing editor felt that the time was not ripe, probably in view of limp public morale, to publicize the story; he told Smalley to write an editorial, keep to generalities, and forget what he had learned. Six weeks later, Meade was given the command. Perhaps the whole mission had had some kind of official inspiration, or its results had been passed upward into some private channel. If Smalley speculated on that possibility at the time, he must have been startled by the story of the violently Democratic *New York World's* Washington man which appeared on May 18th. Stating that "confidential agents from New York" had gone south to feel the army's pulse, it went on:

> One of them, a prominent *Tribune* man, spent a couple of days with the army and went away much astonished. It is stated that, after a long interview with the general commanding one of the corps, he asked: "In case Hooker

> is relieved, who is the proper man to command the army?" The general answered emphatically, "George B. McClellan."

Discretion clearly had its limits. Someone had talked, and the *World* writer had been able to puff a hearsay report into a story favorable to the fading McClellan. Reporters who traveled on private intelligence missions had to keep on the watch for fellow journalists pressed into counter-espionage.[27]

Hooker had one other contact with a *Tribune* correspondent which must have left him with a sense of uneasiness over the damaging possibilities of admitting reporters to camp. In December of 1863, after being transferred to Tennessee and given command of a corps, he found an article in the *Tribune* accusing him of pushing his command, during one part of an operation around Chattanooga, into a barren attack which had cost a thousand needless casualties. Hooker found out that the story came from Charles D. Brigham, a correspondent whom he knew to be an intimate of General W. F. ("Baldy") Smith, a cantankerous Vermont-born West Pointer nearing sixty. Smith had become involved in a sharp dispute with Hooker while they were both in the Army of the Potomac. Now that they had both left it, Hooker wrote in a temperamental letter straight to the Secretary of War, Smith was using the reporter as an instrument in a vendetta, inspiring

[27] War Conduct Committee Report, I, 575-582; Smalley, *Anglo-American Memories*, pp. 158-160; *New York World*, May 18, 1863. See also the *Tribune* for December 24, 1862, January 8, April 18, 1863.

him to send stories which would sap confidence in "Fighting Joe's" abilities. Stanton offered no satisfaction, and Hooker was able only to have Brigham ordered out of the fighting area, meditating darkly meanwhile on what fresh villainy Smith would be plotting against him, and whether a reporter would be its agent.[28]

Happier prospects were in store for *Tribune* correspondents in the camp of Benjamin F. Butler than in any other. Butler, well marinated in nonprofessional realism, knew that a soldier's martial exploits were what contemporary historians made them, and that friendly reporters needed, on occasion, the tender care sometimes bestowed on a doubtful district. In the spring of 1864, when the headquarters of his Army of the James moved ceremoniously down to Fortress Monroe, he saw to it that members of the working press got traveling accommodations on the staff steamer *Greyhound.* Correspondents also had their own headquarters mess, presided over by a Negro named Horace, who knew what to do with his kettles, frying pans, and coffeepot. While less valuable members of the official family pined for fresh fruit and vegetables, Horace passed dishes of cucumbers and onions sliced in vinegar to the newspapermen when they gathered at meals. They must have felt that civilization had made impressive strides in two years. In the early and unenlightened days of the war, correspondents had been left to find rations almost entirely on their own. Junius Browne, at the batttle of Fort

[28] *New York Tribune,* December 9, 1863; *Official Records,* Ser. 1, XXXII, Pt. 2, 467-469.

Donelson, had used up his privately acquired one-day ration, and then been reduced to exploring the confused area just behind the lines for a box of hardtack jolted out of a wagon or abandoned in the excitement. General Butler's forethought in such matters was certain to earn him friends among the working newsmen, who were as willing as anyone to have some of the hell removed from war.[29]

So far as the *Tribune* was concerned, it did Butler no harm either to have a reputation as a thoroughgoing Radical. During the year he had been in command of occupied New Orleans, he had armed Negroes, taken over some of the city's most flossy homes as billets for his officers, arrested foreign consuls suspected of aiding blockade runners, hanged a secessionist or two, and issued an order that patriotic Southern ladies who "insulted" Union officers should be subject to the same arrests and fines as sidewalk tarts. Rumors that he had coined a private fortune by allowing favored friends to traffic in cotton between the lines spread afar, but the Radicals believed firmly that a man in their party should improve his standing in life and promote progress through helping commerce to wax.

It was probably no surprise to Butler to find himself described, then, in the correspondence of the *Tribune*, as "never tiring, ever watchful, prompt, decided . . . the man for an emergency." W. H. Kent, possibly thinking of cucumbers sliced in vinegar, wrote that every contingency

[29] *New York Tribune*, May 9, 24, July 22, September 6, 1864; Junius H. Browne, *Four Years in Secessia* (Hartford, 1865), pp. 55-70.

was "foreseen and provided for by Gen. Butler." Kent was also ready to go into action when he was really needed, during periods in which Butler's military management was clearly showing no returns. In the second week of June, the Army of the James was ordered to dash into Petersburg, the key railroad junction south of Richmond, while Grant was keeping Lee occupied to the northeast of the capital. The attack was bungled, resulting in a bitter nine-month siege of the city. According to the story filed by Kent, however, the fault was entirely that of General Quincy Gillmore, a subordinate commander, and by happy coincidence a regular. Kent wrote that Gillmore had stalled his part of the operation, resulting in its failure despite the fact that "every preparation had been made by Gen. Butler to insure success." Gillmore's relief was hailed by the *Tribune* correspondent as a removal of one obstacle to success.[30]

There were occasional risks to the technique. Shortly afterwards, a new attack on Petersburg failed to gain ground. By that time, the Army of the Potomac was in direct contact with Butler's forces, and Kent pinned the blame, in this case, on the failure of General Winfield S. Hancock to lead his Second Corps in a diversionary demonstration with the proper "spirit and vigor." Hancock got to see this "false and injurious account," wrote a fiery letter to headquarters, and proceeded to get an order from Grant which chased the reporter from the army's lines. As a matter of fact, at just about that time, Kent was

[30] *New York Tribune*, May 9, 14, June 14, 27, 1864.

nearly killed when a wagon which he was passing on a bridge swerved and crowded him over the side. His horse fell on top of him, bruising him badly enough to destroy his usefulness as a leg man for some time. In October, having recovered from his contusions and regained his nerve, he got Butler to write Hancock asking permission for his return. Hancock, a more forgiving officer than, say, Sherman, allowed this, and Butler had the benefit of Kent during the remainder of his command.[31]

In exploring the possibilities of public relations, the correspondents were broadening not only their education but their power. Party managers and generals on the lookout for their fortunes had come to realize that in a modern world, held together in good part by mass communication, public notice was the universally valuable and indispensable coinage which could buy advancement. Many things were possible to the reporters who dispensed it, as they were learning. Among other things, friendly contacts meant more sources, and more copy; and, by coloring a few of the facts in a case to someone's advantage, the reporters were in some instances better able to come by all of them. It was a paradox happily inviting to exploration.

Forthright propaganda filled the *Tribune's* news columns, most of it concerned with Negroes. When thousands of slaves began to come into the camps, fresh from the

[31] *New York Tribune*, July 4, 1864; *Official Records*, Ser. 1, XL, Pt. 2, 567, 583, 593, Pt. 3, 40, 89, XLII, Pt. 3, 203-204.

overrun farms, Greeley was able to offer his emancipation program as simple wartime horse sense. Why should the government, he asked, turn the "contrabands" away and give the enemy "a monopoly of diggers and shovellers without pay?" Obviously a Negro sweating to unload cases of ammunition from a wagon was a problem to the quartermaster who had to scrounge an extra ration for him, but he was also freeing a rifleman for more warlike duties. He might, moreover, have picked up a considerable amount of useful information concerning Confederate forces before making his break for freedom. If there were any worries about the rights of Southern proprietors, they could properly be left among the cares of Jefferson Davis' office; certainly Northern officials should not be concerned.[32]

A correspondent at Fortress Monroe published an account of the "faithful, cheerful and . . . zealous" fugitives making the dirt fly on a railroad under construction by army engineers, selling homemade confections, laundering uniforms and finding enough energy in the evening to cheer up the camps with a touch of plantation harmony. In West Virginia, according to one *Tribune* story, a Negro maid in a local home beckoned a free-talking reporter who was boarding there aside, and begged him to hush his mouth when the conversation waxed military. Her master was a "secesh," waiting to slip off to the Confederates with information. A touching letter from a camp on the Ohio River told of a naked Negro boy, who had just swum

[32] *New York Tribune,* July 23, October 15, November 1, 1861.

the stream, tearfully leaving under guard to be returned to his master, by orders of the regulation-conscious camp commander. Union troops filing off transports to occupy coastal sandspits off South Carolina in December, 1861, were soon joined by slaves who flocked out to the coast. "We've been a waitin' and a prayin' for you, Massa, day and night," one of them told a *Tribune* correspondent, who dutifully recorded the sampling of opinion for interested subscribers.[33]

Tribune readers had the word of its most august correspondents that the Negroes were the Union's truest friends. Albert D. Richardson told them of how, when a column marched through a village such as Harpers Ferry, white townsfolk would ostentatiously slam doors and jerk down blinds, but Negroes would offer mute, grateful greetings with their eyes from corners and doorways. A Missouri correspondent related the saving of an entire scouting party from ambush thanks to the warning of a Negro who slipped into the lines. At Port Royal, in tidewater South Carolina, another reporter revealed that one fugitive, drawing in the sand with a sharp stick, had marked "with perfect distinctness" the Confederate strong points in the area, showing "the location of forces, giving their names and strength, and marking the points of approach." (It might have occurred to cynical readers that few officers in either army below the rank of colonel could duplicate that performance, but Greeley's fundamental appeal

[33] *New York Tribune*, July 27, August 4, 7, 10, September 4, 7, 21, 27, October 8, December 7, 12, 21, 1861.

was to a wide-eyed type of audience.) No less an authority than Samuel Wilkeson himself wrote from the Peninsula to explain that the Union had blown its chance at Richmond by refusing to take the word of runaway slaves, who, "guiding us by day — by night bringing us intelligence upon which our columns could safely march," could have altered the balance. Wilkeson reported "verbatim" the prophecy of a remarkably perceptive slave named Tom, whose special gift was evidently to speak editorial prose:

> *You have got to have us, Mr. W. Our climate will kill your troops. . . . The South is a wilderness. You are ignorant of it, and can be ambushed every day. And . . . if with half a million men you overrun it, it would take a million men to occupy it. . . .* You white men of the North will go into Slavery, unless you take us black men of the South out of Slavery; and, Mr. W., you have not a great deal of time left in which to decide what you will do.[34]

Clearly the *Tribune's* men were covering a different war from that reported by writers for such unhumanitarian journals as the *Herald*. The *Herald* correspondents swore that the "contrabands" were useless idlers, sandbagging an already heavily loaded supply system. Greeley's men were apt to point out, as one did early in 1862, that the slave, equipped in most cases with a manual skill, was a better candidate for membership in a free society than the

[34] *New York Tribune,* October 8, 1862, January 11, 15, May 9, July 14, 1862.

master. Finding a jovial contraband poking through the abandoned fortifications at Manassas, the correspondent asked him whether or not he would starve if set adrift. The Negro grinned; he could raise garden truck and had some skill as a carpenter. He would be "All Right." His former owner, the reporter guessed, might not get along in the world as well.[35]

Given that much of a head start, it was easy for the *Tribune's* men to find nothing but success in the experiment of placing the ex-slaves under arms. The *Tribune's* army correspondence helped soften up opposition in the first place. Stories appeared lauding the slaves as "brave and effective soldiers," given the chance, and asserting that the tough-minded regular army and navy officers, glad of any instrument to end the fighting, were eager to use the "capacity and shrewdness" of the plantation refugees. Later, when the black regiments were organized and sent into the line, *Tribune* notices were glowing. Describing a furious action at Port Hudson, Louisiana, in May of 1863, the paper's New Orleans correspondent said that the ex-slaves "fought like tigers." At Charleston, Negro troops taking part in bitter amphibious operations to reduce the forts around the harbor were reported to be the equals of any white commands. W. H. Kent, at Butler's headquarters, spoke of the conversion of the army to a belief in "negro muscle, dash and endurance," and one *Tribune* observer in the lines around Petersburg recorded a satisfying scene of justice trium-

[35] *New York Tribune,* March 6, 1862.

phant — a sullen South Carolina officer, marching to a prisoners' compound under the shepherding of three armed Negro infantrymen, occasionally encouraging him with respectful comments of "March along dar, Massa—no straggling to de rear — close up dar, Sar?"[36] Day after day in Greeley's paper the Negro appeared, always a stalwart friend of the Union, gradually winning his way into the confidence of the volunteers and even, at last, of the graduates of West Point, the very Babylon of conservatism. Much of the writing was patronizing, much mawkish, and in some of it a political slip or worse was showing, as in an account from Norfolk in 1863 which declared:

> As white men, on the average, are worth a little more than black ones, let us save the country and save all the white men who are worth saving by the aid of a few thousand blacks.[37]

Still, the Negro had cause to thank the *Tribune's* sentimental and carefully directive reporters. A good press of any kind was a luxury that a black man could rarely expect, then and in time to come.

The *Tribune's* corps of correspondents was also at pains to show that the army as a whole favored the Republican program. Each party insisted, whenever it suffered an election setback, that its registered voters were mainly at

[36] *New York Tribune,* March 3, 11, 13, 14, June 9, 22, 29, September 30, 1863, May 30, June 13, 21, 27, 1864.
[37] *New York Tribune,* February 10, 1863.

the front, leaving the field to the opposition's numerous draftdodgers. Greeley, after the Democrats carried New York in November, 1862, judged that of one hundred thousand citizens of the Empire State then with the various armies, two thirds were "ardent Republicans." Reckoning by what *Tribune* reporters had to say, the figure was representative. After the Emancipation Proclamation took effect, Albert D. Richardson, camping along the Rappahannock, wrote that he had not heard a syllable of dissent or harsh language concerning it from any officer or man, though Democratic papers were then running stories such as that of the *Cincinnati Enquirer's* Washington correspondent, who had inside word that whole units of New Jersey troops were ready to resign en masse, unwilling to stay through a war which now "must result in the . . . horrors of negro insurrections." One could find an army to suit one's taste merely by selecting the right journal of fearless and impartial opinion.[38]

The Civil War's common soldier, like most, reserved his best wishes for any program which would return him home in the shortest time. He did, on the other hand, have a number of pungent political opinions, being bred as he was in a ballot-conscious age. The correspondence column of the *Tribune*, however, was not the most unbiased place for the home folks to recapture them. A story from Army of the Potomac headquarters in October of 1863, for example, said that recent Republican triumphs in elections

[38] *New York Tribune,* November 5, 1862, February 19, 1863; *Cincinnati Enquirer,* February 27, 1863.

in Pennsylvania and Ohio had been recognized by the troops as "Union triumphs . . . spoken of in the same tones as Gettysburg and Vicksburg." Moreover, the same story continued, it was no longer a reproach to be called an abolitionist, and the writer had even seen a package of *Liberators* — the fiery Boston abolition journal — on some general's camp table, a discovery which appeared to startle him as much as if he had come across the memoirs of Casanova in a convent. Exciting as this news was, the reporter of it was one William A. Croffut, who had spent the previous winter in Washington, organizing a series of abolitionist lectures held at the Smithsonian Institution. He had also, it was sourly reported by a Democratic paper, been run out of a Minnesota town where opinions were touchy and action quick, for "ultra Abolitionism" in prewar days.[39] (According to Croffut, the fighting men were not only politically knowing but literary-minded. He wrote a stimulating account in later years of entertaining a group of cavalry troopers with whom he was bivouacking one rainy night by reading aloud from a copy of Byron which he carried with him.)

Other *Tribune* men tuned on the editorial A. "There are more friends of the downtrodden negro in the Union ranks than even the most sanguine Abolitionist is apt to suppose," said one story from Nashville. A Cairo correspondent declared that Illinois troops, generally regarded

[39] *New York Tribune,* October 21, 1863; William A. Croffut, "Horace Greeley Knows His Business," *Atlantic Monthly,* CXLV (1939), 228-239; *Cincinnati Enquirer,* January 30, 1862.

as unfruitful targets for emancipation talk because of their many Southern kinfolk, ceased to "sympathize with their 'misguided Southern brethren' when . . . shot at a few times." Western troops were reportedly ready to hang Copperheads to neighborhood trees in wholesale quantities, to credit another *Tribune* reporter's story.[40]

In 1864, some of the correspondents found work ready to their hands in de-emphasizing McClellan, nominated by the Democrats and cutting an awkward figure, with one leg balanced on his military record and the other on a plank calling for an armistice and thereby admitting the war to be a failure up to then. (His personal repudiation of that part of the platform was ignored both by the opposition and by numbers of his own supporters.) A *Tribune* man in Georgia, finding Sherman, after a two-hour search of his "headquarters," wrapped in blankets asleep at the foot of a tree, contrasted the red-bearded general's simplicity with the gorgeous equipage that had surrounded McClellan and his titled staff. His story pointed out, if anybody had forgotten to notice it, that the less showy officer was having more spectacular results in the field. In the Army of the Potomac, according to another *Tribune* account, the popularity of "Little Mac" had vanished. The writer of the story quoted a useful anonymous soldier to the effect that "no man who has served . . . [could] be fooled and trifled with by . . . the . . . platform." At Butler's headquarters, Charles A. Page, a beardless boy in *Tribune* livery, predicted that the troops would

[40] *New York Tribune,* September 1, 3, October 1, 1862.

vote against McClellan solidly, being empty of enthusiasm for what a colleague of Page's described as a "Copperhead, hybrid, double-faced, dough-faced ticket." Page also did his bit for Lincoln by publishing his own incontrovertible proof that McClellan was the Confederates' candidate. He wrote that a "rebel" deserter had confided to him the Southern hope of making peace with the North on satisfactory terms if the Democrats carried the election. General Butler himself vouched for the interpretation, which put a virtually ecclesiastical stamp upon it. How "*horrible*," mused a *Tribune* correspondent whose profession had left him curiously sensitive, that Democrats should be "encouraging . . . the Rebel leaders to the *murder* of their own and *our own* men and brothers" for a "short lived and ignoble *party* success." [41]

The usefulness of this poison-pen reporting was questionable, since the best Republican campaign arguments were being furnished by Sheridan, Sherman and Farragut, who were smiting the Confederates hip and thigh in Georgia, Virginia, and the Gulf of Mexico. It was a bad autumn for the South and the Democrats, with Lincoln gathering in 216 electoral votes to McClellan's 21 in his victory. Still, Greeley's reporters were maintaining the glorious journalistic tradition of the fifties that the two sides of a story were the "right" and the "wrong" ones — and only the "right" one needed to be told, in order to fulfill's a paper's mission of leadership and enlightenment.

[41] *New York Tribune,* July 14, August 30, September 6, 7, 16, 17, October 7, 8, 1864.

Concentrating as it did on the education of the voters in the war's issues, the *Tribune* was occasionally taunted with letting others get the drop on it in collecting news. In May of 1862, the *New York Herald* gleefully ran a story embodying a letter which one of their own men had "found" in camp on the Peninsula. It was allegedly from the *Tribune's* managing editor, Sidney Gay, to Samuel Wilkeson, and ordered him to work more on speed. As it was, Gay had written, they were obliged to copy from the *Herald* in order to get the most up-to-date news. The *Tribune*, in its first angry reaction, accused the *Herald's* correspondent of horse theft. It acknowledged that a recent letter from Wilkeson had complained of the loss of a mount, complete with saddlebags. The *Herald's* publication of a "confidential business letter" to Wilkeson proved that Bennett's paper had a rustler in its employ. The *Tribune* forgot, however, that this accusation had one unfortunate result — it guaranteed the authenticity of the letter. It was necessary to add to the story, and as late as next February Greeley was still boiling, and telling readers that the "extract" from the private letter which it "caused to have stolen is a FORGERY. No such admission was made in it as *The Herald* pretends." [42]

The *Tribune* did work at getting the news more earnestly than its propaganda concerns seemed to show. It was able to spend money freely, which was never harmful. When Gettysburg was fought, Homer Byington, one of the Washington correspondents, trying to locate the army,

[42] *New York Tribune*, May 16, 1862, February 15, 1863.

found that the wires from the telegraph station nearest the battlefield had been cut. He rounded up five men and a handcar, and sent them out to repair the line, with an understanding that he should have a monopoly of the service for two days. Whether or not his monopoly held, he was able to get off the earliest report on the first day's action.

Richardson, covering Missouri in 1861, was so well heeled (either with the *Tribune's* money or his own) that when he met Franc Wilkie of the *Times* returning to St. Louis with an exclusive write-up of an engagement in his pocket, he was able to offer him one hundred and twenty-five dollars in gold for it. Wilkie had, in fact, risked his life for the story. A Confederate force had bottled up the Union-held town of Lexington, and the correspondent of the *Times* had, on a presumption that he was lucky, boldly ridden into the "rebel" lines and announced that he was after information. It was a period in which strangers were shot with great informality, and Wilkie was fortunate in convincing his captors that he was not a spy, as they initially (and ominously) guessed. When Richardson attempted to highjack his story for Greeley's use (knowing that Wilkie was badly in need of money at the time), Wilkie felt that the depths in mistreatment of a less opulent professional brother had been touched. He disliked the *Tribune's* man more heartily than ever thereafter.[43]

[43] Croffut, "Horace Greeley Knows His Business," pp. 228-239; Franc B. Wilkie, *Walks About Chicago* (Chicago, 1869), pp. 122-139.

But Richardson did also have the other ingredient for the success of a reporter — pure nerve. It was no laughing matter to attempt a ride on a provision barge towed by a small and noisy tugboat past the Confederate batteries at Vicksburg, which had spent a long siege in getting the range of everything that moved on the river. But Richardson, Junius Browne, and Richard Colburn (of the *New York World*) did try it in May, 1863, in order to save one day in getting down to Grant's forces working south of the city. A well-placed shell exploded the tug's boiler, turned the barge into a bonfire, and forced the crew to tumble into the Mississippi and eventually Confederate hands.

It was the same kind of risk that Henry Wing, a nineteen-year-old *Tribune* reporter, ran a year later. Grant's army was engaged heavily in the Wilderness, and the line of communications to Washington was unprotected from hard-riding guerrillas. Wing, carrying a pocketful of dispatches, slipped into a rough coat, pants and shoes, and began a seventy-five-mile ride for life. Twice he was held up by Mosby's raiders, trigger-happy and suspicious. Both times he got away, once only a horse's jump ahead of pursuit. He finished the trip by limping afoot along the railroad track to Bull Run, where, in final irony, he had a difficult time convincing the unimaginative Union authorities that he was not a spy for the "rebels." Only after a telegraphic palaver with Stanton himself was he allowed to board a special train for Washington.[44]

[44] Richardson, *Secret Service, Field, Dungeon and Escape*, pp. 337-345; Ida Tarbell, "Lincoln Kissed Him," *Collier's*, LXXIX (January 15, 1927), 17.

That kind of reporting had a future, no matter what the political crystal ball revealed. When the war ended, with the Union "preserved and purified," as Greeley thought, it was inevitable that there should be a place for the adventurous and useful news-gatherer. He was one of the most durable by-products of the war which the *Tribune* thought it had won singlehanded.

CHAPTER VII

Republican Torchbearers

ON December 16, 1862, while the Army of the Potomac was counting losses and discovering that it had suffered over twelve thousand casualties in the week-end battle of Fredericksburg, a telegram was delivered to John Russell Young, managing editor of the *Philadelphia Press*, in his office at the corner of South Fourth and Chestnut Streets. It was from the paper's owner, "Colonel" John W. Forney, and said: "DON'T TREAT THE AFFAIR AT FREDERICKSBURG AS A DISASTER." Young was apparently to use whatever editorial techniques he chose to offset any reports from the field clearly indicating that it *was* a disaster. He chose well, for a week later he got a note from Forney, thanking him with a full heart for his "Burnside article." "It is a splendid tribute," wrote the publisher, "and I know will be appreciated by the administration." [1]

There was no mistaking the truth of that. After months of clamor, Lincoln had removed McClellan from command and replaced him with his showily side-whiskered subordinate, General Ambrose E. Burnside. Within five weeks of taking charge, Burnside, nervously sensible of the pressure on him to keep moving, had led the army into

[1] John Russell Young Papers, Library of Congress, Forney to Young, December 16, 23, 1862.

a thorough defeat. Thus, at the end of one year and eight months of war, the Union had yet to win an important battle in Virginia, and the Democrats had cashed in on the country's discontent in the off-year elections. The administration, therefore, was more than merely "appreciative" of articles which retouched misfortunes here and there, or emphasized bright future prospects with a bond salesman's vigor. Such articles were urgently needed, and, because of that need, editors of Republican papers carried into party councils the prestige of heavy investors at a stockholders' meeting.

Forney was typical of the administration's editorial chiefs. A Pennsylvania political factotum, he lived in the capital and personally edited one of his papers, the *Washington Chronicle*, turning the *Philadelphia Press* over to Young. Young was kept on a relatively short tether, which was not entirely necessary. Though youthful, he was brimful of talents, and at the beginning of a career which would carry him to the editorial high command of the *New York Tribune* and *New York Herald*, the American legation in China, and the post of Librarian of Congress. From time to time, Young went into the field as his own correspondent, and at such times his connection with Forney was a prized professional advantage. When he appeared in Washington just before Bull Run he carried a personal introduction to Irwin McDowell, commanding general in the field, signed by the Secretary of War himself. In October, reporting to the command post of General Nathaniel P. Banks in Maryland, he offered as his passport a note in Forney's own hand requesting that the general treat the correspondent kindly in the name of friendship. Banks, a former Republican Speaker of the House and governor of Massachusetts, would know what that meant. Certain favors in return might reasonably be expected by hard-driven soldiers. Forney could send helpful messages to his Philadelphia lieutenant, such as one ordering him to do "full justice" to McClellan at the time of Antietam, or another telling him to kill dispatches from North Carolina hostile to the commanding general there, or another bespeaking support for Burnside when the outcry after Fredericksburg was loud and restless.[2]

Another journalistic sprig of the reigning party nobility was Joseph Medill, of the *Chicago Tribune*. Although Medill, during the war, merely shared the direction of the paper with William Bross, Charles Ray and John L. Scripps — all charter member Republicans — he was most vociferous among the Radical drumbeaters in the West. Medill was a ferocious disputant, a suitable trait in a man who was to leave his name imperishably linked with the "World's Greatest Newspaper," and when Stanton took over the War Department in January of 1862, Medill took the liberty of warning him:

> You will encounter rottenness and rascality from top to bottom; you will discover scores of lukewarm, half secession officers in command who cannot bear to strike a vigorous blow . . . three fourths of all the "West Point-

[2] Young Papers, Simon Cameron to McDowell, July 20, 1861, Forney to Banks, October 14, 1861, Forney to Young, September 15, December 18, 22, 1862.

> ers" in the army. . . . The country looks to you . . . to infuse vigor, system, honesty and *fight* into the service. The army has lost more men in the past four months from inaction and ennui than it would have done from ten bloody pitched battles.

Medill was then in his thirties and the army needed recruits, but presumably his plight was that of Artemus Ward's friend, the editor of the *Bugle-Horn of Liberty*, who confided: "Ordinarily I should delight to wade in gore, but my bleedin' country bids me stay at home . . . for the purpose of announcin', from week to week, that *our Gov'ment is about to take vigorous measures to put down the rebellion!*" Medill, in fact, was especially able to keep an eye on the Gov'ment's measures to scotch the rebellion. His Washington correspondent, Horace White, was the clerk of the Senate Committee on Military Affairs, a listening post which could hardly have been improved upon. White had earned his own ticket, being a former member of the National Kansas Committee, which forwarded guns to the antislavery forces, and a personal friend to Lincoln. Not yet thirty, he was a cultivated writer and a classical scholar, educated at Beloit College. He was also another young reporter on the way up, eventually to be the *Tribune's* editor in chief, and later an editor of the *New York Post.*[3]

[3] Philip Kinsley, *The Chicago Tribune: Its First Hundred Years* (New York, 1943), I, 11-12, 34-38; Tracey Strevey, "Joseph Medill and the *Chicago Tribune* During the Civil War Period" (unpublished Ph.D. dissertation, Department of History, University of Chicago, 1930), pp. 17-19; Edwin M. Stanton Papers, Library of Congress, Medill to Stanton, January 21, 1862.

Henry J. Raymond, the editor of the *New York Times*, took a furlough from his desk to chair the New York delegation at the convention which nominated Lincoln in 1864. Raymond liked to get away from his editorial cares as well by an occasional trip into the field on his own; he had pioneered as a war correspondent in the Franco-Italian war of 1859, and it gave him a sense of contact to supplement the *Times's* small staff of army reporters; the *Times*, not yet a score of years old, could not spend money as freehandedly as its neighbors, the *Tribune* and *Herald*. When Raymond visited a headquarters, he was treated with due regard for his rank. Going down to Washington on the eve of Bull Run, he got the strategic picture from commanding general Winfield Scott himself, at Scott's own dinner table. When he went from there to Butler's command at Fortress Monroe, he was a personal guest of the bald and slightly cross-eyed general, along with Thurlow Weed, New York's Republican boss, and Senator Henry Wilson of Massachusetts. Just after Fredericksburg, he visited the army again in camp on the Rappahannock. After talking with most of its generals, and personally watching an attempted new move founder in a sleet storm and several inches of mud, he rode back to Washington by ambulance and steamboat in company with Burnside, who felt the need of making a personal report to the White House.[4]

Other correspondents of less exhilarating status were

[4] Francis Brown, *Raymond of the Times* (New York, 1951), pp. 170-174, 203-208, 221-224.

able to secure front-row seats at engagements, partly because of their own deftness — a good reporter in the field lived by his wits as much as a confidence man — but partly, too, because the papers which sent them were widely known to occupy positions where they might be useful. William D. Bickham, of the *Cincinnati Commercial*, was a familiar face around the various headquarters established by General William S. Rosecrans in Kentucky and Tennessee in 1863. Rosecrans himself was an Ohioan with Republican notions, and the *Commercial* spoke up most influentially for the administration in the State. Neither fact was a handicap to Bickham. There was also the case of the private accommodations granted by Andrew H. Foote to Charles Carleton Coffin on the Mississippi River flotilla's flagship early in 1862. Coffin, a solemn, jaundiced Yankee, was the top-ranking army reporter for the *Boston Journal.* He appeared on battlefields ritually equipped with a cape, binoculars and notebook, and would lope over the terrain making sketches, with his bearded face bent close to the ground like an animal snuffling along a trail.[5]

Another *Boston Journal* reporter was able to describe with satisfaction a "dinner for the press" given by a thoughtful staff officer of General Banks in New Orleans during 1862's holiday season. At the battle of Fort Donelson, Joseph B. McCullagh of the Republican *Cincinnati*

[5] J. R. Beatty, *Memoirs of a Volunteer* (New York, 1946), pp. 185, 204; Franc B. Wilkie, *Pen and Powder* (Boston, 1888), p. 117; F. Lauriston Bullard, *Famous War Correspondents* (Boston, 1914), p. 381; *Boston Journal*, March 10, 1862.

Gazette was almost killed with kindness. "Mack" had talked a gunboat captain conscious of the power of the press into permitting him to ride in the pilot house during an offshore bombardment of the fort, which commanded the Tennessee River near its mouth. McCullagh was standing within inches of the helmsman when a loud explosion stunned him. The pilot turned a surprised look in his direction and dropped dead of a chest wound. Sometimes, it seemed, it paid to be *out* of favor — but not over the long haul. A Cincinnati rival of the *Gazette* later in the war ran a long reprint from the correspondence of a Republican paper. A glum editorial blamed the need for borrowing on politics, claiming that a paper which fought the administration was lucky if its reporters were simply allowed to stay with the army.[6]

The reporting which appeared in the Republican press was not entirely homogeneous. There were professional mavericks like the *New York Times's* Franc Wilkie, whose own inclinations were towards a cynicism through which he filtered the whole Republican program; he was an ancestor of the hard-boiled reporter. There were also correspondents who worked at keeping useful contacts happy whatever the political considerations. And besides, there was ample room for difference within the occasionally creaking framework of the party. Only the Radicals were really explicit. The *Chicago Tribune's* Washington corre-

[6] *Boston Journal,* January 2, 1863; Walter B. Stevens, "Joseph B. McCullagh," *Missouri Historical Review,* XXVI (1931), 256-266; *Cincinnati Enquirer,* September 26, 1863.

spondent let slip what was virtually the official extremist view of high command problems in 1862. West Point graduates had not been "over-zealous in hurting the rebels," had no heart in the war, were "intensely pro-slavery . . . essentially aristocratic" and as hostile to "democracy" (as the Radicals saw it) as anyone at Richmond. That took care of most of the Union officers able to command more than a regiment at the beginning of the war. The real candidates for martial honors in Radical papers were the volunteers who warmed to the all-out program which the editors endorsed. As the strongly Democratic *Chicago Times* explained, an "abolition General" could "do no wrong, commit no blunders, make no mistakes, moral, social, or political." He lost battles only by the "treachery, cowardice or ignorance of . . . subordinates." There was a way out even for a West Pointer, however. He had only to

> repent, partake of the sacraments of orthodox abolitionism, put on the white robes of the "loyal" elect, take a harp in his hands to chant the praises of the redeemed nigger and the abolition God, and thereafter he [would] lose no more battles.[7]

That would have been true of Frémont, to judge by the cheers of his Republican press gallery. The *Cincinnati Commercial*, fairly moderate in its ideas of what the war could and should accomplish, had William D. Bickham on the scene in Missouri. Bickham, a bearded Midwesterner, was hardly able to contain his generosity. He wrote

[7] *Chicago Tribune*, February 1, 1862; *Chicago Times*, April 21, 1864.

that "jealous politicians" were denying "fair play" to the Pathfinder, when Frémont's exploratory instincts were failing to find a Confederate army to fight in Missouri. According to Bickham (who was polishing the promotional techniques he used later in the camp of General Rosecrans), Frémont moved slowly only because he was snared in the coils of a "red tape anaconda" devised in Washington. His Olympian isolation from visitors was part of a "workmanlike way of doing business," and his removal would cause nothing less than "*rebellion.*" All the charges against him were "the most palpable lies." A correspondent of the St. Louis *Missouri Democrat* charged these up to "the malignity of domestic hatred," and another was full of "gloomy forbodings" when talk of the general's relief gathered momentum.[8] (The *Missouri Democrat* was a Republican paper, and, to compound the confusion, the other major organ of St. Louis, the *Missouri Republican*, was Democratic. The *Republican*, however, though Democratic, supported the Republican Frémont. The natives of St. Louis, a sturdy lot, were able to thread their way through these arrangements without noticeable frustration.)

Sometimes interference on the local party line produced a novel effect in correspondents' messages. The St. Louis agent of the *Chicago Tribune*, during September of 1861, was an intemperate supporter of Frémont, explaining that his "brilliant military designs" had been nullified by a

[8] *Cincinnati Commercial*, May 16, 1863, October 10, 15, November 13, 1861; *Missouri Democrat*, September 28, October 9, November 8, 1861.

pettifogging War Department, which had held supplies down to such a trickle that even the commander's "genius and energy" were unable to conjure results. Another reporter for the paper, placing his ear to the ground in Kentucky, found that Frémont's "abolition" proclamation had done no harm in the border State at all; rather, its promise "to treat the rebels, slaves and all, according to the *laws of war*" had increased the confidence and thus the influence of Kentucky Unionists.

Yet suddenly, at the end of September, dispatches of this kind disappeared. Instead a "background" story from a reporter at Cairo was printed, almost frigid in its restraint. Declaring that while the "people of the West" had "reasonable confidence in [Frémont's] military ability" — *reasonable* confidence meant nothing in the prose inflation of the sixties — it warned that a few more mishaps would leave the public "fully prepared for his removal."

On the surface this turnabout appeared to be a bid for municipal popularity. Frémont's "mishaps" had included a failure to reinforce a regiment boxed up in Lexington, Missouri, by General Sterling Price, so that it was finally compelled to surrender. As it happened, the regiment was drawn largely from Chicago's Irish wards. However, the *Tribune's* bitter rival, the *Chicago Times*, had a more intriguing suggestion, namely that Lincoln was using the buggy whip of patronage to control Illinois editors who were balky over his treatment of Frémont. "How sweet are the drippings of the Chicago postoffice! and Abraham Lincoln dispenses those drippings!" was the *Times's* way of putting it. The *New York Tribune*, angry that its Chicago namesake had broken the Frémont ranks, interestingly placed the responsibility on the army correspondents. Certain *Chicago Tribune* reporters, it said, had not received from the general "that consideration to which they thought their importance had entitled them," and instead of sallying out to the field to be numbed with admiration by Frémont's exploits, they had spent their time "hugger-muggering with disappointed contractors and bar-room politicians" who had turned on the commander.[9] Whether they made policy or followed it, the correspondents had to keep an eye open for quick changes.

McClellan at first did surprisingly well even with the generality of the Republican press, in part because the country genuinely yearned for a hero in the Eastern theater of war, and editors were reluctant to give up on one so patently tailor-made. Bickham, writing in the *Cincinnati Commercial*, found McClellan to be a "first class military genius" when the general was harrying the Confederates out of the steep valleys of what afterwards was West Virginia. At that time, in the summer of 1861, neither the idea nor the language was especially original. On the Peninsula, however, Bickham noted that the policy of guarding private property in noncombat zones was a sound one, since a license to "plunder" would "demoralize and destroy the army." That was not the way the Com-

[9] *Chicago Tribune*, September 20, 22, 30, 1861; *Chicago Times*, November 13, 1861, October 14, 1862; *New York Tribune*, February 25, 1862.

mittee on the Conduct of the War saw it. The *Commercial* was a temperate paper, however, and even printed Bickham's singularly forgiving observations on the loyalties of West Point graduates. Most of them, the correspondent wrote, were "pro-slavery," but at least "ninety-nine per cent . . . would fight under the old flag . . . gallantly" no matter what policy the government adopted. Wayward as the regulars were, they had hearts of gold after all, beneath their double rows of gilt buttons.[10]

Even the *Chicago Tribune* ran one petulant letter from the Army of the Potomac after McClellan's relief, complaining that the soldiers' most preferred leader had been needlessly shelved. The *Boston Journal's* Washington observer, Benjamin Poore, thought that no commander since Washington had been so "beloved and honored" — a statement which, to some extremists of the Republican side, was almost pure secession doctrine. A correspondent of the *Philadelphia Press*, with a style even more lacy than was then popular, applauded the modesty of "little George," whose "ornaments [were] the victories he won." [11]

Other correspondents, however, had a hand in the undermining of the young Napoleon. While McClellan was receiving the grudging support of most pro-Lincoln papers during the campaign of Antietam, a letter appeared in the fine-printed columns of the *Cincinnati Gazette* from its Washington correspondent, "Agate." "Agate" was, in fact, Whitelaw Reid, a slender, dark-haired young man of

[10] *Cincinnati Commercial*, July 20, 1861, June 13, July 7, 1862.

[11] *Chicago Tribune*, November 20, 1862; *Boston Journal*, September 11, 1862; *Philadelphia Press*, June 25, July 31, 1862.

twenty-five, native to Xenia, Ohio. Reid, like John Russell Young, was making of war correspondence an apprenticeship for bigger things. As fortune had it, he was to succeed Young, in 1869, as managing editor of the *New York Tribune;* where Young went to China as an envoy, Reid was minister to France and later ambassador to England; while Young eventually became Librarian of Congress, Reid served as one of the commisioners to negotiate peace with Spain.

Reid's story from the capital claimed nothing less than the discovery of the secret of McClellan's prized popularity with the common soldiers in the army. When his veteran divisions swung through Washington to head off Lee in Maryland, according to Reid, the commanding general took care to have the line of march run past headquarters, where he placed himself in full view, mounted and wearing his familiar fatigue cap. As the men tramping by recognized McClellan, they sent up cheers, which he acknowledged by raising the cap. But soon a regiment came past in "moody silence." Little Mac knew what to do about that; looking over the heads of the officers into the ranks, he asked: "What regiment is this?"

> "The Third Vermont," was the reply. "*And a gallant regiment it is*," exclaimed the young General, with an enthusiasm apparently as natural as if it were the very regiment over whose services he felt the proudest.

Out burst the whoops of the complimented foot soldiers in response to this, and another demonstration for the popular leader went into the regimental histories. Such tactics, thought "Agate," explained McClellan's snug grip on the army's affections "in spite of his disastrous failure on the Peninsula." [12]

The Committee on the Conduct of the War gave another newspaperman disenchanted with McClellan a day in court on July 10, 1862. It called to the stand Mr. Uriah H. Painter, of West Chester, Pennsylvania, who had been, for a year past, war correspondent for the *Philadelphia Inquirer*. Painter's sizzling testimony, presumably based on his role as an eyewitness, seemed to rivet down the anti-McClellan case. The Confederates had, he said, been greatly outnumbered throughout the Peninsula fighting, a fact which demolished McClellan's excuse for an indifferent showing. The commanding general (he deposed further) had never been present at an engagement. Only two of his corps commanders could "indorse" his plan of campaign. His nicety in guarding the homes of Virginians had been so scrupulous that the troops had occasionally been denied such simple comforts as a drink of water from a well. In another case wounded men had been laid in a pigpen while a large, airy building next door with a wooden floor was reserved for "rebel privates." [13]

As if that were not enough, a *New York Times* correspondent, William Swinton, was able to tap a source in

[12] *Cincinnati Gazette*, quoted in *Cincinnati Commercial*, September 12, 1862.

[13] "Report of the Joint Committee on the Conduct of the War," *Senate Reports*, 37th Congress, 3d Session, No. 108 (Washington, 1863), I, 283-294.

the highest and most confidential levels of the War Department for information with which to blast McClellan during his Presidential race. Swinton was a confidant of General Ethan Allen Hitchcock, a ponderous, intellectual career soldier, given to writing volumes of abstract philosophy in moments of respite from his military duties. Hitchcock, functioning as a kind of special consultant to the Secretary of War, had been convinced by Stanton of "the astonishing incompetency of General McClellan" as early as March, 1862. When, in 1864, Swinton readied a series of bitter articles with the self-explanatory title "The Exposure of McClellan" for the *Times*, he requisitioned ammunition from private notes of Hitchcock, which the general had been "kind enough" to place in his hands. Reporters could be persistent and influential enemies, as well as useful auxiliaries.[14]

General Buell had an even worse time of it with sections of the Republican press. By late 1862, McCullagh, now with the *Cincinnati Commercial*, was piping the keynote for his colleagues on the paper when he asked how long an army of lions was to be commanded by a jackass. "Mack" reported that most of Buell's subordinates were "disgusted" with his campaign, but a less professional judgment by another *Commercial* reporter lit up the real reason for Buell's failure to impress proadministration editors. In briskly enforcing an early general order compelling the return of runaway slaves to their masters, he had, as

[14] Ethan Allen Hitchcock, *Fifty Years in Camp and Field* (New York, 1909), pp. 440, 461-462.

the correspondent put it, demonstrated less "love for the Union than . . . for the 'peculiar institution,'" and his "failures" arose because his men were "as largely employed in guarding houses, fields, [and] fences" as in chasing Confederate General Braxton Bragg. An army writer for the *Chicago Tribune* at Louisville compared Buell to the nursery-rhyme king who marched his troops uphill and down without any accomplishment; the godly Mr. Coffin of the *Boston Journal* noted significantly that "every secessionist" spoke well of Buell; a war correspondent for the *Missouri Democrat* published a reportedly inside story which declared Buell to be so hopelessly cautious that he had threatened to arrest Grant for capturing Nashville in advance of schedule. All of this fire was replied to in volume and with spirit by reporters for papers hostile to the high-riding Radicals.[15]

Sometimes the way to a paper's heart was geographical; a general had merely to be a favorite son. When Lincoln, late in 1862, attempted to conciliate a restive opposition in his own Illinois, by giving a special command to Major General John A. McClernand, the latter was marked down by the *New York Tribune's* sharp-eyed reporter Henry Villard as a political officer "who sought glory as much through army correspondents as by feats of war." Among the correspondents contributing to his glory was Albert H. Bodman, a Chicagoan with the well-fed air of a

[15] *Cincinnati Commercial,* July 25, 30, September 30, October 22, 29, 1862; *Chicago Tribune,* September 28, October 4, 1862; *Boston Journal,* August 1, October 24, 1862; *Missouri Democrat,* March 28, 1862.

successful restaurant operator, working for the *Chicago Tribune*. Bodman wrote glowingly of McClernand's "laurels" earned in the spring battles of 1863 around Vicksburg, and when the onetime legislator had been ousted by Grant, for demonstrated incompetence and arrogance, the *Tribune's* field correspondence asked sulkily whether "General Grant, like Jehovah, [could] do no wrong." Horace White, intent to catch any cloakroom whispers in Washington, suggested that Grant and Sherman were trying to deprive McClernand of his share in the glory of taking Vicksburg. Neither White nor Bodman was likely to have forgotten that Lincoln had made the appointment, and that the *Tribune* was a complaining but steady supporter of the President in Illinois.[16]

A general who combined political good form with special care for a pet correspondent was almost sure to acquire a pleasing scrapbook. General William S. Rosecrans took command of the Western theater from Buell, in the second year of the war, with a sound reputation and high ambitions. Although he already had been labeled "a true genius for war" by the *New York Herald*, the mid-fortyish commander was looking for support from more rewarding sources than the opposition could offer. In February of 1863, answering a vote of thanks by the Ohio legislature, he sent them a public letter which ostentatiously pointed out that anyone then thinking of peace was "fit only to be

[16] *Cincinnati Commercial*, January 12, 1863; Henry Villard, *Memoirs* (New York, 1904), I, 272; Lloyd Lewis, *Sherman, Fighting Prophet* (New York, 1932), p. 282; Wilkie, *Pen and Powder*, p. 85; *Chicago Tribune*, January 22, May 28, June 8, 1863.

a slave . . . a traitor . . . who deserve[d] the scorn and contempt of all honorable men." A good many Ohio valley Democrats were still hoping audibly for "peaceful restoration of the Union," based on what they called "compromise with honor," so there was little question of Rosecrans's aim; he was out for selection as the Radicals' two-fisted military hero, and he did awaken enough interest for Horace Greeley to send out a reporter to interview him on the emancipation question, a sure test for soundness of doctrine. Rosecrans wrecked his own boom, first by laying a critical tongue indiscriminately on too many of his superiors and subordinates alike, and then by leading the army into what nearly became a disastrous rout, at Chickamauga in September of 1863. In the interim, however, he was able to count on "constructive" correspondence in the Radical press; one of Greeley's men described him as "calm, cheerful and confident," when he first came into his new command, and a *Chicago Tribune* correspondent assured the public of his "coolness and courage in battle." [17]

Since he was both "loyal" and approachable — a genial, ruddy man, fond of a good cigar or a game of chess with one of his staff — Rosecrans might safely have left his public relations to chance. To make assurance doubly sure, however, he undertook certain personal arrangements with Bickham of the *Cincinnati Commercial.* Bickham was the

[17] *New York Herald,* June 15, 1863; *Cincinnati Enquirer,* February 12, 1863; Ralph R. Fahrney, *Horace Greeley and the Tribune in the Civil War* (Cedar Rapids, 1936), pp. 167-168; Villard, *Memoirs,* II, 67, 211; *New York Tribune,* January 12, 1863; *Chicago Tribune,* January 9, 25, 1863.

general's protean "volunteer aide-de-camp," with an assimilated rank of captain. His major duties were clearly understood by his colleagues and by officers who knew their way around headquarters. Henry Villard, irritated by Rosecrans's attentions designed to earn favorable notice in the *New York Tribune*, wrote:

> There was a correspondent attached to his headquarters, W. D. Bickham, who did that sort of work for him very willingly. . . . "Old Rosey," as the puffer in question nicknamed him, tried to make me help in pointing him out as the great and only hope of the country . . .

Villard was not the only one to be rankled by the situation. An officer of a division which had been criticized in one of the *Commercial's* army reports took his case to the *Chicago Tribune* in a public letter explaining that any knowing member of the army discounted Bickham's "twaddle and falsehood"; the reporter would have been beneath notice except that he lived at Rosecrans's headquarters and was "supposed . . . to reflect his sentiments." The *Tribune* ran a later report that troopers of the offended division had threatened Bickham with a beating-up and driven him from their camp area.[18]

Bickham did his share. Describing the conduct of "Old Rosey" at one battle, he was thorough enough in his praises.

> There can be no mistake that in coolness, readiness, fertility of resource, celerity of thought and decision, and

[18] *New York Herald,* October 29, 1863; *Cincinnati Commercial,* September 4, 1863; *Official Records,* Ser. 1, XX, Pt. 2, 215; Villard, *Memoirs,* II, 67; *Chicago Tribune,* October 24, November 11, 1862.

> comprehensive grasp of mind in the midst of the most trying situations of peril, personal and military, Gen. Rosecrans . . . proved himself perfectly equal to the tremendous responsibility which devolved upon him. You rarely found practical skill, profound strategy and executive faculty with a mind which grasps general principles, and eagerly inquires into, and handles remote details, embodied in one character, and yet Gen. Rosecrans has demonstrated that he combines all.

The rest of his dispatches, whenever they referred to Rosecrans, took the same tone; a mid-nineteenth-century writer did nothing by halves. Eager to expand the audience somewhat, Bickham published a "history" in May of 1863 with Moore, Wilstach & Keys, of Cincinnati. Entitled *Rosecrans's Campaign With the Fourteenth Army Corps or the Army of the Cumberland: A Narrative of Personal Observations, by "W.D.B." of the Cincinnati Commercial*, it made certain that no one forgot which Union general had coolness, readiness, fertility of resource and celerity of thought. Bickham, in the end, wrapped up his career so thoroughly with Rosecrans that when the general was relieved his own active service with the army came to an end. While a fellow *Commercial* reporter suggested, from Nashville, that Rosecrans's reputation would survive post-mortem smears, since "like fine gold" it became brighter when rubbed, "W.D.B." evidently felt that his own fair fame would prosper most in a new setting. He retired in good order on Dayton, to become the owner-editor of the *Dayton Journal* and to reap the royalties from his history, available at a dollar in a paper binding and at a dollar and a quarter in muslin.[19]

Making heroes was in some respects a natural preoccupation for the correspondents. The country fidgeted over the morning papers impatiently, looking for the one man with the ready answer or short cut which would bring a quick return out of the growing national investment in man power, energy and cash. In the age of the open frontier, Americans were used to fast results, to things which *got done*. They could not accept then — in fact, they never did learn to accept — the notion of a war to be won by long and bloody campaigns of strangulation. The faith in the coming of a "genius" who would carry matters through with one master stroke died hard. The reporters who became barkers for these "geniuses" were no more gullible than most, but their position made their errors more damaging. Besides, in flattering officers for personal or political motives, they were depressing their newborn profession to the hurdy-gurdy-playing levels of army "public relations." Always ready with a sneering word, the *Chicago Tribune*, in 1862, wrote that much of the laudatory writing of the war was emitted by "army correspondents, with bellies full from the mess tables of Major Generals . . . the dissonant few being swallowed up like Pharaoh's lean kine by the well-kept bullocks who form the majority." [20]

[19] *Cincinnati Commercial*, January 14, May 16, October 14, 28, 1863; Z. L. White, "Western Journalism," *Harper's Magazine*, LXXVII (1888), 678-699.
[20] *Chicago Tribune*, November 12, 1862.

Most of the correspondents were apparently as willing to state political opinions as a party guest with a comic monologue to perform. They could not avoid the emancipation question if they tried, what with each day of march bringing companies and batteries into bivouacs on abandoned plantation grounds, and few of them seemed to try. As the Democratic journals acridly pointed out, the Negro was "chin capital" for the Republican press. In that press, the Negroes were painted as a band of brothers, knit by a universal desire for legalized freedom. "Ah, master," one of them reportedly said in a *Cincinnati Commercial* correspondent, "dey tells you white folks we don't want freedom. We don't want nuffin else." Joseph McCullagh, writing his daily stint for the same *Commercial* at Lagrange, Tennessee, struck at the footlight conception of the slave as a creature content with his banjo, his possum, and the loving assurances of Old Massa's protection. To a "plantation darkey," he said, a cotton field was "the *acme* of all that is horrible and repulsive." Elsewhere in Tennessee, a *Chicago Tribune* reporter took note of the arrival in camp of a Negro who guilelessly declared: "I 'spec' I belongs to you gemmen." The reporter, George P. Upton, was something of a scholar — a musician, with a Master of Arts degree from Brown. In his observations, conclusion flowed from premise as smoothly and imperturbably as in a theme in Logic:

> He did really belong to us by all rules of war, of business, and of common sense. His owner was in arms against the government. . . . He had delivered himself up and

> now let him go to work as a free man for the government into whose hands he had fallen, the consequence is as palpable as the result of a simple addition.[21]

"History will record," William Bickham wrote from the Peninsula, that "the only friends of the Union found by this army in Eastern Virginia [were] negro slaves." He went on to say that one of the army's topographical engineers had acknowledged the best maps of the region to be those which he made on the basis of information given by the slaves. So eager were the fugitives to do their bit, according to a *New York Post* correspondent in Louisiana, that when a thousand of them were asked, at one camp, if they would work their old plantations for pay, the show of hands was unanimous. A good many conservative orators were frightening laboring audiences with the warning that the Negroes were all too willing to work. If set free, the argument ran, they would drift northward and crowd white men out of jobs. An army correspondent of the *Chicago Tribune* stepped into the breach with the answer to that. Relying on his observations in the zone of operations, he assured readers that the Negroes did

> not wish to remove to the cold and frigid North. This climate is more genial, and here is their home. Only give them a fair remuneration for their labor, and strike off their shackles, and the good people of Illinois need not trouble themselves at the prospect of negro immigration.[22]

[21] *Cincinnati Commercial,* March 21, November 14, 1862; *Chicago Tribune,* April 19, 1862.
[22] *Cincinnati Commercial,* June 28, 1862; *New York Post,* quoted in *Boston Journal,* April 24, 1862; *Chicago Tribune,* November 29, 1862.

The army was in sympathy with the trend of things, according to the Republican notes from what editors then liked to call the tented field. Early in the war, General Halleck had issued a notorious General Order Number Three, his one significant accomplishment during his tenure in the Western theater command. It ordered all responsible officers of units sheltering escaped slaves to return them to their owners on claim. A *Cincinnati Commercial* correspondent in northern Missouri reported that majors and colonels with a high regard for their own dignity objected to "peering into tents and wagons . . . or playing 'nigger hunter,' and finding out the *pedigree* of the sable gentlemen who black boots and groom horses." In effect, that was the kind of research necessary to prove the legitimate title of a Southerner who came into camp and pointed out a Negro as his own.

As a matter of fact, many officers and men were genuinely opposed to releasing "contrabands" from camp on practical as well as political or sentimental grounds. Three war correspondents, sweating through the siege of Corinth, Mississippi, in mid-1862, had domestic arrangements typical of many members of the expedition. They shared the services of Bob and Johnny, two Negro youths who blacked boots, pressed clothes, cooked, ran errands and more or less gentled their employers' condition for monthly wages totaling six and twelve dollars. Charles Coffin and Albert Richardson, at the same locale, made joint use of a tent and an "African factotum" who awoke them to the hardships of a campaign each morning with a call of "Breakfast is ready." Newspapermen at Ben Butler's headquarters were saved from the ravages of vitamin deficiency by the care of a black chef who dealt out fresh vegetables to them in the mess tent. Helping the contraband was an especially attractive brand of humanitarianism. Soldiers were as easily able as the correspondents to find that out. In many cases the discovery reinforced existing abolition leanings. The "loyal" reporters tried to make it appear that those inclinations were as commonplace as the desire to go home; a *Boston Journal* correspondent was typical in reporting from McClellan's army that the men were "all turning Abolitionists" and said that "they did not come . . . to catch niggers." [23]

In forthright electioneering, correspondents favored vigor over subtlety. Army reporters for the *Cincinnati Commercial*, in addition to their military duties, lent a hand in the Ohio gubernatorial campaign of 1863. The race matched John Brough against Clement Vallandigham, most bitter and outspoken among the Midwestern "peace Democrats" in Congress. It was bound to have an effect on the families at home if it could be shown that Ohio men then serving with the forces were not having any of Vallandigham's assertion that he would, if elected, bring them back from an unsuccessful "abolition" war with honor. The *Commercial* therefore featured promi-

[23] *Cincinnati Commercial*, February 20, 1862; *Philadelphia Press*, May 13, 1862; Richardson, *The Secret Service, The Field, The Dungeon and The Escape* (Hartford, 1866), p. 256; *Boston Journal*, October 24, 1862.

nently the letter of a correspondent with the Ohio units at Vicksburg, in which he declared that the men detested the "*nasty little traitorous impostor and gabbler of sedition.*" Another *Commercial* "special" in Kentucky endeared himself to the State's Republican committees by revealing that no one was "more obnoxious to the army than this arch-traitor." News of Vallandigham's nomination had provoked "universal indignation," according to another source, and one reporter, taking a straw vote among Buckeye veterans in Alabama, discovered no support whatever for the Democratic choice, since any soldier disloyal enough to "go for Vallandigham" automatically became disloyal enough to desert. Not all of this was political moonshine, for when the soldiers were allowed to vote by absentee ballot they did give the victorious Brough over nine thousand votes to some two hundred and fifty for Vallandigham, according to a count which ran in the non-Republican *New York Herald*. The receipt of the election returns, according to "Mack," caused "genuine, hearty cheering," which it might well have, since General Rosecrans had thoughtfully sent word for "three times three" throughout the camps most heavily tenanted by Ohioans.[24]

Stories in the "loyal" press also did much to dispel the gloomy picture of the war's prospects painted by the opposition, which never failed to insist that emancipation

[24] *Cincinnati Commercial,* March 7, April 10, May 18, June 20, September 15, October 21, 22, 1863; *New York Herald,* October 19, 1863; *Chicago Tribune,* October 28, 1863.

meant war to the bitter end, and that the bitter end could only be a stalemate, rather than total victory. Correspondents of Cincinnati and Boston papers gave prominent place in their dispatches of early 1863 to rumors of a wholesale cleanup in the high command to replace generals who were openly unhappy over the Emancipation Proclamation. The imputation was that these officers of tepid loyalty had been responsible for defeats up to then; therefore, matters were bound to improve with their departure. Other field reporters were more or less scornful of Confederate resolves to die in the last ditch. Near Vicksburg a *Cincinnati Commercial* man rode through the back country with a colonel and stopped in for a call at a plantation. One of the ladies present angrily told them that if the defenders of Vicksburg surrendered, their wives and daughters would carry on the fight. " 'Well madam,' replied the urbane colonel, 'whenever the women *present arms*, we'll fall in.' "[25]

During the 1864 campaign the fighting on all fronts had reached a crescendo, and the casualty lists occasionally took up half of a front page: "28th Massachusetts: Peter English, face, shell; John Smith, leg fractured; Joseph Cosseth, foot fractured; John Fitzgibbon, breast; J. H. Purcell, mortal, since died." It was not always easy to write (or believe), as Charles Carleton Coffin did in July, "prospects of crushing the rebellion never have been so bright as at the present." Yet it was desperately neces-

[25] *Cincinnati Commercial,* March 12, 17, 1863; *Boston Journal,* February 28, 1863.

sary for the Republicans to prove that, whatever the cost, victory was near, and that the only hope of the "rebels," indeed, was the election of McClellan, who would never be able to wash out the damned spot of the Democratic peace platform. That was one reason for the *Boston Journal's* welcome to a correspondent's dispatch relating a chat with a three-man commission from the Confederate side, sent to negotiate concerning prisoner exchange. They were, according to the report, "very anxious as to McClellan's prospects." It was to offset "defeatism" by showing the allegedly Southern origins of peace talk that the *Chicago Tribune* ran an "interview" by one of its correspondents with some freshly captured enemy deserters.

> Q: How long do you think the leaders will hold out?
>
> A: Till after the Presidential election; they think a peace man will be elected and the Union armies will be withdrawn.
>
> Q: What do they think of McClellan?
>
> A: They say he is all right . . .
>
> Q: What, in your opinion, will be the effect in the masses of the army if Lincoln is successful?
>
> A: They will stand no longer; they will tell their officers they have been deceived, and the mutiny will be so general, that it will be a success.

This was supposedly enough to make it clear that "Little Mac" was the genuine choice of the Confederate army; the Union troops had switched to more attractive names. As one *Cincinnati Commercial* man insisted, "McClellan stock" was "below par," and would be "as worthless as Confederate currency" after election day. It was.[26]

Trained as shock troops in the operations to create a secure base of public opinion for the war, the correspondents were garnering side experiences which would be useful as they pursued their calling through the more devious quarters which politics and business opened up to them in an age of enterprise. They came out of the war on more familiar terms than ever with the special weapons available to them — the careful touches and highlights by which reputations were built up, the condemnation from the mouth of a nameless informant, the carefully placed rumor from "confidential sources." Some chose to use them irresponsibly, while others made at least the pretense of discarding them from the armory. One thing was certain, however. During the years of actual fighting, reporters for the leading Republican papers had occupied unquestionably superior terrain on which to maneuver politically. They had the bulk of patronage, wealth and respectability on their side. A correspondent might be a crusader, or a hard-shell sinner believing in nothing but deadlines; either way, he could do better when given an inside track to the authorities. The military men were, after all, right; nothing was so good as a secure line of communications. Any editor or correspondent of a Democratic paper, often left in outer darkness, could have vouched for that.

[26] *Boston Journal*, July 21, August 25, October 6, 1864; *Chicago Tribune*, September 28, 1864; *Cincinnati Commercial*, October 22, November 9, 1864.

CHAPTER VIII

Our Democratic "Contemporaries"

IN March of 1863 the editor of the *Cincinnati Enquirer*, a paper thoroughly cankered in its opposition to Lincoln, sent a reporter to army headquarters in Nashville. He was to obtain a pass and accompany the troops in a drive on Chattanooga. Soon after his arrival the correspondent, over his pen name "Quill," sent back a letter explaining that he had been fouled at the starting line. "Letters of recommendation from editors of prominent Republican or Abolition journals possess the charm of a talisman," he wrote, "and expedite in a remarkable degree the business of procuring the necessary papers." No talisman, no stories. No Republican connections, no talisman. It was all very clear and very bleak.[1]

The Democratic press had its trials in covering the war, just as the entire Northern wing of the party had its ordeals in remaining alive and useful. At the outbreak of the war, many of the younger leaders joined the Union ranks, and within months were shooting at men with whom they had raised the fraternal war whoop in party conventions only a short time previously. Others remained in Congress to vote war credits, but their support was always somewhat conditional. The war aim of the Northern Democrats was a set-

[1] *Cincinnati Enquirer*, March 14, 1863.

tlement which would restore the South to the Union with its original political independence. Abstract considerations of justice and constitutionalism aside, it was only in that way that they could count on the return of their Southern associates, without whom they remained a powerless minority. The Union had to be restored if the party was to be restored. It was a lesser, but still compelling, motive for fighting.

For that reason, the Democrats insisted on a "proper" kind of struggle — one which would lead to a compromise peace. To almost all of them, this meant no tampering with slavery. Meantime they scrambled for issues in the conduct of the war. Lincoln was assuming too much power; the wrong generals were being chosen; campaigns were mismanaged; above all, the growing determination to free the slaves meant that the South could be brought back to the Union only as a prisoner, beaten to exhaustion and bound hand and foot, and the North did not have the strength for that kind of war.

The trouble was that an orator could become a captive of this kind of line. From insisting on "guarantees to Southern institutions" one could slip downward into a morass of racial mudslinging. In trying to show that negotiation was the only realistic path to peace, one could disparage Union military successes with a gusto that propagandists in Richmond might envy. The result was to leave an impression that the party was predominantly white-livered or treacherous, a stereotype with which Republican campaign speakers made hay for a full generation after the war's end.

There was difficulty enough for editors of Democratic papers in following this party line during the emotional heat of wartime. Besides that, the papers richest in circulation, prestige and access to the mighty were Republican. Barring the *New York Herald* (which was independent, rather than purely Democratic), few of the antiadministration journals seemed able to mount, feed and pay a staff of correspondents. No consistently Democratic paper "owned" a star reporter.

Standing high among the big-city Democratic organs were the *Chicago Times*, *Cincinnati Enquirer* and *New York World*. The *Times* was edited by Wilbur F. Storey, a powerfully built and eccentric man, with a sulphurous pen that dripped ridicule on the entire war effort day after day. According to one veteran reporter of the *Times*, furloughed servicemen in Chicago sometimes bustled in, ready to mop up the floor with whoever had written some piece that sneered particularly at their outfits. A look at Storey's forbidding figure discouraged them, but the editorial office nevertheless was in the perpetual tension of a combat zone. Storey, whose married life gave him private miseries to add to his political discontents, occasionally got away from it all by provoking a rancorous argument with his staff and then disappearing on a drunk of several days' duration. With all this, the *Times* remained a lively concern, and its war correspondence from the Western armies was moderately plentiful and always gamy.[2]

[2]Franc B. Wilkie, *Thirty-five Years of Journalism* (Chicago, 1891), pp. 40-120.

The *Cincinnati Enquirer* spoke for a number of disgruntled Ohio valley Democrats plagued by the continuance of the war. With the Southern markets closed, Midwestern farmers had little choice except to ship their produce by rail to east-coast ports. Freights were high. Taxes were high, and part of the reason was clearly to be found in the inflated prices paid by the government to Eastern contractors — virtual subsidies to manufacturing. State banks, long-time sources of easy credit for hard-pressed Westerners, were being squeezed out of existence. The tariff was climbing. It seemed to a good many residents of the Western States, Republicans and Democrats alike, that the loaves and fishes of the 1860 victory had not been evenly distributed. Some of the Democrats, at least, felt that the situation called for a quick restoration of peace and a reexamination of affairs. Besides all this, many settlers of the Ohio valley shared with their numerous Southern cousins a distaste for the Negro, both as a human being and as a possible low-priced competitor for laborers' jobs. The *Enquirer*, therefore, despite tempests of criticism, always managed to find an audience for its jeremiads on the war, and its editors, James Faran and Washington MacLean, could afford to keep at least a few correspondents in the field.[3]

In New York, the opposition to the war crystallized around shippers and cotton merchants pining for the quick

[3] Charles R. Wilson, "The *Cincinnati Daily Enquirer* and Civil War Politics" (unpublished Ph.D. dissertation, Department of History, University of Chicago, 1934), pp. 1-30.

return of the Southern trade, and Irish workingmen poisonously suspicious of the Negro. The group found a spokesman in the *New York World.* The *World* had begun, shortly before the war, as a religious journal, and it originally supported Lincoln. Its correspondent in Cairo, Nathan Shepherd, was in fact described by Franc Wilkie as "a saintly product." But in the winter of 1861-1862 the paper fell onto the financial rocks and was tugged off by a syndicate of Democratic backers. By the second summer of the war it was snarling at the administration and had become, as one wag put it, " 'the *World,* the flesh and the devil' rolled into one." It was captained by a youthful newspaperman, Manton Marble.[4]

Papers of this skeptical fraternity did not enjoy many placid moments during the war. They got little help from official agencies in placing their men. In 1864, Phil Ripley, a *New York World* correspondent in New Orleans, was arrested by the provost marshal for some infraction of the rules. Marble wrote to the commanding general, Nathaniel P. Banks, asking for some assistance, and was flatly turned down. At almost the same time, another of the *World's* men, a Mr. Francis, riding back from Grant's forward outposts with dispatches, was taken prisoner by the businesslike Confederate guerrillas roving the rear areas. Marble applied to Assistant Secretary of War Dana, and requested an official hand in getting his reporter exchanged. Dana, formerly the managing editor of the rival *New York Tribune,*

[4] *Chicago Tribune,* October 15, 1862; Wilkie, *Pen and Powder* (Boston, 1888), pp. 84-85; *Cincinnati Commercial,* June 8, 1863.

wrote back with poorly concealed enjoyment that nothing could be done, and added a final fling: "It seems to me that Mr. Francis ought not to be treated with uncommon severity by the rebel authorities." Marble swallowed this and in December tried once again, this time applying to have a correspondent, Jerome B. Stillson, accredited to Sherman's army. Dana refused once more, this time declaring that the Secretary of War himself did "not consider that paper a proper one to receive such facilities." [5]

The wonder of it was that a paper like the *World* could keep reporters with the armies at all. In its early, or pious and loyal, phase, it had enjoyed the services of Edmund Clarence Stedman, another correspondent of literary pretensions (like the *Tribune's* Bayard Taylor) who was later to achieve some reputation as a parlor poet, while prudently looking to his mundane affairs in a Wall Street broker's office. Stedman left the *World* early in the war, after publishing a widely read account of Bull Run. Marble's enemies passed the word that the departure was caused by Stedman's inability to stomach the shift in the paper's loyalties. The correspondent did not make any public statement to nourish this viewpoint, but, in a still genial letter to Marble in November of 1862, he asked: "[Y]ou are affording aid and comfort to Secesh — aren't you?" [6] With correspondents decamping on their own initiative, and others

[5] Manton Marble Papers, Library of Congress, Banks to Marble, June 8, 1864, Dana to Marble, November 29, 1864, Stillson to D. G. Croly, December 8, 1864; *New York World*, June 8, 1864.

[6] Marble Papers, Stedman to Marble, December 9, 1861, November 24, 1862.

unable to be salvaged after loss because of calcified hostility in the high command, Marble must have felt heavily the burdens of service as editor of a wartime opposition paper.

One reporter whom Marble *did* manage to reclaim from Confederate hands, however, was Richard T. Colburn, a ruddy, thickset Englishman who was on the same army supply barge as Richardson and Browne, of the *Tribune*, when it was sunk in the Mississippi by gunfire in 1863. (The correspondents raced each other from battlefields to telegraph offices in furious rivalry to file their stories first, but they went into action companionably enough.) Colburn was quickly exchanged, with a firsthand report from inside the Confederacy to show for the experience. He was also one of the few men to earn the respect of Franc B. Wilkie. When Colburn first joined the newspaper writers' informal unit at the siege of Corinth, Wilkie took him for a ride beyond the forward outposts, expecting maliciously to enjoy a greenhorn's first fright in battle. As they trotted along a plank road through a swamp, shots tore the tree branches overhead and kicked up a column of muddy water at their feet, but Colburn's face remained as expressionless as a new-shelled clam. Suddenly a Union column of horses and wagons, choking the road in full flight, burst out of the woods ahead, coming straight in their direction. "You blasted idiot!" shouted Wilkie, "If you don't run, I will." He wheeled his horse into a gallop, with Colburn, apparently still unruffled, following just behind. Courage was a useful part of a war correspondent's equipment, and

Colburn's supply was far more than the prescribed allowance.[7]

Even with reporters of established mettle at work, however, the troubles of an opposition paper were not over. Sometimes commanders of military departments, their nostrils always wide for a sniff of subversion, used their discretionary authority to clamp off the circulation of "disloyal" journals. The *New York Journal of Commerce* ran afoul of Secretary Stanton himself in March of 1862; the *Chicago Times* was suppressed in February and again in June of 1863; the *Cincinnati Enquirer* was barred from Kentucky by the military satrap there early in 1863; and New York's *World* and *Journal of Commerce* had their presses padlocked in May of 1864. In the last case, their error had been to print a proclamation, alleged to have been signed by Lincoln, which called for a day of national fasting and prayer. The effect of such a call would have been to spread like a brush fire the impression that the game was up in Virginia and that the White House knew it. As it happened, the proclamation was a hoax, passed off on the editors of the two papers with some skill as an Associated Press dispatch. Rumor had it that the affair was a war correspondent's prank, conceived by Joseph Howard, a pale and bespectacled man who wrote for the *New York Times*. All the suppressions were temporary. The Administration had no intention of giving the Democrats a Zenger case to exploit. There was, nevertheless, a certain precariousness to the job of getting out a daily edition of a

[7] *New York World,* May 26, 1863; Wilkie, *Pen and Powder,* pp. 163-170.

newspaper which bucked the tide of wartime opinion.[8]

"Loyal" reporters, particularly on days when the army had few printable items to offer, were fond of stimulating their readers with an occasional reminder of the iniquities of the "enemy press." The idea was to show that the Democratic papers were the intellectual nourishment of the Confederate masses. Joseph McCullagh wrote from Tennessee, late in 1862, that a captured "rebel" surgeon, having extracted permission from the authorities to return to the Southern army which needed him badly, was caught in the act of departing with a packet of editorials clipped from the *Chicago Times* in the bottom of his medicine chest. "Mack" also insisted that he knew a Union secret agent who, on a mission behind enemy lines, had gotten access to various Confederate officials by producing copies of the *Cincinnati Enquirer* and forged letters of introduction from its editors. The *Enquirer* took a special beating from its "loyal" rivals. During a period in 1863 when the army was on short rations, "Mack" wrote of how a half-starved jackass, tired of gnawing wagon tongues and hitching posts, had eaten "an *Enquirer* . . . full of prospective Democratic victories" and died at once. Another *Cincinnati Commercial* correspondent observed that

> Whenever we see a long-haired, long-eared, black-tan skinned, gaunt, spindle shanked secessionist behind a cotton bale, or a wood pile, or in some obscure corner, read-

[8] *Cincinnati Commercial*, March 26, 1862; *Official Records*, Ser. 1, XXIV, Pt. 3, 41, 50, Ser. 2, V, 724, 741; *Cincinnati Commercial*, April 22, 1863; *New York World*, May 23, 1864; William A. Croffut, *An American Procession* (Boston, 1931), pp. 264-265.

> ing a newspaper, we know . . . that he is feasting his diminutive soul on . . . the *Cincinnati Enquirer.*

New York, Boston, Philadelphia, Chicago and St. Louis papers were practiced hands at the same technique. The Democratic papers were far from shrinking, and they fought back with as little truth and with as much gusto. They could never quite command as much righteousness.[9]

Badgered by unfriendly officials and working in the face of general suspiciousness, the correspondents of the opposition had little freedom of maneuver. They were critics at a time when the market demand was for heroes rather than goats, and they had to bellow requests to stop and consider above the blare of marching bands. They played heavily to local loyalties and prejudices, and gratefully accepted the hospitality of camps where they were at least regarded with nothing more than the well-bred distaste of a diplomatic colony for the minister of a newly recognized revolutionary government.

One cause in which the Democratic journals could be rhapsodic was that of McClellan. A reading of the army correspondence of the *Chicago Times* and *New York World* alone offered compensation to his supporters for all the vicissitudes of an unjust world in which the Stantons and Lincolns held the upper hand. The Washington correspondent of the *Times* gave subscribers early warning that "abolitionists" were pursuing McClellan "with the malignity of fiends," and that the Confederate defenses in Vir-

[9] *Cincinnati Commercial,* July 30, November 22, 1862; October 20, 26, 1863.

ginia, before which the army lay inactive through the entire autumn of 1861, were "literally impregnable." When McClellan spent his early weeks on the Peninsula in time-consuming siege operations, the same Washington reporter explained that no fewer than 75,000 Confederate troops were available to oppose him; obviously, any sudden move would invite disaster. Several weeks later, a correspondent with the army put the total of the enemy forces at over 200,000, a figure which handsomely supported the general's persistent claim of being outnumbered rather than outgeneraled. The army needed, according to the correspondent, no fewer than 75,000 reinforcements, and the failure of Washington to provide them was part of an "outrageous plot . . . in pursuance of which the fruits of McClellan's patient labors for ten months [were] to be snatched from him." When the week-long battle in the first week of July had forced McClellan into making his costly and unproductive change of base, the faithful reporter, soggy with fatigue and strain, asked bitterly if the army was to be "annihilated in order to gratify the revenge, the malice, or the envy of Edwin M. Stanton." [10]

McClellan's claim on such loyalty from the *Chicago Times* was a slim one. He was the hero of anyone who opposed the administration, and he had, to be sure, held a position in the Illinois Central Railroad system during his peacetime period of retirement. There seemed to be a much better reason for the excellent press which he re-

[10] *Chicago Times,* February 12, March 18, April 12, 15, June 5, 13, 20, July 9, 1862.

ceived in the *New York World.* One of his most cherished friends and lieutenants was General Fitz-John Porter, a handsome regular from New Hampshire. During the Peninsula fighting, Porter was addressing letters swimming with chatty and amiable gossip to Manton Marble, the *World's* editor. Several of them would have gone far to confirm the most horrible suspicions of the regulars' conservatism entertained by the Committee on the Conduct of the War. Porter confided to Marble his discovery that "treason" was "at work and the abolition element . . . working with southern rebels to produce dissentions [*sic*] and break up our army." He also wrote:

> I everywhere hear good opinions expressed of the President and the most kindly feelings . . . for him . . . I do not hear a flattering one of the Secretary. At times I have opportunities to overhear remarks of the men and . . . if members of Congress and Senators could hear them — could only listen unseen — I believe many would tremble for the probable fall of their political party. All wish an end to this war — death to the tyrants and demagogues at the South, and death to the demagogues of the North.[11]

When McClellan was under the prod of virtually the entire Radical press to pursue Lee into Virginia after Antietam, the *Chicago Times's* Washington operative, scandalized, declared that the cries for action were no more

[11] Marble Papers, Porter to Marble, March 17, April 26, July 20, 22, 1862. Two of the letters are signed "F.J.P." and one "You Know Who," while another is unsigned. However, they are unmistakably from the same hand, and internal evidence ties them clearly to Porter — to whom they are assigned by the cataloguers of the Library of Congress's Manuscript Division.

than the "yelping of village curs." He wrote that "fanatical politicians" — the village curs of the capital — were blocking the assignment of reinforcements to the army, hoping to involve McClellan in a defeat. Meantime, the other member of the *Times* team, the correspondent with the army in Maryland, wrote feelingly of the unreadiness of the troops for operations. Figuratively blowing on his hands and stamping as he wrote, he told of regiments that were "barefooted and shivering." A *New York World* correspondent completed the engraving of Valley Forge, in describing groups of men sheltered under nothing better than huts made of tree branches, waiting patiently for new uniforms to replace their tatters and fresh ammunition for their weapons. It was prose guaranteed to make Washington supply authorities feel delinquent. It had no special effect on the War Department, however; McClellan went out in November. The *Chicago Times's* man saw the handwriting on the wall. Frémont would now be made chief commander, and arms issued to the Southern slaves for a war of extermination. "Hung be the heavens in black when these steps shall be taken," wrote the overwrought oracle of the Midwestern press, "for they will, indeed, mark THE BEGINNING OF THE END." Fidelity could do no more than unveil heavy caps for McClellan's epitaph.[12]

The conservative press, as the war went on, did not have many more opportunities to shine in journalism of this heady genre. A correspondent for the *Chicago Times* who

[12] *Chicago Times*, September 29, October 4, 8, November 10, 19, 1862; *New York World*, October 9, 10, November 14, 1862.

wrote over the signature "Donelson" dedicated a long series of letters to the defense of General Buell late in 1862. He labeled the austere general's cautious tactics as grand strategy of a high order, and in a righteous fling at his fellow newspapermen insisted that reports of mismanagement in the army were fashioned by correspondents who sat in hotels in Louisville, far from any fighting, "playing euchre or poker and drinking whisky." They were in league with "the malignants . . . moving heaven and earth" to get rid of Buell, who was "not prosecuting any anti-slavery crusade" as they wished. The technique of disposing of him was to have the Republican press write up his campaigns using pens "tipped with gall." [13]

It was easier to produce effects by tipping a pen with gall, after all, and the correspondents for the opposition were able to furnish more spectacular copy when they could let the lightnings fly at some commander who had been received into the true church of "abolitionism." General Butler, who constantly drew fire by his own flambuoyant politicking, received the full treatment from correspondents of the *New York World*. Early in 1863 the paper ran a three-column exclusive from its New Orleans correspondent, describing how Butler's subordinates had fleeced the planters of occupied Louisiana by forcing them to sell sugar and cotton to chosen "friends" at bankruptcy prices. Those who had not played the game were denounced as secessionists and sent to jail. When the War

[13] *Chicago Times*, September 22, 30, October 3, 5, 21, 29, 1862; *Cincinnati Enquirer*, December 14, 1862.

Department moved Butler to Virginia, the *World's* enmity pursued him relentlessly. Marble had a correspondent at Norfolk — clearly a place where a newspaperman would not need to rely on the hospitality of headquarters — and from such a sound defensive position it was possible for him to file a story, in 1864, which assured the *World's* public:

> *The general has never been under fire since the commencement of the war, and never will be even by accident* . . . but he is immense in his onslaughts upon rebels in petticoats in general and rebel property in particular.

Short raids into the interior of Virginia and North Carolina, the *World* man wrote, had "merely served to *advertise* the commanding general," who was, as a matter of fact, the very man to appreciate the value of advertising. Other New York correspondents covering his campaign had been bought out-and-out.

> I fear that the pens of these "historians of the war" have been controlled by General Butler, and through them it is not likely to be known that the counties of Gloucester and Mathews have been raided . . . until, from being among the richest localities in Virginia, they are now the poorest and most desolate. . . . [Norfolk] is filled with spies of the most despicable character. Detectives . . . swarm the streets and frequent every place of public resort. Women prostitute themselves to this kind of work, and there is not a day passes but someone is arrested upon the testimony of these irresponsible vagabonds and subjected to indignities. . . . Old Point is . . . the mecca of mendicant politicians of the Butler stamp. . . . [T]he

plans of the ensuing presidential campaign are being arranged. . . . Butler wants to get before a Presidential convention. His vanity demands nothing else.[14]

That was the kind of counterattack which the reporters who were left frigid by the cause of freedom could mount. In the battle of the generals, honors were evenly divided so far as vigor in manhandling facts was concerned; it was simply a case of the heavy battalions being on the side of orthodoxy.

When all was said and done, however, the loyalties of newspapermen towards generals were not always predictable in the light of politics. Republicans were known to climb aboard the McClellan bandwagon, and the Democratic *Missouri Republican* waved the flag for Frémont during his royal progress through the State. A pass to the camp, a "U.S."-branded horse obligingly "loaned" by a quartermaster, or a seat on an empty ration box at a headquarters mess tent — these things won friends and influenced people of every political shading among the reporters. But in covering the role of the Negroes with the army, the correspondents for Republican and Democratic papers left no room for doubt that the differences between them were deep and beyond bridging at the time. They proved as well that objective reporting of the subject was too much to expect of the sixties.

In their choice of popular issues some Democrats felt

[14] *New York World,* February 4, 17, April 28, 1863, April 2, 1864.

the need of an appeal with enough bite to offset the persuasive humanitarianism of the antislavery crusade, and they found the answer in a line of racial propaganda that would have appeared reactionary in a place like Mississippi ninety years later. Certain Democratic editors talked less about the thievery of bankers than they did about the "infernal nigger," and their mistake was tactical as well as moral. There were voters who might have cheered lusty attacks on the economic drift of the times towards business hegemony. They were, however, unimpressed when they heard from Northern Democrats nothing more than the same paleolithic States' rights and proslavery arguments which had cozened the South out of the Union. It was easy for the Republicans to win counties with the charge that all Democrats were tools of Richmond when some Democratic spellbinders insisted on sounding like Richmond. Racism was not altogether unpopular in the North, but it had only a limited pay-off at the ballot box.

A few Democratic papers had yet to learn that fact during the fighting, and their correspondents either were sent or went willingly to work demonstrating that the Republicans' war was nothing more than "a vast John Brown raid." The abolitionists were not only practicing an especially noisome kind of political rascality in dragging out the issue, but they were subverting the natural law plainly declaring that it was a white man's country. As a *Chicago Times* reporter noted in penning a kindly paragraph for General Halleck, who firmly returned fugitive slaves to their owners, the general intended to "preserve the government for the benefit of the white race, whose ancestors framed it." [15]

The value of the plantation slave as an intelligence agent, so highly touted by Republican correspondents, was mythical, according to observers for the opposition. One *Missouri Republican* writer said that the Negro whose "imagination stretched the most" generally won the reputation for being most truthful. A *Chicago Times* reporter aboard a gunboat in the Mississippi wondered why "abolition correspondents," who had complained for years of the ignorance in which Southern masters kept their slaves, seized upon information brought by those slaves and labeled it as premium-grade intelligence. A *Cincinnati Enquirer* man in Tennessee had a sneer for fugitives, unable to tell a regiment from a squad, who spoke "as glibly as so many 'Patent-office Reports'" about military dispositions and were believed because they were "the color of an old meerschaum pipe." [16]

As for the argument that the Negroes could be used as the backbone of an auxiliary pick-and-shovel corps to free more men for the front, it was hollow. There was, for example, the testimony of Warren P. Isham, of the *Chicago Times*, who was covering the war in Tennessee during 1862. (Isham was a case of nepotism in the newspaper world — he was the brother-in-law of Wilbur Storey, the *Times's* editor.) Isham observed that Negroes working for

[15] *Chicago Times*, April 28, 1862.

[16] *Missouri Republican*, February 19, June 4, 1862; *Chicago Times*, April 30, 1862; *Cincinnati Enquirer*, December 5, 1862.

pay were worthless, even under the system by which plantation owners had occasionally allowed extra hands to hire themselves out on odd jobs, keeping all or a portion of their wages. He, Isham, knew of a man who had to pay a white gardener thirty dollars a month while a lazy Negro boy sauntered, hands in pockets, about the grounds. The same family had "hired out" a Negro cook from her owner, but she was so useless that a white replacement had been hustled into the breach. The men who wrote glowingly of the ex-slaves' services to freedom were "little counter-jumping warriors," now "waited upon by ebony servitors," or foot-weary infantrymen who, "seeing a stout nigger by the roadside [could] not well resist the temptation of loading their knapsacks and guns upon him, and trotting him along as a pack-horse." Another *Times* dispatch from Tennessee said that abandoned plantations were already going to seed from neglect, due to the Negroes' "indolence, love of ease, and incapacity to manage." "'Contrabands' . . . flock like carrion crows about the beef barrels in camps," wrote a *New York World* correspondent in New Orleans, referring to the runaway slaves as clearly "worthless, good-for-nothing vagabonds." [17]

Sometimes the embattled newspapermen fired into each others' ranks. There were reporters who could not view the hard life of the fugitive without dabbing at their eyes with their pocket handkerchiefs; camp servants led "a dog's life from which . . . they were glad to run away and re-

[17] *Chicago Times*, March 14, June 3, November 30, 1862; *New York World*, February 2, 1863.

turn to their masters," wrote one *Chicago Times* man. Graveyards in the wake of the army were full of Negroes, "once happy and contented," who had fallen ill and died when they fled to the transitory comforts of a Union camp in which "niggers [were] good to kick and cuff around," according to a Cincinnati correspondent. These stories, however, made curious reading in the light of reports that the Negroes were being "coddled." At Memphis, ran a story to the *Times*, "Every train that passes is crowded and loaded down with fugitives . . . [while] sick and foot-sore Union soldiers are denied transportation, and compelled to . . . drag wearily along." Near Vicksburg, it was reported, a Union general found that the only way to move his own sick and wounded to base hospitals was to commandeer a railroad train and expel the Negroes who had crammed themselves aboard it. "NIGGERS IN AMBULANCES AND SOLDIERS ON FOOT — NIGGERS ON FULL RATIONS AND SOLDIERS ON HALF" were the *Times's* one-column headlines over these accounts. Whether a reader felt paternal or resentful towards the Negroes did not matter. There was some news for every taste, and a contradiction now and then apparently only whetted the curiosity for more information and new editions.[18]

Correspondents of the *Times* had dark warnings, too, for any registered voters of Illinois likely to miss the implications of "abolitionism." At Memphis one of them saw

[18] *Chicago Times*, April 2, 1862, February 10, 17, March 28, 1863; *Cincinnati Enquirer*, October 1, 1862, February 27, 1863; *Milwaukie News*, quoted in *Cincinnati Enquirer*, April 10, 1863.

streams of Negroes preparing to move northward. In Washington, a place where Eastern skulduggery was always to be watched for, the vigilant *Times* man, flinging syntax to the winds, exposed the work of the "negroes' friends in Congress" who were

> devising means to set him free in all the states; they provide him with meat, drink, and raiment, cotton handkerchiefs with the declaration of independence printed thereon, woolen shirts, and straw hats; they invite them to the lectures at the Smithsonian Institute, and to come into Gautier's and eat ice-cream with them.

A *Cincinnati Enquirer* army correspondent at Cairo had already found that the "negro element" had "taken possession" there as if they were "themselves fully equal to the white men, if not superior." It was evident from the testimony of these reporters, therefore, that the entire North had better take steps, or else steady its nerves for the spectacle of Negroes eating ice cream and attending lectures side by side with their betters throughout the country.[19]

The reaction of all-out Democratic papers and their reporters to the arming of escaped slaves was typified in the story sent in by the *Chicago Times's* Washington correspondent, never a man for understatement, when the bill authorizing the step appeared in Congress. It was

> an invitation to a carnival of barbarities — a solicitation that negroes [should] apply the torch to the homes and dip their knives in the heart's blood of white men — a

[19] *Chicago Times,* October 4, 30, 1862; *Cincinnati Enquirer,* July 28, 1861.

> bugle call rousing the baser passions of the black race to surfeit themselves in the ravishment of the white mothers and daughters of the South.

The reporters with the army who watched the experiment firsthand could not match the voltage of prose like that. A fighting zone was evidently not so full of incitements to ferocity as Washington. They were not especially hospitable to the notion, however, and they occasionally dropped in a report calculated to bring home readers angrily off their parlor chairs. There was one *Times* story of a captain who had "ordered a white man to be tied and whipped by a negro," palpably "the legitimate fruit of the negro equality doctrines of abolitionism." Another of Storey's correspondents at Cairo during the 1864 election campaign said that a white veteran who hurrahed McClellan had been arrested and imprisoned by "a nigger soldier." This was Lincoln's doing, naturally, and a plain reason to "consign the putrid leper to the ignominious fate he so richly merits." Under the circumstances, it was to be expected that the actual performance of the Negro units was ignored. When they talked about ex-slaves in uniform, reporters for both political camps had higher ends in view than mere facts could hope to serve.[20]

While the Democratic editors glumly surveyed the progress of "abolitionism" from their office stools, hints came from the field, like the croaking of ravens, that the war, under Lincolnian management, was a failure. The men, for

[20] *Chicago Times,* May 22, 1862, June 10, 1863, October 13, 1864.

one thing, were purportedly losing heart because of the political manipulation which had switched the war aims after their enlistment. According to a *Cincinnati Enquirer* correspondent in Tennessee, the men "did not take up arms to carry out the behests of the demi-gods of Abolitionism." In fact, "sooner than be the anti-slavery propagandists of Abraham Lincoln," they would "ask Jeff. Davis to hoist the American flag, and receive them under his banners." The antislavery propagandists supposedly had few friends among the veterans. A *Chicago Times* story triumphantly told of a captain who had run a small public opinion sampling in his own company. Seven discriminating privates and noncoms out of every ten had preferred to be listed as Democrats. It was scarcely any wonder that they resented an abolitionist crusade. Early in 1863, the Washington reporter of the *Chicago Times* passed on a rumor that New Jersey troops were murmuring ominously that they did not intend to remain much longer in service, prosecuting "a war which . . . must result in the . . . horrors of negro insurrections." In Tennessee, another *Times* newsgatherer said that the men, "heartily sick of the fighting [and] shabby imbecility and treason in high places," were deserting "in flocks." During the winter of 1862-1863, some of the newly chosen Democratic legislatures of the Ohio valley States passed resolutions calling for the restoration of peace by compromise. Promptly a number of indignant memorials were sent in, signed by the men of units in the field, denouncing this stab in the back; Republican papers cheerfully gave them front-page layouts. But according to one *Cincinnati Enquirer* correspondent with an Indiana regiment, parliamentary procedure had been roughly dealt with in obtaining the resolutions. The colonel of the outfit — the 83rd Indiana — had lined up the men, read to them a paragraph drafted by himself condemning the "peace legislature," and asked for objections. Under those conditions no officer or soldier who knew his way around an army was likely to speak up, and the resolve was "unanimously adopted." [21]

The pessimism of the eyewitness reports from opposition correspondents deepened when the political and military campaigns of 1864 merged. The *Chicago Times's* Washington man, over the pseudonym of "X," spent the discouraging summer of the year playing furiously on the apprehensions of readers. He pointed up the failure of General Butler's campaign on the James, and morbidly noted that, even if Atlanta and Richmond fell, the end of the war was still as far off as it had been in 1862. The South had come nowhere near to exhausting its resources, and "the conquest and subjugation of a people of ten million souls" was impossible. "As long as Abraham Lincoln is President," warned "X," getting to what was transparently the heart of the matter for him, "they will never lay down their arms." In August he had a warning for Grant, who was then besieging Petersburg with 100,000 men. The place was "impregnable." The army should be divided, and part of it sent into more fruitful operations. Within a

[21] *Cincinnati Enquirer*, April 3, 1862, February 27, 1863; *Chicago Times*, August 10, 1862, February 2, 19, 26, 1863.

week, it had come to the notice of "X" that the army *was* to be withdrawn from Petersburg. Without waiting to find out that the story was untrue, editor Storey's prophet of ill omen sounded the alarm:

> . . . We have lost 30,000 men of the flower of our troops — fathers, husbands, sons — for nothing.
>
> The finger of history will point with unerring certainty to Abraham Lincoln.
>
> No more crowing is heard here over either Mobile or Atlanta. The next news from both those places is looked for with unconcealed uneasiness.

It was a good time for the planting of seeds of despair. The Army of the Potomac had reported some 55,000 casualties in the six weeks beginning on May 5th. Casualty lists took up two or three columns of fine print once a week in many papers, and in some, macabre advertisements appeared listing the addresses in New York, Cincinnati, Chicago, St. Louis and Rochester of "U.S. Government Artificial Leg Depots," where amputees were furnished with limbs made to government specifications free of charge.[22]

While administration spokesmen were trying to convince the world that the end was in sight, a Boston paper ran a correspondent's account of an interview with Confederate prisoners, calculated to raise despondency even among the most ruddy of Republican optimists:

> Q: Then you think the South are determined upon independence at all hazards, do you?

[22] *Chicago Times,* May 25, July 6, August 17, 22, 1864; Charles A. Dana, *Recollections of the Civil War* (New York, 1902), pp. 210-211; *Cincinnati Commercial,* October 15, 1864.

A: Yes, sir, the people of the South are now more determined to succeed than ever before. They are ready to sacrifice more than they were three years ago.

Q: If they can't be conquered they can be starved out, can't they?

A: Oh, no sir; there's where you make a great mistake. We always had plenty to eat there, sir — as good fare as ever soldier need ask. There is no lack of food.

There was a hope, though, revealed by the *Cincinnati Enquirer's* correspondent "Gulielmus," who reported an interrogation of a Confederate officer captured before Atlanta. He told his captors that "the Confederate army would never . . . cease to fight while Abraham Lincoln was at the head of affairs, but if a Democratic President were elected there would be no trouble in getting the South to lay down their arms." [23]

Even the successes of the autumn of the year did not altogether quiet the opposition. The editor of the *Cincinnati Enquirer* believed that the capture of Atlanta was a "piddling success," with no more significance than there would be in the capture of Columbus, Ohio (which contained nothing more valuable than the Republican State administration). The *New York World's* Washington man, "Druid," maintained that Confederate General Jubal Early could keep himself afoot indefinitely in the Shenandoah valley, a location from which it was possible to swoop into Washington in some unguarded moment when the entire Eastern army of the Union was busy elsewhere. There was

[23] *Boston Post,* quoted in *Cincinnati Enquirer,* June 27, 1864.

something to be said for the observation of the *New York Herald*, a paper certainly not blinded by Republican loyalty, that Democratic papers went far out of their way to minimize victories:

> Though a Union victory may be demonstrated by such an overthrow of the enemy as puts an army out of existence, they cannot see it, but let ever so small a repulse result from any movement of our forces, and then indeed the democratic journalists have eyes — then they can see wonderfully.

Or as one of Petroleum V. Nasby's characters put it, a Kentuckian whose hostility to abolitionism was preserved in corn liquor:

> He confest that he wuz a week mortel. He hed his ups and downs, bad. It was ruff on him. Wenever Grant and Sherman had a success his faith faled him, and sumtimes he hed difficulty in cumin to time even when Lee whipt Grant.[24]

The Democratic reporters were not only working under professional disadvantages, but they had the double handicap of operating as propagandists for a losing side. The "peace Democrats" had guessed wrong on the strength of the sentiment for an armistice, on the staying power of the South, on the amount of affection remaining for McClellan in 1864, and on the issues worth making a fight over.

[24] Wilson, "The *Cincinnati Enquirer* and Civil War Politics," p. 297; *New York World*, September 3, 1864; *New York Herald*, November 2, 1864; *Hancock Jeffersonian*, quoted in *Cincinnati Commercial*, August 26, 1864.

Slavery and constitutional guarantees did not carry the old magic. But the correspondents had not lost all; they had received invaluable training and indoctrination in capturing and mesmerizing an audience, and in ferreting out the news from the places where it bred. There was a future for reporters, if not for proslavery Democrats.

Yet the odds against which they worked had, perhaps, taken a toll after all. None of the reporters for the opposition press rose during the war to the public eminence of a Whitelaw Reid, a John Russell Young, an Albert D. Richardson, a George Alfred Townsend or a Thomas Knox. The best of the correspondents outspokenly cynical about the administration and its works was Franc B. Wilkie, who drifted from small-town Iowa journalism to the front. After the war he gained prominence as a feature writer for the Chicago press, when a job was suddenly opened for him in the *Chicago Times's* editorial office by the loss of one of the paper's men in a steamboat accident on the Great Lakes. Wilkie won some reputation as a special correspondent in the war, filing his material over the penname of "Galway." But he won it by writing battle reports from the Western theater for Henry J. Raymond's stoutly and incontestably Republican *New York Times!*

CHAPTER IX

Datelines and Democracy

IN March, 1863, the *Cincinnati Commercial* printed a letter that had been written in one of the tents on the western bank of the Mississippi, opposite Vicksburg. The Union army there had come through a long winter of discontent. Months of hard work, sickness and fighting had not brought the capture of the city noticeably closer. The camp around Vicksburg could not have been improved upon as a breeding ground for irascibility, and there was a glut of it in the *Commercial's* letter-to-the-editor:

> The newspaper correspondents now following the Federal forces in the West are, as a class, peculiarly free from . . . "want of confidence in their own ability" . . . [O]*ur own specials* endeavor, by great bravery of assertion, to exact from the public, who do not know them, a confidence and credit denied them by those who do . . .
>
> . . . .
>
> . . . With what pleasant assurance they date their letters at these "headquarters" and on that "gunboat," while themselves wrapt in soothing sloth, far from enemies at the St. Charles or Gayoso, button-hole from straggling soldiers and dyspeptic officers their fragmentary falsehoods for tomorrow's mails. [The St. Charles and Gayoso were Cairo and Memphis hotels.] The worthy rogues are too lazy even to individualize their own bosh, and by

> mutual interchange of lies, present the same brazen surface in all their letters.[1]

The writer was most probably one of the many disgruntled officers who found in the correspondent a new and entirely unwelcome arrival in the tradition-bound world of the army. As he fought his way into recognition, the army reporter, swimming with curiosity, strong opinions and youthful conceit, was bound to draw fire from professionals who were not accustomed to accounting for their actions to the uninitiated public at large. General Alexander McCook, taking leave of his 20th Army Corps late in 1863, spoke up feelingly on the matter. "You have been slandered and maligned," he told his veterans, "by news-scribblers, who, unfortunately in our country, mould the public mind." An admiral in retirement later added a naval postscript. Obviously thinking uncomplimentary thoughts about the political officers who had entered on military service with a more lively awareness of the value of public notice, he observed mournfully:

> It must be admitted that the Army and Navy officers under a republican form of government cannot expect much protection . . . when attacked by the public press. . . . Men who controlled the press, and who had a capital of political influence, often . . . obtained positions . . . for which they were by no means qualified. Against them, a regular officer without influence could have little hope for a fair show.[2]

[1] *Cincinnati Commercial,* March 2, 1863.
[2] *Cincinnati Commercial,* October 16, 1863; H. Walke, *Naval Scenes and Reminiscences of the Civil War in the United States* (New York, 1877), p. 329.

The generals and admirals, undergoing a hard education in the special problems of serving an occasionally ungrateful republican government, were understandably curdled. Public figures who had felt the effect of a hostile write-up were not apt to be reverent about the role of the press. Some of the correspondents, however, fed the guns of their opponents by obviously placing a market value on their good opinion. The *Chicago Tribune* sourly called attention in 1862 to army correspondents, entertained freely at the mess tables of major generals, whose sweetened accounts were for sale. A Washington newspaperman publicly sneered at colleagues who hung "about the back entrance to the General's headquarters or live[d] on the charity of some officer" while supposedly doing an objective job of reporting. A correspondent with the Western army admitted unhappily that he had confreres who were guilty of "puffing . . . any officer . . . green enough to pay for it by . . . a dinner or a drink." [3]

Sometimes a correspondent was driven into such arrangements by the necessities of field soldiering. There was no system of accreditation, and frequently no official recognition of a reporter's existence. A newspaperman in a camp far from any base city needed friends if he expected not to starve to death. When William D. Bickham, the Boswell of General Rosecrans, was covering the Peninsula campaign for the *Cincinnati Commercial*, he discovered that money was "utterly useless to a man in these inhos-

[3] *Chicago Tribune*, November 12, 1862, June 28, 1864; *Chicago Times*, February 15, 1862.

pitable wastes." In a war fought largely in inhospitable wastes, one had to look out for oneself. Yet there was no escaping the fact that reporters were earning, in some circles, a reputation as literary streetwalkers. In 1862, the Committee on the Conduct of the War, grilling a New Hampshire colonel on certain military matters, asked if he did not think that press reports from the front were unreliable, because newspaper writers were "so well cared for by the commanders." The witness figuratively raised a knowing eyebrow. "The gentlemen of the committee," he said heavily, "can draw their inference as well as I can." [4]

A few correspondents also managed to curdle relations with the army by spectacular displays of cheek. Some were plainly carried away by the notion that eager thousands were waiting for their weekly and twice-weekly letters, and went in for highhanded methods of collecting the news; William Swinton, of the *New York Times*, caught red-handed — or at any rate red-eared — eavesdropping on a private conference between Grant and his subordinate commanders during the battle of the Wilderness; Thomas Knox, of the *New York Herald*, flouting Sherman's censorship virtually to his face, and emerging safely from a court-martial. The record was held, however, by two correspondents who approached Colonel Jacob D. Cox in West Virginia early in the war, and demanded to accompany him as aides-de-camp. The request was refused, and the

[4] *Cincinnati Commercial*, April 25, 1862; "Report of the Joint Committee on the Conduct of the War" *Senate Reports*, 37th Congress, 3d Session, No. 108 (Washington, 1863), I, 300-301.

newspapermen bustled off to write letters which presently appeared, describing the colonel's troops as "a rabble of ruffians, burning houses, ravishing women, robbing and destroying property." (The effect was especially harrowing to Cox, whose promotion to brigadier general was then before the Senate.) The attitude of the more intransigent correspondents was put in capsule form by one of them, reacting to an order of Sherman's deploring the presence of reporters in camp. He said it gave "every stuckup jackanapes of an officer" the privilege "to insult gentlemen, and men of learning." [5]

A few of the newspaper writers themselves found some of the other working newsmen unpleasantly pompous. On the Peninsula, George Alfred Townsend was driven into fits of irritability by a Western correspondent whose paper, he suspected, headlined his dispatches with such outbursts as: "*Tremendous Battle at* ROANOKE! *The Correspondent of* THE BLUNDERBUSS *hoists the* NATIONAL FLAG *above the* REBEL RAMPARTS!!!" A *Chicago Times* man in Kentucky called attention to a professional hazard, in the person of

> the correspondent of the *Bungtown Gazette.* He is a very important personage, and must be treated with becoming consideration by all with whom he comes in contact, and especially be patronized by the superior officers, who are expected to furnish him with a horse and detail a servant

[5] Jacob D. Cox, "McClellan in West Virginia" in *Battles and Leaders of the Civil War* (C. C. Buel and R. U. Johnson, eds., New York, 1884-1887), I, 141-142; David P. Conyngham, *Sherman's March Through the South* (New York, 1865), p. 74.

> to take care of it. All plans of battles and general movements should be submitted to his inspection. He should be admitted to all military councils, and be furnished in advance with a copy of every order, general or special. . . . "Our correspondent" holds a rod of terror suspended over the heads of all officers, whom he threatens with a severe writing down if they fail to pay him due deference. He invariably hangs around the officers' quarters, eaves-dropping for private conversations when not openly admitted, or seeking opportunities to pillage official documents.

A small-town paper mocked the pontifical style of the correspondents based on Washington, by running its own inside dispatch from the capital.

> We have the means of knowing that our troops in and about Washington number 201,977½, mostly men, women and children. . . . We have means of knowing that the plan (suggested by us) is as follows — although, according to agreement, we must request our readers not to mention it. . . . A force of 100,000 men will . . . leave for the Pacific Coast, and marching via Pike's Peak, Kansas, Missouri and Kentucky, enter Virginia and attack the rebel army in the rear. If . . . these plans fail, either the slaves will be declared free or the masters declared slaves. . . . And in any event, and under all circumstances, we hope, should nothing prevent, that this will prove true; we shall see what we shall see, be the same more or less.[6]

[6] George Alfred Townsend, *Campaigns of a Non-Combatant* (New York, 1866), p. 184; *Chicago Times*, February 17, 1862; *Warsaw New Yorker*, quoted in *Boston Journal*, January 14, 1862.

To give still more ammunition to the opponents of the press, some reporters left themselves open to charges of outright hoax in their filed stories. The best of the correspondents acknowledged that they had tainted brethren in their midst. Benjamin Perley Poore uncharitably described a number of newspapermen as "mere news-scavengers" who wrote up whatever rumors they could extract from rear echelon sources and sent them on to be committed to print. Charles Carleton Coffin charged that a few correspondents printed lying reports of disaster, to push down the market price of gold and assist speculators selling short.[7]

While they were about it, they carried their frauds off with style. An issue of the *New York Herald* in June, 1863, thrilled the faithful with an account of the battle of Port Hudson, Louisiana. It was written, ostensibly, from a vantage point in "a high tree, within less than one hundred rods of the first line of rebel defences." When the story got back to Philip Ripley, the *New York World's* man in New Orleans, he snorted, reached for a pen and paper, and hurried to explain to editor Manton Marble how he had been scooped. The *Herald's* writer, a certain Johnson, had been at sea, bound for New Orleans, when the engagement took place. He had arrived just after the battle and built his story, complete with tree, from interviews with a witness. Marble himself was in no position to fling up his arms virtuously. The year before, the *World*

[7] *Cincinnati Commercial*, June 10, 1863; Poore, *Reminiscences of Sixty Years in the National Capital* (Boston, 1886), II, 126-127; Coffin, *Four Years of Fighting* (Boston, 1866), p. 138.

had carried a dispatch from the battlefield of Pea Ridge, Arkansas, where the Union forces had finally met up with the Confederates whom they had hunted through Missouri. The *World's* reporter had galloped head-on and breathlessly into his story:

> Even now, while I attempt to collect my blurred and disconnected thoughts, the sound of booming cannon and the crack of the rifle rings in my ears, while visions of carnage and the flames of battle hover before my sight. Three days of constant watching, without food or sleep, and the excitements of the struggle, have quite unstrung my nerves.

As it happened, nothing but a bad hotel accommodation could have unstrung the writer's nerves at that particular time. The only New York reporter at the battle was Thomas Knox, of the *Herald*. "Two New York journalists" — one of them Junius Browne of the *New York Tribune*, and the other presumably the *World* reporter — had gotten wind of the fight and proceeded to the telegraph station at Rolla, Missouri, some two hundred miles from the field. Working with what information they already had about the order of battle of the Union forces, they had pieced their ripsnorting accounts together, like jigsaw puzzles, from the bulletins which came in over the wire.[8]

[8] *New York Herald*, June 27, 1863; Manton Marble Papers, Library of Congress, Ripley to Marble, July 16, 1863; *New York World*, March 19, 1862; Albert D. Richardson, *The Secret Service, The Field, The Dungeon and the Escape* (Hartford, 1866), pp. 270-271; Franc B. Wilkie, *Pen and Powder* (Boston, 1888), pp. 124-126; Thomas W. Knox, *Campfire and Cotton-Field* (New York, 1865), p. 138. Wilkie, Richardson and Knox all agree that only one New York reporter was actually at the battle, and

Those who were suspicious of the pressmen had, perhaps, been touched lightly with the prophetic spirit. They sensed, in their bones, what a future full of reporters might see in the way of scandal hawking, press agents' antics at their worst, and undeclared war on privacy. But there was a good deal to be said on the correspondents' side. They were, so far as the purposes of wartime history went, the only men in a campaign sufficiently disentangled from unit and personal loyalties to offer balanced stories. If they were cocky as a group, they could hardly be blamed when a paper like the puissant *New York Tribune* itself assured the world that "the government of this country" lay, not in Washington, but "in this City of New York, with its wealth, and its energy, and its — above all else — its Press." Diffidence never made much headway in the newspaper calling, dedicated to the loud pursuit of certainty.[9]

Besides, some of the correspondents had developed their truculence in what they took to be a legitimate battle for status. Men like Junius Browne and Thomas W. Knox believed that as reporters they had a mission. As Browne put it, the correspondent

> is at his post to relate what he sees; to applaud valor and merit wherever found; to point out abuses and blunders

it was quite evidently Knox himself. He claims it, Wilkie seconds him, and Richardson says nothing. Wilkie only refers to Junius Browne as the author of the fictitious report, but Richardson names "two New York journalists." Unless the *World* had an out-of-town reporter writing for it under the title of "our special," it is fairly clear that the collective leg of New York was being pulled by the *World's* bloodshot-eyed account.

[9] *New York Tribune,* December 24, 1862, August 27, 1863.

> that would not otherwise be reached, save through the endless duration of military investigations and courts-martial.

A seconding speech to that might have been clipped from a *Philadelphia Press* editorial which observed that families had been "relieved a thousand times by the early reports of correspondents," and that the pressmen, moreover, had "traced mismanagement and defect to its proper source quite as thoroughly and more quickly than Congressional committees." There was scarcely more to say. Knox concluded his lengthy memoir of the war with a long exhortation to the authorities to create some fixed place for correspondents in the tables of organizations used in any future campaigns. The language of both Browne and Knox was sententious, but behind it lay the conviction that members of the press were specially anointed by Providence to keep an eye on public servants at work. The idea was the germ cell of a code of professional standards. Some of the reporters for the Union seemed to be steering journalism toward the wastelands of ballyhoo, but others were pointing the way towards crusading newspaperdom at its effervescent best.[10]

One thing was certain: the army reporter's job was not a simple magnet for notoriety-seekers. It was hard and occasionally dangerous, and its pay had no special allurements. Salaries hovered around twenty-five dollars weekly,

[10] Junius H. Browne, *Four Years in Secessia* (New York, 1865), pp. 1-17; Knox, *Campfire and Cotton-Field*, pp. 482-490; *Philadelphia Press*, May 13, 1862.

with expenses sometimes thrown in. That was the sum which a top-seeded correspondent such as the *Boston Journal's* Charles Carleton Coffin got at the beginning of the war. Work by the line offered little more. Franc B. Wilkie risked his neck by becoming a voluntary prisoner of the Confederates in Missouri in 1861. The story which he got would, he estimated, run to some five columns in the *New York Times*, for which he could expect $7.50 a column, a total of $37.50. Even an editor, such as D. G. Croly of the *New York World*, had to dun his employers for a *raise* to thirty dollars a week late in 1864. It was fairly good pay for the eighteen-sixties, but in an era about to give birth to Rockefellers and Goulds it was clear that journalism was not the road to wealth for a young man.[11] (Henry Villard was an exception, but newspaper work was a way station for him.)

The writing was done under conditions which set up discouraging hurdles to inspiration. When the troops were on the move, correspondents who got as little sleep as any infantryman had to write their daily stint in whatever few moments the army could take to rest. Reporters scribbled handwritten letters of four and five thousand words on stumps, on ration boxes, or on portfolios balanced on knees; hustling back to file stories they dashed off page after page of copy in jerking railroad coaches. Thomas Knox said that some correspondents reached their home of-

[11] Oliver Gramling, *AP: The Story of News* (New York, 1940), p. 42; W. E. Griffis, *Charles Carleton Coffin* (Boston, 1898), p. 83; Wilkie, *Pen and Powder*, pp. 43-44; Marble Papers, Croly to Marble, April 20, 1864.

fices so thoroughly done in that they could not hold pens in their hands; shorthand reporters had to be called in to take down the text.[12]

The risks were the inevitable ones of war. Not many correspondents were killed or wounded, but they were captured almost regularly. From Wilkie, confined overnight in a barbershop in Lexington, Missouri, early in the war, to Browne and Richardson struggling barefoot and half-starved through the snow-piled back country of the Blue Ridge mountains in December, 1864, to escape after nineteen months of Confederate prison camps, a long line of newspapermen tasted captivity. Their adventures varied. Finley Anderson, of the *Herald*, had a year in jail. Joseph B. McCullagh had to walk eighty miles back to the Union lines after Confederate guerrillas had picked him up in Kentucky and forced him to remain with them for a time. A *New York Tribune* man who signed himself "J.B.H." was taken by the lynch-minded irregulars of Mosby in Virginia. His identification papers were found on him, and he was on the verge of being strung to a tree as an "abolition liar for Horace Greeley" when the timely intervention of a Union cavalry patrol saved him. Other unlucky newsmen from time to time lost pants, watches, shoes, notebooks, horses and their liberties for transient periods.[13]

It took considerable dedication to follow a calling of so

[12] *Chicago Tribune*, September 6, 1864; *Cincinnati Commercial*, January 23, 1863; Knox, *Campfire and Cotton-Field*, pp. 482-490.

[13] Franc B. Wilkie, *Walks About Chicago* (Chicago, 1869), pp. 122-139; Richardson, *Secret Service, Field, Dungeon and Escape*, pp. 347-509; *Cincinnati Commercial*, September 6, 1862; *New York Herald*, March 6, 1863; *New York Tribune*, August 19, 1864.

many unexpected vicissitudes. Besides the Confederates, there were always the more terrible-tempered generals to look out for. Sherman was the worst, trying to hang Knox on the grounds of his palpable disrespect for orders barring correspondents from the lines. General Meade devised a less lethal but picturesque punishment for Edward Cropsey of the *Philadelphia Inquirer*. Cropsey had written a story from the Army of the Potomac claiming that, after the first day of the battle of the Wilderness, Grant had ordered a further advance only over the objections of Meade, who thought it would be prudent to fall back and presumably begin later with a refreshed army and fewer risks. Meade, outraged at the figure which he cut in the dispatch, had Cropsey walked out of the camp on a horse which bore a placard reading LIBELLER OF THE PRESS.[14]

The newspapermen felt that this kind of treatment was doubly insulting when they themselves rarely passed up a chance to serve as volunteer scouts for the army. In September, 1862, Lee was marching into Maryland, with Jeb Stuart's cavalry screening the movement. Some of Stuart's troopers captured Uriah H. Painter, the correspondent of the *Philadelphia Inquirer*, and then let him slip away. Painter, who had picked up the invasion plan by keeping his ears open, made haste to Washington to warn the War Department of what was afoot. The department ignored him, and continued insisting publicly that everything was under control, until the first Confederate patrols had crossed

[14] *Official Records*, Ser. 1, XXXVI, Pt. 3, 670, 751, XLII, Pt. 3, 484-486; *New York Herald*, June 10, July 13, 1864.

the Potomac and cut the Baltimore & Ohio railroad from the West.

Painter's frustration was a match for that of Homer Byington, who normally helped to cover the Washington scene for the *New York Tribune*. Byington left the capital to see the battle of Gettysburg for himself, and after the fighting was over galloped alone after the bruised Confederates. He found them crowded into a bend of the Potomac, which heavy rains had made unfordable. Hurriedly, the correspondent found an old man with a horse and wagon, and sent him off to Meade's headquarters with the message that the Confederate army — men, horses, wagons and guns — was waiting to be bagged. If Meade got any such message, however, its effect was not noticeable. He huddled his own combat-weary units off the field cautiously, while Lee made good his escape.

But Henry Wing, the youthful reporter for the *Tribune*, who rode, swam and walked seventy-five miles through guerrilla country and was nearly hanged as a spy before he could clear his identity with the War Department, succeeded in bringing dispatches from Grant's army. As it happened, Grant had completely cut his communications in moving out from his base camp to start the fighting in the Wilderness. He knew that the best way to be close-mouthed about an operation was to keep Washington out of it, and he had no urge to be nagged by the War Department. The result was that for the first three days of the battle the capital knew nothing whatever of the army, and Wing brought the first assurance that Grant and his men had not been wiped out to the last drummer boy. Wing was personally taken to the White House to repeat his stories (having already wired a hasty bulletin to Greeley's office), and legend has it that the President impulsively pulled the nineteen-year-old reporter to him and kissed his forehead.[15]

As a partial result of sharing dangers of this sort, the correspondents did begin to develop a clear *esprit de corps.* They wrote political diatribes against each other's papers, and foundered horses trying to beat each other to telegraph offices. But they did present a more or less united front to the generals, and to the scorn of the old-school-tie dignitaries who found something too plebeian in the new journalism. They were hungry, wet, cold and frightened together. In the midst of mud and wagons and contrabands, overturned ration boxes, discarded equipment, dead animals, boredom and profanity, the "newspaper writers" of the fifties began to be welded into a loose professional kinship. They were turning from literary gentlemen, of strong political leanings, into regulars who were narrow-eyed, inquisitive, and willing to work under any banner for a chance at good stories and a reasonable weekly check.

While they were about it, they were setting up a romantic tradition good enough to last into the age of Hollywood. Shortly after Bull Run, a Philadelphia youngster wrote palpitatingly to John Russell Young, begging for a corre-

[15] Coffin, *Four Years of Fighting,* p. 112; *New York Tribune,* July 7, 1863; William A. Croffut, "Horace Greeley Knows His Business," *Atlantic Monthly,* CXLV (1939), 228-230; Ida Tarbell, "Lincoln Kissed Him," *Collier's,* LXXIX (January 15, 1927), 17.

spondent's berth. "Let me go," he panted. "I fear nothing. Should death overtake me, I am content, should I return, who can doubt that I can claim a fair girl's hand." Even experienced reporters were caught up in the swirl. Just before going up the Red River, on his impromptu gunboat expedition in 1863, Finley Anderson of the *New York Herald* wrote to Frederic Hudson that he was making the risky trip "to see, just for my own gratification, what kind of stuff I am made of." He had time to think over the question as a prisoner, after the vessel on which he had posted himself was captured with him on board. Young men of the sixties liked nothing better than to strike poses, but there *was* a zesty flavor of adventure in a war correspondent's job, and the breakneck accomplishments of the best of them, well aired in their own papers, went far to increase it. Richard Harding Davis and platoons of derring-do war reporters of fact and fiction could have traced their literary bloodlines back to the army correspondents of the Civil War.[16]

The correspondents made no lasting contributions to American letters, which was not surprising in view of the fact that journalism at best is a perishable art form. In 1863, an order was issued requiring all reporters with the Army of the Potomac to sign their letters with their full signatures, or with pen names registered at headquarters.

[16] John Russell Young Papers, Library of Congress, John Norcross to Young, N.D., 1861; James Gordon Bennett Papers, Library of Congress, Anderson to Hudson, February 10, 1863.

The idea was primarily to keep a rein on correspondents who played loose with security regulations. Two *New York Herald* reporters, however, protested the decree. They said that they did not mind being held responsible for the content of their stories, but that they were embarrassed to be known as authors of such hasty and unpolished prose as was necessitated by the early deadlines.[17] Most of the paragraphs ground out by the correspondents were cursed by the mid-century affectation of "high-tone" style. They dragged a clanking chain of moralities after them like Marley's ghost. Type was small and columns were long, so that there was little need for writers to be herded into terseness. Wherever foursquare statements could be replaced by euphemism, the substitution was made, apparently on the theory that a naked fact was an indecent affront to sensitive subscribers.

"The sounds of the advance are in my ears," wrote a *New York Herald* observer just before moving on to Bull Run. "I go to join it. God protect the right." A typical descriptive passage by a Chicago reporter burst hoarsely into the present tense.

> Our extreme right reaches beyond the enemy's front, it rapidly closes in, and pours murderous volleys into his flank. He stops short, turns and flees. Our boys rapidly pursue, cheering and firing as they go. They have stemmed the torrent and turned the tide of battle.

Confronted with death on the field, a correspondent as seasoned as Charles Coffin wallowed in bathos.

[17] *New York Herald,* May 7, 1863.

"Do not weep," he said; "it is God's will. I wish you to write to my father and tell him that *I have tried to do my duty to my country and to God.* . . . I have a good many friends, schoolmates and companions. They will want to know where I am. . . . You can let them know that I am gone, and that I die content. And, Chaplain, the boys in the regiment — I want you to tell them to *stand by the dear old flag!* And there is my brother in the navy — write to him and tell him to *stand by the flag and cling to the cross of Christ!*" [18]

On the other hand, a reporter occasionally broke through with a piece of writing that would have earned respect in any school of realism. When the campaign of the Wilderness was going on, the *New York Tribune's* Samuel Wilkeson paid a visit to Fredericksburg, a major collecting point for casualties of the operation. He wrote:

. . . Where are not these wounded? In yards where pumps are, they get water and sit on the earth and moisten their bandages and cool their burning. In all the many wooden tenements vacated by the bombardment and stripped afterward of doors, windows and weather-boarding up to the second story, they are to be seen sitting and having the appearance of waiting, either in weariness or expectation or uncertainty; making no parade of naked arms bloodily bandaged, and of bloody bandages shown through great holes slit with knives in their trousers, and left unpinned to let in cold water and cool air, and of black-bandaged hands and feet taking on a glossy crust outside the cloth — the measure of the length of neg-

[18] *New York Herald,* July 22, 1861; *Chicago Tribune,* October 17, 1862; *Boston Journal,* July 1, 1864.

lect. On every side-walk men pass you strengthening a wounded and bandaged leg as they go, with a pole on which they lean their whole weight, and as it were propel themselves. They sit bandaged on door steps. Bandaged and muddy and weary, with only canteens of water beside them, they sit on curb-stones in every street. Everywhere men in Federal blue, and with some mark of blood and battle upon them, walk slowly with canes, freshly cut in the woods, and inquire for corps hospitals. . . .

Every church in the city is a hospital, and every one is full. Outside of each are wounded soldiers ready to take the places of those who die within, or are sent to Belle Plain. Every public building is a hospital, and is full. All the large dwellings are hospitals. In small houses all over the city our wounded are to be found. The warehouses, large and free in the lower story, especially built for the great trade in agricultural manures, are occupied by soldiers lying in rows, upon muddy and bloody blankets, and nurses go up and down the alleys of these maimed or helpless ones with pails of ice-water. . . .[19]

A *Boston Journal* man following Sherman's army into Georgia, gave a graphic picture of what the war was doing to the South.

Georgia, as seen from Chattanooga to Marietta — about 150 miles . . . is totally swept of its male inhabitants. In the still standing cottages (mostly near the depots), and selling peaches, apples and pies around the cars, you see the lean, lank, yellow-skinned women of the lower class, with their tow-headed children — a few boys under twelve, and some unmanageable girls — all clad in the commonest of female or of homespun male garments; but

[19] *New York Tribune,* May 18, 1864.

> never by any chance, excepting near the lines, and then *very* rarely, an able-bodied man! Every able-bodied man wears the Federal uniform. Every able-bodied Negro is in the service of the army. Georgia here is abandoned excepting by its women. All — *every* man — of the adult male population is in the Southern army.
>
> . . . .
>
> All along the railroad you see the black embers and charred timbers, and chimneys standing alone, that show where houses have been burned down by Johnston's or our army. The few little villages that there are on the road are utterly deserted. You see large hotels, all open, with broken panes of glass, doors and blinds (of these last a few only) off their hinges, emptied of furniture from cellar to ceiling. So of all the stores, excepting those occupied by our troops or the Sanitary Commission.
>
> At every bridge, however small the stream it crosses, there is a block house or stockade built or building, and a guard of soldiers. It was dark when we reached Marietta.

To get that story the reporter had ridden his hundred and fifty miles sitting on a platform of three planks laid lengthwise along the top of a railroad car. There were no interior accommodations; nothing moved on the road, under the watchful eye of Sherman's chief supply officer, except troops and supplies. The *Journal's* representative took his chances with soot, splinters and rain in a light summer suit. He was one man who was able to write with feeling about the horrid effects of war.[20]

If a battlefield, to a run-of-the-mill correspondent, was a place where God protected the right and murderous volleys

[20] *Boston Journal*, August 26, 1864.

were poured (with cheers) into the fleeing foe, it was something else to an observant writer for the *New York World*, who filed a report on the appearance of Gettysburg one week after the battle. Picking out small details, he built up a picture in which there was no gilding.

> . . . The dead, though buried in every part of the field I have yet seen, are placed so very close to the surface that an odor of insufferable sickliness pervades the whole atmosphere. . . . No doubt the quantities of dead horses, on whom the flies are at work by millions, contribute largely to this pestilential effluvia . . .
>
> . . . .
>
> It is hard to say where to begin. Shall it be with the muskets, lying about rusty and broken, without bayonets or ramrods, and often with the butt-end broken off by some . . . heavy ammunition wagon. Not far from the broken musket may generally be seen the bayonet or ramrod stuck in the ground at some small angle, the latter twisted at the thin end by trampling, the former foul with clay or blood. Shall we go on and speak of the countless shells lying about, some exploded and split into all kinds of fragments, others lying apparently harmless on the ground . . . round pine-shaped cone-shaped rockets, grape-shot and goodness knows what beside . . .
>
> . . . .
>
> . . . By the rifle-pits in the heights lay the mementoes of the artillerymen's occupation . . . Some few boxes of ammunition still lie unopened . . . Close by are innumerable proofs of the long hours . . . stood in action — fragments of biscuits, bones of meat, grounds of coffee . . . parcels of half-used wadding, damp with the mist and rain. . . .

> . . . As we trod our way . . . there lay at our feet, dirty and trampled, a Bible, still nearly entire, which some pious soldier must have brought with him on the field. Soon after we found a mass-book, thumbed and much trampled on. It opened for itself at the litany of the saints — calling on all angels and saints, and virgins and confessors, each by their name, to "pray for us." [21]

There was nothing fustian about writing like that. It might have done for captions under the photographs of Brady, whose camera, unable to remember classroom lessons in rhetoric, was easily the best reporter of the war.

One other service the correspondent could render was in the role of atrocity-monger, and he was ready to take it up from the moment of mobilization. A good many passionate newspaper writers had been sharpening their eyes in the prewar days of thrust and parry, and the coming of war removed at least two restraints. For one thing, unconfirmed reports from the South could not be challenged by anyone on the spot, and for another, the argument that tales of blood and slaughter fomented sectional disunity collapsed like a concertina. Sectional disunity was, after April 12, 1861, obviously beyond anyone's capacity to repair peacefully for some time, and open season could safely be declared on truth even in normally hesitant quarters. Among other things, atrocity stories gave respectable subscribers a chance to enjoy rightfully the forbidden thrills of penny-dreadful writing.

[21] *New York World,* July 14, 1863.

The *New York Herald's* coverage of Bull Run included a report that wounded men had been trampled on and ambulances fired into intentionally. The *New York World's* correspondent at the battle said that the faces of the dead were beaten in with muskets, casualties bayoneted, and "helpless prisoners stripped and tortured." "We were prepared for fiendishness," said the reporter, whose paper had not yet gone Democratic, "but not for ferocity." The next spring, after Union forces had reoccupied the old field, another *World* man interviewed a local resident who assured him that corpses had been dug up, the flesh boiled from the bones, and the bones passed out among the Confederate soldiers as "mementoes of southern conquest." Stories of that particular kind made such headway that the Committee on the Conduct of the War ran a special "investigation" of them, confirmed their apostolic truth, and embodied them in an efficiently publicized report which did no harm whatever to the Radical cause before the electorate.[22]

The stories played no favorites in geographical areas. A *Cincinnati Commercial* correspondent originated a report that a gunboat sailor, wandering along the shore of the Mississippi, had been seized by some Arkansas troops who bound him, "*deliberately cut his bowels out with a dirk knife . . . cut his heart out and hung it upon a tree.*" In the same zone of operations, a *New York Herald* reporter said, a group of "rebels" had hung an eighty-year-

[22] *New York Herald,* July 24, 1861; *New York World,* July 25, 1861, March 15, 1862.

old woman in her own front yard for speaking un-Confederate sentiments. On the Peninsula, it was charged, Union prisoners were shot and clubbed to death when they fell out of line, on the way to collecting points, to get water. Wounded men at Vicksburg were allegedly bayoneted. A Union man who surrendered to a Confederate cavalry force conducting a spectacular raid in southern Ohio had his "brains knocked out with a musket" by one of the riders, "maddened by the sight of blood or crazy with liquor." In Missouri, according to another story published in the *Herald*, a dead artillery private was brought in with his face mashed into a pulp of blood and cartilage by boot heels. A *Chicago Tribune* front-line dispatch said that the Confederates, before evacuating Chattanooga, had deliberately hospitalized smallpox cases in homes where the incoming Yankees would probably be billeted — a rough-and-ready kind of bacteriological warfare. In Kentucky, according to the same Chicago paper, a member of Nathan Bedford Forrest's cavalry was captured taking home a Northern scalp to his children. There was special popularity in the scalping charge; in Georgia, correspondents of both the *New York Tribune* and *Herald* reported almost in unison that the Confederates were lifting the hair of the dead and wounded, and had even hung some of their "reeking" trophies on tree limbs, with slips of paper pinned to them asking "How do you like this?" [23]

[23] *New York World*, August 11, 1862; *Cincinnati Commercial*, June 4, July 16, 1863; *New York Herald*, January 26, 1863; *Chicago Tribune*, September 23, 1863, April 3, 1864; *New York Tribune*, June 1, 1864; *New York Herald*, June 2, 1864.

The *New York Tribune* specialized, as in prewar years, in the nameless horrors inflicted on victims of the Slave Power in darkest secessionland. An Arkansas correspondent of the paper told of Union sympathizers who were kidnapped in the dead of night by guerrillas. Next morning, "a corpse . . . with bullet-pierced heart, or cloven skull" would be found by the roadside. Another of Greeley's men, aboard Farragut's flagship in the Mississippi, told of a woman left in charge of a plantation who had tied up two Negro children and set dogs on them. In South Carolina another *Tribune* operative unearthed the story of a woman in Charleston who had been shot for waving at the Stars and Stripes when a flag-of-truce boat pulled into a landing. In New Orleans, a writer for the *Boston Traveller* bid strongly for honors in the department of naked horror with a grand-slam account gathered from Unionist refugees freshly arrived from Texas. They reported that an antislavery man had been lynched in a small town there. His heart was cut out and placed in a pickle jar full of whiskey, which was kept on display in the window of a local drug and paint store. His fat had been "tried out from the flesh" and divided among the neighboring menfolk "for the oiling of their firearms." A doctor had taken home the head, boiled the flesh from it, and confided with satisfaction to his wife that he had "long desired an abolitionist's skull for his study, and now he had got one." Obviously the only way to improve on the appeal of a tale such as that was to provide one in which horror was embellished with a touch of sex. The *Chicago Tribune* qualified with a letter from its correspondent in Cairo. It described a raid by guerrillas on the home of a Missouri Unionist. Finding the man absent they had seized his wife, stripped her, and lashed her with switches.[24]

The residents of the occupied territory were given a thorough working over by some of the reporters, whose antirebellion urges were reinforced by the discomforts of campaigning in the Southern back country. The "rebels," civilian and military, were pictured as "long, gaunt, cadaverous, blear-eyed . . . ignorant, thriftless and unambitious . . . scum and offscouring . . . gamblers, murderers, horse-thieves, hags, land-pirates and desperadoes." One of Greeley's men in Virginia explained to readers that the typical enlisted man of Lee's army was "long haired, small snaky eyes, [with] high cheek bones . . . sunken breast and stooping gait." The "F.F.V. *officer*" showed the effects of having been "nursed by 'negro mammys,' papped on whisky, [and] coddled on tobacco." [25]

The vote-getting purpose in much of this was evident, and a rule of thumb seemed to be that the more revolting a story sounded, the better billing it was likely to get in the extreme Radical press. Halfway through the 1864 campaign the *Chicago Tribune* gave an entire page to one of its staff writers for a lengthy article which was a compendium of the best ones produced by three years of the war. After

[24] *New York Tribune*, March 20, July 18, December 26, 1862; *Boston Traveller*, quoted in *New York Tribune*, February 20, 1863; *Chicago Tribune*, January 10, 1863.

[25] *New York Herald*, January 25, 1862; *Missouri Democrat*, October 21, 1862; *New York World*, July 3, 1862; *New York Tribune*, September 2, 1864.

each new instance of depravity, there was a sardonic insert in italics — the plank in the Democratic platform, nailed in by the party's peace faction, calling for "*immediate efforts . . . toward a cessation of hostilities.*" The *Chicago Tribune* was never the newspaper to make a point delicately.[26]

On April 7, 1865, the skeleton of Lee's army was almost cornered at Appomattox. In New York, James Gordon Bennett was restless — a characteristic feeling. The official end was a matter of days away, but Bennett felt that the time had come for curtain calls and future announcements. A long special editorial appeared on the front page of the paper — which, on that day, had an announced circulation of 133,200 — pointing proudly to the "large corps of trained and able men," numbering some "thirty or forty historians," who had brought the war to the breakfast tables of *Herald* readers. They had collected information which would be "invaluable and indispensable to the future Macaulay," while piecing together the "earliest and most graphic pictures of battles, marches, sieges, scouts and skirmishes." Rising to the enthusiastic heights of a nominating address, the editorial credited the correspondents with "intelligence . . . quickness and closeness of observation. . . capacity for literature and for business, . . . and an appreciation of the importance of their position." The inevitable question was, of course, what would be done with them now. Bennett had the answer.

[26] *Chicago Tribune,* September 29, 1864.

> We shall send them as our ambassadors to all the great capitals of the world. . . . Just as there is a "*Herald's* headquarters" tent with every army, and a *Herald* bureau in Washington, so there shall be a *Herald* legation in all the chief cities from Melbourne to Spitzbergen. Using the Atlantic cable and the Russian telegraph, these correspondents, who have acquired experience, tact and vigor in the school of this war, will send us every item of our intelligence throughout the world, so that we shall place before our readers in every morning's *Herald* a complete photograph of the world of the previous day, and can issue extras with the news of a revolution in Pekin or the discovery of Sir John Franklin at the North Pole before the event happens, if allowance be made for the difference in time. . . . What we have done is a guarantee of what we shall do. The United States, the city of New York and the *New York Herald* have a future compared to which the present is as nothing.

Bennett was riding, as always, the main stream of American thought, forever convinced that there was a future compared to which the present would be nothing. As the sound of the guns faded, the roar of drills, forges and furnaces grew louder. The great boom, the headlong rush to convert the land into an industrial Brobdingnag, was under way. The newspaper world would be carried along, sharing the excitement and the morning-after headaches. Presses would grow larger and spin faster; circulation figures would surge upwards. Headlines would burst out of one-column imprisonment, and photoengraving, cartoons and color would change the face of the front page. Consolidation would have its day. Small dailies would die.

"Yellow journalism" would become a battle cry shouted at men named Pulitzer, Scripps and Hearst. The idea of civic service would carry newspapers further into the political ring. In a few decades, there would be doubters to ask whether independent journalism had died in the machine age, killed by its own search for the utmost in circulation and advertising revenue. Like democracy itself, the press had to cope with the acquisitive spirit, the dynamo and the contest between mass and individual.

The correspondent would be recording it all, and asking many of the questions. He had a place in the new world; he brought it to life every morning from police blotters, mimeographed handouts of government secretaries, and strips of tape in the teletype rooms. He could be cynical or tragic or bombastic or mechanical, but whatever he felt was important because it impressed itself on millions of Americans. And millions had first learned to gather impressions from the news columns in the heady days of sectional struggle and Civil War. Out of the jousts with the censors, the political pleading, the races to make morning issues, the cheers and hisses for selected generals — out of all this had come an acceptance of the news writer as a permanent part of the scene — a man with a profession (if not a calling) and with influence.

The *Philadelphia Press*, on May 13, 1862, trying to weigh the role of the reporters during the war, had made one striking statement in an editorial, possibly penned by John Russell Young, who had been to the field himself and knew.

> Their mission has not been all a mercenary one, but a labor of enthusiasm which the outside world can scarcely understand. It may be appreciated by the historian, who cannot complete his record of the times without giving a long chapter to the correspondents.

In their wartime work the correspondents had helped to bring to maturity a relationship worth thinking about — a mobile, influential, three-cornered relationship between the world, the reporter, and the reader. Through the reporters, still one more feature of modern times had been unveiled as a surprise result of the war for the Union.

Index